DEB MARTIN

JIM PETERSEN

LIVING PROOF

NAVPRESS

A MINISTRY OF THE NAVIGATORS
P.O. BOX 35001, COLORADO SPRINGS, COLORADO 80935

The Navigators is an international Christian organization. Jesus Christ gave His followers the Great Commission to go and make disciples (Matthew 28:19). The aim of The Navigators is to help fulfill that commission by multiplying laborers for Christ in every nation.

NavPress is the publishing ministry of The Navigators. NavPress publications are tools to help Christians grow. Although publications alone cannot make disciples or change lives, they can help believers learn biblical discipleship, and apply what they learn to their lives and ministries.

Ninth printing, 1994

(Originally published as *Evangelism as a Lifestyle* © 1980 by Jim Petersen, and as *Evangelism for Our Generation* © 1985 by Jim Petersen.)

Unless otherwise noted, Scripture quotations in this publication are from the *Holy Bible: New International Version* (NIV). Copyright © 1973, 1978, 1984, International Bible Society. Used by permission of Zondervan Bible Publishers. Other versions used are the *Revised Standard Version Bible* (RSV), copyright 1946, 1952, 1971, by the Division of Christian Education of the National Council of the Churches of Christ in the USA, used by permission, all rights reserved; and *The New Testament in Modern English* (PH), J.B Phillips Translator, © J.B. Phillips 1958, 1960, 1972, used by permission of Macmillan Publishing Company.

Printed in the United States of America

CONTENTS

AUTHOR

Jim Petersen is currently part of a four-man executive team that leads the international work of The Navigators.

Jim grew up in a Christian home in Minneapolis, Minnesota, and graduated from the University of Minnesota. He also studied at Northwestern Bible College and Bethel College.

When Jim was twenty-one God became the most important influence in his life and Jim began a consuming search for a better personal knowledge of Him. The following year he approached Ed Reis, a Navigator representative, for more personal help. Jim attributes acquiring the vision and the skills needed to match his personal desire to be used by God to Ed's influence in his life.

Jim served as an area representative in Minneapolis-St. Paul from 1958 to 1961. Following a brief assignment at the Navigator international headquarters in Colorado Springs, Colorado, Jim and his wife, Marge, moved to Brazil in 1963 to open the Navigator ministry there. Jim became the Latin American Navigators Divisional Director in 1972, and served in that position until 1985 when the Petersons moved to Colorado Springs, where The Navigators' international headquarters is located. In 1988 Jim began leading an international leadership development project, the Scriptural Roots of Ministry (SRM).

The material in *Living Proof* is also available as a video training course. Jim has also written *Church Without Walls* (NavPress, 1992) and *Lifestyle Discipleship* (NavPress, 1993).

He and his wife have four children, Michelle, Todd, Raquel, and Rochelle.

FROM THE AUTHOR

Living Proof is really two books, *Evangelism as a Lifestyle* and *Evangelism for Our Generation*, revised and combined into one. I think I owe an explanation to you, reader, as to how this came about. We'll start at the beginning.

In the mid-70s we returned to the United States for a two-year assignment after ten years in Brazil. When you step back into a familiar place after being away for a time, the changes leap out at you. We were struck by changes in attitudes and values, especially among the unchurched in our society. America was more secular. For example, the idea that there might be absolutes that would govern a society or one's personal behavior was unthinkable for many. Relativism had become a common basic assumption.

Since we had spent those ten years working fruitfully among Brazilian university students and young professionals, who had largely abandoned their religious tradition to embrace secular philosophies, we believed that such people could also be reached in the United States. I was also aware of the radical cooling of the spiritual climate that was taking place in Europe. The same forces that were propelling that climate change were evident in the United States. This too concerned me. Prompted by these factors, I decided that during the two years we were scheduled to be in the country, I would focus my public speaking on this issue. I talked about it everywhere I went. My message was simple: almost half of our society is unchurched, and we Christians are not communicating with them; the people in that half will not come to us or to our programs, but they are reachable; we need to learn to bring Christ to them on their turf.

Well, I thought it was simple. But often the response was blank stares. I felt as though I was trying to describe an invisible world as I talked.

When after two years we returned to Brazil, my concern had grown. By then I felt I had verified my first impressions of a shift in spiritual climate, and I had managed enough personal involvement with unchurched people to be convinced of their openness to Christ. But I knew I had not managed to communicate what I was seeing and feeling. That was when I decided to write *Evangelism as a Lifestyle*. I thought that if I could lay the whole thing out in a book, I might get my message across. I wrote the book, committed it to God and to the publisher, and went on to other things. I thought I had said what I had to say about evangelism.

Then letters started coming. Apparently I had transmitted my basic message to the readers, but I had not provided enough practical guidance for anyone to be able to do anything about it. I was glad we were living 7,000 miles away! Then I received a many-paged letter from a Navigator in California, Peter Gerhard. I had never met him. His letter consisted of one "how-to" question after another. As I read it I thought, *It will take another book to answer this letter!* That's when I wrote *Evangelism for Our Generation.*

Soon after *Evangelism for Our Generation* was published, Joe Coggeshall of CBMC (Christian Businessmen's Committee) wrote me about using the two books as the basis for a video seminar. He told me NavPress and CBMC were interested in doing this as a joint project. It took me over a year to warm up to the idea. Then when I did, Pat McMillan suggested that it would sure be nice if I would integrate both books into a single text! That suggestion wasn't entirely new, as I had already heard it from a few seminary professors. But with my current responsibilities, it just seemed impossible. I turned to Jake Barnett.

Jake has worked with me line by line in the writing of both *Evangelism as a Lifestyle* and *Evangelism for Our Generation*. Without Jake's encouragement and deft assistance, I doubt that I would ever have produced anything in writing. Jake offered to integrate the two texts for me. He teamed up with my old mentor, Ed Reis, and shortly they presented me with a rough draft. I disappeared with the draft, worked it over, and then got back to Jake. Together we gave it a final polishing. *Living Proof* has emerged out of this process.

The material in this book is the product of thirty years of doing a lot of things wrong and a few things right. My sources have been the Bible, my nonbelieving friends (and foes), my colleagues, and a few good books. I can't sign off without mentioning a few very special friends who were fellow-learners with me: Ken Lottis, Osvaldo Simóes, Aldo Berndt, Fernando Gonzalez and Mário Nitsche. Any one of these people could have written this book.

NEW INSIGHTS ON TRADITIONAL EVANGELISM

Evangelism Bound by Tradition

In 1963 my family traveled by ship from the United States to Brazil. The trip marked a new beginning. We expected that. We did not expect that the sixteen days aboard ship would, in themselves, mark the beginning of discoveries that are still going on. This book is an attempt to pass on what I have been learning about evangelism since that trip.

There were 120 passengers on the ship. Half were tourists, and half were missionaries—including us. Sixty missionaries and sixty tourists! A one-to-one ratio for sixteen days. Since there isn't much to do aboard ship other than walk, read, or converse, I couldn't imagine how any tourist could get through that trip without receiving a thorough exposure to the Christian message. More ideal conditions for evangelism couldn't exist.

During the first three days, my wife and I spent our time relating to the other passengers. Conversations were unhurried, and soon we found ourselves deeply involved in discussing Christ with our new acquaintances.

On the third day, I thought that if the other fifty-eight missionaries were doing what we were, we would have a serious case of overkill. I decided to check with the others about coordinating our efforts. My first opportunity came when I encountered six missionaries sitting together on the deck. I joined them and expressed my concern, suggesting we get our signals straight so we wouldn't overwhelm the passengers.

I had totally misjudged the problem. When I explained what was on my mind, the six just looked at one another. Apparently, it hadn't occurred to them to talk to the other sixty passengers about Christ. Finally one said, "We just graduated from seminary and didn't learn how to do that sort of

thing there." Another said, "I don't know. I have sort of a built-in reservation against the idea of conversion." A third said, "I've been a pastor for
three years, but I've never personally evangelized anyone. I don't think I
know how either."

I remember saying that if we, in sixteen days and with a one-to-one
ratio, couldn't awaken these sixty people to the gospel, we might as well
forget about the ninety-five million Brazilians. Perhaps it would be just as
well if we would all catch the next boat north.

A few hours later there was a knock on our cabin door. I opened it to
find three of the six I had just been talking to. They had come to tell me that
they had obtained permission from the captain to conduct a Sunday
service for the ship's crew and that they wanted me to preach the sermon.

As they elaborated on their plan, I was reminded of a conversation I'd
had three weeks before with a friend's pastor. The pastor told me his
congregation had recently begun witnessing. He said the young people
were going to the old folks' home each Sunday to conduct a service. Some
of the men were holding weekly jail services, after which they would
counsel prisoners individually.

Obviously, there is nothing wrong with conducting services in jails
and rest homes, but if such things alone constitute the main evangelistic
thrust of a body of Christians it raises a problem. I asked the pastor, "Aren't
you running the risk of teaching your congregation that the gospel is only
for those in unfortunate circumstances—for those who are relatively
unthreatening to us? Shouldn't Christians learn to carry the message to
their peers, to go after people on their own level?"

I expressed the same concern to the three missionaries in my cabin.
We could slip into the same mental trap aboard ship. I said, "Your consciences were pricked by what we talked about. So now you've spotted the
unfortunate sailors who never go to church and have planned a service for
them. That is good, but I don't think we can escape from our responsibility
to the passengers."

They got the point, but they had already committed themselves to
conducting a service for the crew. The captain posted a notice in the crew's
quarters, and arrangements had been made to use the galley. I agreed to
attend, but not to speak.

The four of us arrived in the galley on schedule. It was empty.
Occasionally a sailor would have to go through the room in the course of
his duties. He would dart through quickly, obviously intent on not getting
caught. Finally, one sailor came in and sat down. He was a Baptist. So we
had the service: four missionaries and one Baptist sailor!

After that, my three friends began to think in terms of going to the
tourists.

There was an elderly Christian couple among the passengers. It was the husband's birthday, so the three missionaries organized an old-fashioned sing to commemorate the occasion. Sensing what was coming and not wanting to jeopardize my relationships with the people I was getting to know, I felt it wiser to stay away. When the time came for the program, I was up on the third deck. One other passenger was up there enjoying the night air. We began discussing the New Testament I had taken along to read.

Down below we could hear the old songs: "Suwannee River"; "My Old Kentucky Home"; then it was "Rock of Ages," another hymn, a pause. And so it went: hymns, then testimonies, and finally a message.

When it was over my three friends were euphoric. They had succeeded in "preaching" to virtually all the passengers. Naturally, they called another sing for two nights later. Once again I went to the third deck, but this time there were sixty others up there with me. They weren't about to get caught twice!

As I later reflected on those sixteen days aboard ship, it occurred to me that this situation represented a microcosm of the church in the world. Traditional methods and activities that are meaningful to us are often not effective in reaching the world around us. Subsequent years of adapting to a new culture and language for the sake of the gospel have confirmed that realization.

One benefit of taking the gospel across cultural and linguistic frontiers is that many of my best and most unassailable ideas were destroyed in the process. Few of my methods survived the transition, and those that did probably shouldn't have. Stripped, I discovered my ignorance, which lay buried all along. This was an extremely valuable experience, for awakening to one's ignorance is the dawn of learning.

All of this has set me on a quest that continues to this day—to determine what it really means to take the gospel into the world. Over these years I have considered many questions relating to the mobility of the gospel. Many remain unanswered (including some of those I will list), but I have learned enough to realize that I have sometimes been oblivious to some major biblical truths. Consequently, these have been years of searching. My desire is to enlist you in this search, so that together we may contribute to the progress of the gospel in the world.

Here are some of the questions I've faced:

What about the world we live in? How accurate is our perception of it? Do we understand what is really going on in the minds of those around us? Are we aware of where modern man's philosophy has taken him? Do we know where he is emotionally?

What about secularization? Do we know the extent to which the world around us has become secularized? How do we communicate with the secularized? Is it even possible?

What is genuine communication? To what degree do we have to consider differences in mentality when we share Christ? How can we know the gospel has been communicated? When we fail to communicate, who is responsible? Just how do we adapt to our hearers?

What did Jesus mean when He said the gospel is to be preached to "every creature" and in "all the world"? At what point have we fulfilled this command? Is it when we have proclaimed the terms of the contract to someone, or is there more to it than that? Are evangelism and "reaping" synonymous?

What did Jesus mean when He told us we are to be "in the world"? How do we reconcile this with "coming out from among them"? What is the balance between involvement with the world and isolation? Are we in the world as Jesus intended, or are we ghetto-ized?

What about the great things that are happening in the church today: the big crusades, the seminars, the super-churches? Given time and adequate manpower, will they not accomplish the commands of Christ? Will our programs and institutions fill the need? If not, what's missing?

Who is responsible for the advance of the gospel in the world? Is it realistic to expect every Christian to be involved? Or are we loading our brothers with false guilt? What about personal evangelism? Is that the answer? Is personal evangelism only for the gifted few? Where does the community of believers fit into the picture?

As I searched for answers, I realized that the Christian mission is far more complex and varied than we are willing to admit. Our limited success in communicating across the frontiers of different mentalities and cultures convinced me that we must be overlooking some major scriptural truths in this matter of communicating the gospel to the world. We are not effectively communicating with the secularized men and women of Western cultures or with the billions of others outside of the normal scope of our proclamation.

Our Western society is becoming less receptive to approaches that were effective in the past. At the same time, we have so simplified our understanding of evangelism and have become so accustomed to our ineffectiveness that we continue busily in our established patterns and are nearly unaware of the unreached world that surrounds us.

Our evangelism is primarily among the strays from our own fold, people who have grown up in our churches. Caring for them, together with attending to the internal needs of our churches, is enough to keep us busy. Consequently, there is little time to pause to reflect on the fact that we are not doing well at reaching out to the unbelieving world around us. In a sense, we are talking to ourselves and don't even realize it.

Ken Lottis, who was my colleague in Brazil for twenty years, has provided a good illustration of this. In recounting the adventures of one of his furloughs, he told me the following story.

As I drove up to the coffee shop that afternoon, I really didn't know what to expect. I hadn't seen Pastor Ellsworth in over twenty years. Now, after all this time, he had tracked me down with a letter and some phone calls. With his wife, he was driving 165 miles to have a cup of coffee with my wife and me.

When we had first become acquainted, he was newly married, recently ordained, and holding his first pastorate. I, too, was recently married at that time, involved in a Navigator ministry, and attending his church. Now, twenty years later, we were about to meet in a hotel coffee shop. My wife wondered as we walked in the door, "Do you suppose we will even recognize them?" We did, probably because they were something of a mirror image of us: a bit of gray hair, a few extra pounds, and some wrinkles around the eyes.

As we began our discussion, we mostly reminisced and talked about our families. Then the conversation shifted to the ministries we had been involved in during those twenty years. Pastor Ellsworth had held several different pastorates, each a bit larger than the previous one. His current church in a midwestern town was typical middle America—farmers, ranchers, etc.

My twenty years had been spent in a Navigator ministry in Brazil. When I mentioned some of our experiences in communicating the gospel to young Brazilians, he responded by saying, "In every congregation I have been in, I have tried the traditional methods of evangelism: crusades, house-to-house calling, personal evangelism seminars. I picked up *Evangelism as a Lifestyle* because I knew it was about your work with Jim Petersen in Brazil. As I began to read, I suddenly had the feeling that I was finding some explanations for my frustration in my attempts to evangelize the people in our community.

"Our church is a Bible-believing, Bible-preaching church like hundreds of others in the Midwest. The community is small, with a population under ten thousand. Last year I had a week-long series of evangelistic meetings. The evangelist was good and the meetings were well attended, but mostly by people from our own congregation.

"In reading about things you did in Brazil among the secularized, I finally realized that there were many people in my community also who were secularized. They were not intellectuals; they were simply people for whom the Church and its message no longer held any interest. They were never going to walk through the doors of my church. I am now asking myself what I have to do to reach them."

This story illustrates several difficulties we Christians have in communicating with those around us. We are often oblivious of the gap between ourselves and them. Our methods do not lead to genuine communication with those who most need to hear. We can be unaware of this failure, and even when made aware we are at a loss to know what to do about it.

It does not have to be that way. It is possible to communicate the gospel effectively to all kinds of people. But to do so, we must expand our understanding of what the Scriptures teach about evangelism. That is the purpose of this book: to awaken our awareness to the world of people around us and to call our attention to some biblical truths we have been neglecting. We will demonstrate that a complete definition of evangelism as described by Jesus and expanded in the epistles involves two aspects:

1. The *proclamation* of the gospel: an *action* through which the nonChristian receives a clear statement of the essential message.
2. The *affirmation* of the gospel: a *process* of modeling and explaining the Christian message.

We will find that both aspects are essential if we are to reach all kinds of people. But both are also limited. We are more familiar with the first, often treating it as the comprehensive means of evangelism. Proclamation is essential, but is only one phase in the complete process. It may be an initial phase, as when the Apostle Paul entered a city, went to a synagogue, and talked to people. Or it may be a later phase in the context of affirmation. In the past we have focused on proclamation and have almost ignored affirmation.

With a scriptural definition of evangelism, we will find that much more of our society is reachable than we imagine—although these people may not be immediately reapable. It is time to begin actively trusting God that we can liberate more people from slavery to darkness than we are now. It can be done, but it will demand change.

PART ONE

ANALYSIS OF THE TIMES

ONE

UNDERSTANDING THE TIMES
A World of Unprecedented Change

THERE WERE ONCE "men of Issachar, who understood the times and knew what Israel should do" (1 Chronicles 12:32).

Men of Issachar, where are you now?

The Western world is in a cultural shift that offers a bewildering challenge to those who would understand it. To grasp the nature and significance of what has already happened is an elusive task. To read the trends and understand where they are taking us is even more difficult.

Futurologists are proliferating the racks with books and periodicals containing a broad range of interpretations and predictions. This makes interesting and enlightening reading. But the changes are coming so fast that often what these writers have to say is dated by the time it reaches the reader. To add to the confusion, there are fundamental differences in their perceptions.

It is not my intention to add one more analysis of our society to those already in existence. Rather, it is to identify, with the broadest of brush strokes, the prevailing trends that characterize our society. My purpose in this chapter is not so much to inform the reader of what is happening as it is to sensitize him to the *fact* of change—that our society *is* in flux.

Change tends to get past us unnoticed, while we carry on with business as usual. But for the sake of Christ's command to "go into all the world" (Mark 16:15), we cannot afford to let this happen. We who are Christians are commissioned to work as co-laborers with God in this world. We must, therefore, seek to understand the times, for the people we were sent to reach are caught up in them. If we fail to understand this basic

17

reality, then we will fail to communicate. We will be talking to people as they once were, before they moved on. We must be alert!

PERCEPTIONS OF THE TRENDS:
WHAT ARE THE ANALYSTS SAYING?

Predictions concerning the spiritual climate of our society vary widely. Some foresee a period of unusual receptivity to spiritual values. Others are predicting the opposite.

The optimists. Rifkin and Howard make some very optimistic projections for the growth of the Church. They say, "A growing number of historians, ecologists, economists and anthropologists ask: What will replace materialism? Most agree that . . . the focus of human existence will change from the horizontal plane of materialism to the vertical plane of spiritualism. Only a massive spiritual upheaval, they argue, can provide both the elements of a new world view and the faith and discipline needed to put it into practice."[1] This is indeed a positive note.

In the same vein, John Naisbitt says the United States is undergoing a revival in religious belief and church attendance. This is happening because "during turbulent times many people need structure—not ambiguity—in their lives."[2] People need something to hang on to, to provide an anchor during a transitional age.

George Gallup conducted a religious survey of Americans in 1977. He observed that "the cumulative evidence suggests that the late seventies could, in fact, mark the beginning of a religious revival in America."[3]

These observers of a positive religious trend rely on a common set of indicators to document their analysis. They call attention to the fact that "42 percent of all adults in America attend religious services at least once a week"; that "nearly one in every three Americans now claim to have been 'born again'"; that today "1300 radio stations—one out of every seven in America—is Christian owned and operated"; and that evangelical publishers now account for a third of the total domestic commercial book sales.[4]

It is true! There *is* a boom in evangelical Christianity in America. Anyone can verify this fact by the simple exercise of working his way through the Sunday morning traffic jam surrounding any one of the many super-churches that dot the American scene. The euphoria that seems to characterize these churches, as the overworked pastoral staffs attempt to cope with their own success, gives little occasion to pause and reflect on the bigger picture. Every success indicator confirms that things have never been better.

So Howard and Rifkin conclude, "Of two things we can be sure: a massive religious awakening is in the offing and the first rumblings of this change can already be heard."[5] Are they right?

The pessimists. But there are dissonant evaluations of the religious future of America, made with equal certainty and with equally impressive documentation. These other voices must sound very strange indeed to Christians who are engrossed in the church growth described above. Kenneth Kantzer, former editor of *Christianity Today*, states, "We may well stand at the end of an era extending from the Reformation to the Russian revolution. A religious ice age is drifting down over Europe and North America (though with significant exceptions in the form of pockets of evangelical vigor). Materialistic paganism has become the dominant world view. This growing secularism, which fashions a culture alien to Christianity, erodes the biblical values in our society and penetrates the church."[6]

What is Kantzer talking about? I believe he is seeing things that have been ignored by the more optimistic observers. He is addressing the bigger picture. The religious trend we just described, impressive as it may be, is not mainstream. It is a countercurrent that is decidedly distinct from the broad flow of society. In terms of size and impact, the secularized mainstream exerts an overwhelming influence.

Rifkin and Howard recognize the precariousness of the present situation. They observe that "America . . . is made up of two cultures which exist in a carefully structured relationship to one another. . . . The Reformation culture of John Calvin [which] remains the basis [and] its bastard-ized successor, the liberal ethos, superimposed on top."[7] According to them, the question is "whether the new evangelical revival will reshape the American climacteric, or rather be reshaped and absorbed by the secular culture."[8]

Different authors say it in different ways, but most agree that a good part of the world, particularly the Western world, is caught up in this cultural shift. One way of life is dying; it is being replaced by another.

How this shift will affect the spiritual receptivity of the people of our generation is impossible to predict. Much depends on how alert we Christians are to what is happening, and whether or not we will have the flexibility necessary to respond appropriately.

Christopher Lasch identifies the direction he believes society is taking with the title of his book *The Culture of Narcissism*. In it he summarizes the factors that signal the death of what he calls "the culture of competitive individualism," and the emergence of its logical successor, "the pursuit of happiness to the dead end of a narcissistic preoccupation with the self."[9]

Lasch observes that our political theories have lost their capacity to explain events, that our economic theories have suffered the same fate, and that the sciences, once so confident of their ability to provide answers to life, now make it clear that they are not to be looked to for the resolution of the social problems.

The humanities, he says, are as bankrupt as the rest, making the "general admission that humanistic study has nothing to contribute to an understanding of the modern world. Philosophers no longer explain the nature of things or pretend to tell us how to live." The arts claim only to reflect "the artist's inner state of mind." Historians themselves are warning us to beware the "lessons" of history—that they are "not merely irrelevant but dangerous."[10]

Anxiety has added to disillusionment, as society contemplates the consequences of the depletion of our natural resources and the well-founded predictions of ecological disasters. Irrational acts of terrorism and dangerous localized wars make the threat of nuclear annihilation an everyday concern. Inflation renders financial security a tenuous matter. Even the family has lost its earlier function of providing a common life and of child rearing. Social relationships have become tentative and superficial.

Lasch goes on to observe, "As the twentieth century approaches its end, the conviction grows that many other things are ending too. Storm warnings, portents, hints of catastrophe haunt our times. The 'sense of an ending'. . . now pervades the popular imagination."[11]

Since tomorrow is too dubious or too fearsome to contemplate, we absorb ourselves instead in our own private performance. "To live for the moment is the prevailing passion—to live for yourself, not for your predecessors or posterity. . . . Having no hope of improving their lives in any of the ways that matter, people have convinced themselves that what matters is psychic self-improvement: getting in touch with their feelings, eating health food, taking lessons in ballet, immersing themselves in the wisdom of the East, jogging, learning how to 'relate,'" and so on.[12]

And the truth is somewhere in between. The perceptive reader will realize that the optimistic projection of a massive spiritual awakening and the pessimistic prediction of a society imploding into narcissism are both proving to be unrealistic polarizations. Both are overstatements. Both trends continue to be in evidence, but neither gives a balanced picture of what is, in fact, taking place.

In many ways, life seems to be strikingly normal. America's youth continue to pursue their traditional goal: success. They are studying; they are concerned about maximizing their potential for success; they are hustling for the financially profitable jobs. There is even a reassuring, though modest, display of concern for politics and social issues.

It almost feels like the "good old days" are back. After the convulsions brought upon us by the generation of the sixties and the indifference and self-gratification that marked the seventies, the scene today seems to be a decided improvement. We finally have a generation that does not seem bent on destroying its own habitat. But this generation is the offspring of the sixties and seventies. Beneath the surface lies the heritage of those two decades. Allan Bloom, in his opening sentence in *The Closing of the American Mind* says, "There is one thing a professor can be absolutely certain of: almost every student entering the university believes, or says he believes, that truth is relative."[13] Bloom's thesis is that since openness is perceived as being the highest virtue among our educators, the relativity of truth has become a moral postulate. But once we embrace this postulate we cannot really think at all. "Thus what is advertised as a great opening is a great closing."[14]

Bloom goes on to make some observations that are highly relevant to the subject of this chapter. He describes how, in his early years as a university professor, students "could be counted on to know the Bible," but now "real religion and knowledge of the Bible have diminished to the vanishing point."[15] Consequently, with its gradual disappearance, "Fathers and mothers have lost the idea that the highest aspiration they might have for their children is for them to be wise . . . [and] without the book even the idea of the order of the whole is lost."[16]

If the idea of absolute truth is missing, as Bloom maintains, right and wrong become something the individual, together with his society, decides for himself. Anything goes! Consequently, the foundations of this generation are more pagan than anything else. The ease with which we accept abortion, our readiness to divorce and remarry, our indifference to the psychological health of our children; characteristics such as these are pagan, not Christian. As long as such attitudes prevail, there is little room for debate about the true value system of our society.

This brief vignette of our society should serve to demonstrate the fundamental incompatibility that exists between the belief system of the mainstream of our society and the belief system of those of us in the Christian countercurrent. While the Christian ethic is rooted in faith, hope, and love, the prevailing systems are characterized by self-centeredness. Wanda Urbanska, the author of *The Singular Generation*, says "We are singular—the first generation of Americans who aspire to be self-sufficient—and who, almost instinctively, commit ourselves to a lifelong dynamic relationship with ourselves."[17] Self-fulfillment is the driving value of our generation.

The people of the mainstream are not really seeking our spiritual values. The idea that the Christian faith could serve as a basis for living never even crosses the minds of most people. Instead, they attempt to satisfy their feelings of inner emptiness and malaise by pursuing experiences that provide momentary illusions of well-being. As one friend of mine put it, "My life consists of going from one experience to another, none of which lasts longer than the time it takes to live it."

WHAT IS SECULARIZATION?

Although *secularism* and *secularization* have joined the list of household words used to describe the prevailing world view of our society, our understanding of these terms is often vague. Most of the definitions of secularization center on one idea, that the secularized person has declared, consciously or perhaps unconsciously, his independence from God. Since secularization permeates our society, a careful definition is necessary.

According to the dictionary definition, *secular* is "pertaining to worldly things, or to things that are not regarded as religious, spiritual, or sacred." *Secularized* is "made secular, separate from religions or spiritual connection or influences, made worldly or unspiritual." The first definition reflects a focus of life, the second implies that there has been a transformation from one focus to another.

Os Guinness makes a helpful distinction between secularism, secularization, and the secularized. *Secularism* is a philosophy. As such it can be analyzed and defined with precision. *Secularization* is a process by which religious ideas become less and "less meaningful and religious institutions more marginal."[18] Secularization rubs off on people. Unlike the philosophy, it is contagious, so that wherever modernization goes, some degree of infection is inevitable. The *secularized* are the people who have been infected. There are different degrees of infection, and Christians are not immune to its influences.

The secularized comprise a large segment of the Western world's population. Expressed in Paul's words in Ephesians 2:12, they are "without God in the world." Their personal philosophy of life does not include God. He is not considered a vital part of their existence.

This would include those who have never experienced a God-oriented philosophy, as well as those who have "become" secularized, who have made a transition from a God-oriented philosophy to one without Him. A few may have made this transition within their own lifetimes. More often the transition involves several generations of subtle change. Many of these people are at least a generation removed from experiencing life in relationship to God. They do not regard God as a valid basis for a personal philosophy.

The secularized may not, in the ultimate sense, be characterized as "non-religious." If religion is defined as a set of beliefs upon which life is based, then all men are religious. This is conspicuously true of the atheist, the agnostic, the Marxist, or the philosophical humanist. Often a quasi-religious ideology is based on faith in science, economics, and technology; the secularized man looks to these to answer man's questions and meet society's needs. In reality, man has been created incorrigibly religious, and secularism functions as a religion, as a set of convictions that form the foundation of life.

Secularism can function as a religion, but just as its more formal expression in humanism, it is inadequate to meet man's needs. The present trends within our society toward the mystical Eastern religions, conscious self-worship, the occult, and Satan worship are indications that secularism is in reality a transitional stage. The "New Age" movement is an example of the pseudo-religion which secularism will inevitably generate.

The varying degrees of secularization that Guinness describes tend to confuse us. We like to polarize things to extremes. We define things in terms of black and white: people are either religious or secularized. As a result, we usually fail to recognize secularization, except when we encounter an individual who is suffering from a terminal infection.

Frequently, I get the impression that when people think of a "secularized" person, they get a mental image of someone who is off-beat. Such a strange person can most easily be found in a spiritually resistant pocket of the country, in a place like San Francisco or New York, and lives some sort of an alternative lifestyle. As one person put it, "I would really like to become involved with secularized people, but I don't think we have any around here."

The secularized people of our society are usually not off-beat at all. They shave. They go to the hairdresser. They wear suits and ties. They car-pool our kids, run our local businesses, and farm our land. We are surrounded by the secularized. Middle America *is* secularized.

A dozen years ago, we were living in the U.S., where one acquaintance described his personal philosophy as "hang loose, avoid commitments, do your thing, and let others do theirs." One of our current neighbors described his view of life in similar terms. "Life," he said, "is like the butterflies. They spend their time flitting from flower to flower. When it's over, it's over. The idea is to look as pretty as you can while you flit."

Our present neighborhood in a midwestern suburb is characterized by divorces and unmarried couples. Across the way, the couple completed their house, installed the lawn, then put the house up for sale. Divorce. The identical thing happened farther down the block. A single man lives in the corner house, and three small children spend the weekends with him. Another family consists of a couple, both fresh from divorces, bringing their children together for the first time. One husband is in prison, charged with the attempted murder of his wife.

These things are the inevitable result of being "without God in the world." In the absence of a meaningful philosophy of life, the relativism that grows out of secularism is being lived out in our society with devastating effects.

GETTING AHEAD OF THE TRENDS

The implications of these trends are multiple and far-reaching, but within the scope of this book one question stands out: What will the effect of all this be on the progress of the gospel in the world?

I believe the answer will be determined by *the manner of our response.* If we continue to carry on and repeat our old success patterns as if the world just described didn't exist, the results will be very easy to predict. But if we respond with understanding and adapt accordingly, we could find the situation serving to the *advantage* of the gospel.

The cultural shift we are discussing is occurring at a rapid pace. In *Idols of Destruction,* Herb Schlossberg notes that some "social scientists assign the shift to despair to a single decade: the 1960s."[19] No matter when it first occurred, this negative shift is now readily observable.

I am affiliated with the Christian organization known as The Navigators. Our ministry is primarily among the lost with the aim of equipping those we win to labor among their peers. This obviously means that we are working at the grass-roots level, where the early signs of social changes are first perceived.

The trends seem to be running from east to west in the Western world. Europe is being affected first, with the United States following suit. Our European colleagues were among the first to detect the shift to despair.

Changes in approach, content, and expectations were forced on our staff in Holland within a five-year period. In an unpublished paper, Dutch Navigator Gert Doornenbal observed, "The young people of today are not like those we were reaching ten years ago. More and more children are growing up in one-parent homes. Often they lack love and attention."

In Sweden, family counselors talk about "never children." They have never heard anyone say "I love you." They live with unmet emotional needs, wrestling with loneliness and insecurity. They are incapable of normal emotional expression and relationships.[20]

Rinus Baljeu, a Dutch Navigator ministering in Sweden, expands on the implication of this situation. He observes, "The '80s started with the shocking discovery that in several countries our evangelism had become a scramble for the very few. We are on our way to becoming a non-religious society. Eighty-five to ninety percent of today's teenagers regard questions like 'Did Jesus live?' or 'Was he the Son of God?' as irrelevant and unimportant."[21]

A British Navigator colleague, John Mulholland, did a limited survey in an effort to understand the extent of secularization among students in England. He said, "The results came as something of a surprise. Students are more secularized than we thought. We have to decide where we should labor: among the relatively few prepared people close to the Kingdom of God or among the more secularized. Obviously, the prepared should be reaped, but others are active in reaping this small harvest. Given that those on the secular half of the scale outnumber those on the more biblical half by five to one, the majority of people are substantially secularized. If we are to equip our laborers to work relevantly in the harvest, it is imperative that we learn to work effectively among the secularized and train others to do the same."[22] Every fall this same scramble for "the small harvest among the prepared" is repeated by Christian student organizations on campuses across the United States.

Failure to understand the trends has reduced the effectiveness of many churches and Christian groups in reaching the world around them. Many spiritual leaders have become greatly discouraged because they feel they are struggling against an overpowering tide. As they become exhausted, motivation drops, and doubts about their calling or their doctrine often develop. They begin to feel irrelevant. The simple thing for them to do is to turn their backs on this baffling world and engross themselves in the familiar, comfortable Christian environment.

Long-established institutions especially suffer these stresses. That which seemed so effective, relevant, and successful a few years ago is not effective today. This kind of declining effectiveness is threatening to any organization. It is also a clear-cut sign that something must be done.

Baljeu observes, "For most countries in Europe today, the adaptations we face are not just minor modifications. A major re-evaluation of our whole style and structure is needed. Our patterns of fellowship, our special emphasis and terminology, our organizations, our views on discipleship and standards of conduct—all these need to be reworked so that our ministry, in fact, deals with the needs of those we seek to reach. . . . This is not a matter of becoming more effective. It is a matter of our survival in the 1980s."[23] Anyone who gets a close look at the problems from the vantage of a Christian organization can recognize the urgency and the gravity of the situation.

So the effects of secularization are already upon us. We are not forecasting; we are simply addressing influences that today are powerfully affecting the Church and its mission in the world. The mainstream is rapidly moving away from biblical values. But that is no reason for us to give up or to entertain the idea of abandoning certain segments of the population. *Our response should be to work toward understanding the trends and to seek to make them work in favor of the growth of the gospel.* We have a long way to go before that happens. Most of us do not know how to proceed to influence our nonChristian contemporaries with the gospel.

A VERY TYPICAL STORY

The contrast between the secular world and the Christian subculture is becoming progressively apparent and uncomfortable to many people. A friend of mine described this dilemma in personal terms:

> I was working for a bank in Houston, Texas. I was also a member of a local Baptist church, where I was integrated into a singles group; there were six of us in the group. So my life was made up of two different contexts: my friends from the church and my friends from the bank. Most of my friends at work had a church background, which they had rejected and forsaken. Some didn't have that much. I had a strong desire to bring them to Christ, but every effort resulted in frustration.
>
> Our working relationship was good, and I tried to develop social relationships too. I would attend the bank parties and participate in as many social activities as possible, but there were deep differences between us. In fact, we had so little in common that there was no real communication.
>
> Since I was a relative newcomer in town, some of these friends took the initiative on several occasions to include me in their activities. Once they took me with them to watch the Houston Oilers. But I did not feel comfortable with them. They, of course, sensed this, and it wasn't long before their invitations ceased. My world was the Christian subculture. When I'd leave it, I'd feel insecure and it was easier to go back to my friends from the church.
>
> So that is just what I did. I involved myself in a couple of activities in order to satisfy my desire to be involved in evangelism. For a while I teamed up with a group that visited the local campus to witness to whomever we encountered. Then I participated in the "Here's Life" campaign, evangelizing by telephone. Both efforts produced some response, but the experiences were inconsequential for my own spiritual development. They did nothing to enrich my own walk with God, because they did not result in an enduring involvement with people who were my peers.

Today, as I look back on this experience, I recognize the distance that existed between myself and my friends at the bank. When I was in the middle of it, I couldn't see it. Although they were my peers both socially and intellectually, there was not enough rapport between us for me to be able to sit down and share the gospel openly with them.

This story is so typical. It could certainly be multiplied thousands of times. Fundamental differences that we don't really understand make us fearful and insecure around the nonChristian. Because we feel such a distance between "us and them," we carry on as if such people didn't exist. Efforts at evangelism are often either an unannounced assault on a stranger, or little more than being nice to someone.

WHERE IS OUR OFFENSE?

Christian leaders and writers are addressing the fact of secularization. Indeed, it is difficult to pick up a Christian magazine that does not contain some reference to secularization and its effects. The problem is that, almost without exception, the objective of such articles is to make us aware of threats against our religious liberties and human rights.

As secularization moves our society away from theistic religion, humanism—faith in man himself—rushes in to fill the vacuum, undermining Christian ethics and values. Thus, *humanism* has become a household word among Christians. It is understood as being the foremost philosophical alternative to Christianity, the great contemporary enemy.

I would agree that this threat is real, and that we are indebted to those who are alerting us to the encroachments of secularization and its consequences. But it seems to me that something is missing in much of what is being said. We are skilled at spelling out the distance between the positions. We are clear in our warnings and counsel related to endangered rights and freedoms on private and political levels. In short, we are building a great defense. But *where is our offense?*

We are not dealing merely with ideas and philosophies; we are dealing with *people*. Ideas find their existence only in people's minds. In the zeal of our battle against ideas, we Christians often confuse matters by placing ourselves in a position of war against those who hold to those ideas. But we must always remember that we are sent to such people.

A similar situation apparently existed in the first century between the Christians and the Jews. Michael Green points out that Christianity was not distinct from Jewish culture for at least a couple of decades after Jesus' resurrection. Jewish Christians had no thought of separating themselves from the rest of Israel. The Messiah had come! They hoped Israel would come to share this conviction about Jesus. Although the seeds of division were there from the beginning, the Christians of the first century still held on to the hope of winning Israel.

Green observes, "Though violent at times, the Christian approach was inflamed by love . . . and longing to see [Israel] acknowledging their Messiah. But successive turning points . . . changed [this attitude] to one of hatred and antipathy. It was no longer evangelism among the Jews but apologetic against the Jews which interested Christians."[24]

We Christians are running the risk of falling short of the grace of God in the same way today. This book is written with the prayer that we will look upon the people of our time as Christ does—with compassion on those who are "harassed and helpless, like sheep without a shepherd" (Matthew 9:36). Although it may be necessary to understand the distances between the secular and the Christian positions, our main concern is with building bridges.

NOTES:

1. Jeremy Rifkin with Ted Howard, *The Emerging Order* (New York: G.P. Putnam's Sons, 1979), page 95.
2. John Naisbitt, *Megatrends* (New York: Warner Books, 1982), page 240.
3. Rifkin, page 99.
4. Rifkin, pages 99, 101, 105, 112.
5. Rifkin, page 96.
6. Kenneth Kantzer, "Evangelicalism: Mid-Course Self-Appraisal," *Christianity Today* (January 7, 1983), page 11.
7. Rifkin, page 129.
8. Rifkin, page 126.
9. Christopher Lasch, *The Culture of Narcissism* (New York: W.W. Norton & Co., Inc., 1979), page xxv.
10. Lasch, page xxiv.
11. Lasch, page 3.
12. Lasch, pages 5, 4.
13. Allan Bloom, *The Closing of the American Mind* (New York: Simon and Schuster, 1987), page 25.
14. Bloom, page 34.
15. Bloom, page 54.
16. Bloom, page 58.
17. Wanda Urbanska, *The Singular Generation* (New York: Doubleday, 1986), page xl.
18. Os Guinness, *The Gravedigger File* (London: Hodder and Stoughton, 1983), pages 52-53.
19. Herbert Schlossberg, *Idols of Destruction* (Nashville: Thomas Nelson Publishers, 1983), page 3.
20. Gert Doornenbal, "Knowing the People of Our Time" (January 1982), page 2.
21. Rinus Baljeu, "Evangelism: Secularization and The Navigators" (August 1982), page 1.
22. John Mulholland and Gary Pryke, "Secularization and Student Evangelism," Reading, Great Britain (September 1983), page 9.
23. Baljeu, page 3.
24. Michael Green, *Evangelism in the Early Church* (Grand Rapids: Eerdmans, 1970), page 105.

TWO

UNDERSTANDING THE PEOPLE OF OUR GENERATION

Creatures in Rebellion

WHENEVER A CULTURAL shift takes place, we know that on the practical level people are changing. For Christians who make up the countercurrent and are not caught up in the change, this can be unsettling. We find ourselves surrounded by people we really do not understand. Our most common response is to ignore or deny the reality of these cultural differences. "After all," we reason, "people are people, and the gospel is the gospel." But effective communication presupposes an understanding between communicator and receiver. And when we make little effort to truly understand, we lose communication.

What are the people of our generation really like? What makes them different from the people of previous generations? In what ways are they different from their Christian contemporaries? How are they similar?

There are three primary factors in man's make-up that determine the answers to these questions. Two of them are constant; they have not altered since the beginning of human history. The third differentiates the people of one generation or culture from another. In one sense it is correct to say that "man is man" the world over. There is a sameness about man wherever and under whatever circumstances he is found. But those who call our attention to the differences between generations and peoples are closer to the whole truth. There are profound differences that categorically separate one people from another.

We need to understand these three characteristics in their proper relationship if we are to communicate effectively beyond the perimeters of our own sub-groups. The three primary factors are:

1. Man is created in God's image.
2. Man is fallen.
3. Man is influenced by his society.

MAN IS CREATED IN GOD'S IMAGE.

Then God said, "Let us make man in our image, in our likeness. . . ."
So God created man in his own image, in the image of God he
created him; male and female he created them. (Genesis 1:26-27)

When God created man, he made him in the likeness of God. He
created them male and female and blessed them. And when they
were created, he called them "man." . . . [Adam] had a son in his
own likeness, in his own image; and he named him Seth. (Genesis
5:1-3)

"In [God] we live and move and have our being." As some of your
own poets have said, "We are his offspring."
    Therefore since we are God's offspring, we should not think
that the divine being is like . . . an image made by man's design and
skill. (Acts 17:28-29)

These are the three principal passages in the Bible about man being
made *in God's image.* What does being made in His image really mean?
Perhaps someone somewhere is satisfied that he has plumbed the depths
of this concept, but I feel that I am still on the surface of it.
    We can make a few fragmentary observations based on the above and
related passages: Man is unique and significant. He bears certain resem-
blances to the God who created him.
    Then we can go on to speculate on the specifics of those resem-
blances: God is a person, possessing the ability to plan, decide, and act. He
has personality, with specific attitudes like love and hate. He communicates, and He exercises creativity and headship.
    Being created in the image of God differentiates man from the rest of
creation. It makes him conscious of his own uniqueness. Man understands
that God has made him different from the rest of the universe. He can
relate to God in a way no other part of creation can. Since God is personal,
and since man is in His image, the nature of this relationship is also
personal. But I suspect the significance of this truth goes much deeper.
    In his last major work before his death, historian Arnold Toynbee
made some observations about man's uniqueness that help broaden the
horizons of our considerations. His observations are especially interesting

because they were made from an avowed nonChristian position. He prefaced his comments with the statement, "It is now hardly possible any longer to believe that the phenomena of which a human being is conscious have been called into existence by the fiat of a human-like creator god."[1]

With this statement Toynbee dismissed Christianity as an invalid source of insight. Consequently, he arrived at his conclusions by observing and contemplating man and life, without reference to God or God's revelation. Then he continued, "But, so far, this no longer tenable traditional hypothesis [of a creator god] has not been replaced by any convincing alternative. . . . The increase in our knowledge . . . has not brought with it an understanding of the nature or the purpose (if there is a purpose) of life and consciousness themselves."[2]

As Toynbee discarded the idea of a Creator God and also the Darwinian thesis, he spelled out the dimensions of the human dilemma: "Every live human being . . . is a conscious purposeful spirit that is physically alive in a material body. None of these components [a conscious spirit and a material body] have ever been encountered apart from the rest. They are always found in association with each other; yet their relation to each other is incomprehensible."[3]

Then Toynbee wondered at the "possession of consciousness and . . . the ability to make plans," and at the ability of human beings to deliberately choose. He asked, "What is the source of these ethical judgments, which apparently are intrinsic to human nature but are foreign to the nature of non-human species? . . . What is the situation and the significance in the Universe of a conscious, purposeful human being, imbued with this sense of the distinction between right and wrong and impelled . . . to do what seems to him to be right? A human being feels as if he is the center of the Universe because his own consciousness is, for him, the point from which he views the . . . panorama. . . . [Yet] his conscience . . . tells him that, in so far as he gives way to his self-centeredness, he is putting himself morally, as well as intellectually, in the wrong."[4]

Probably all of these very perceptive observations on the uniqueness of man-nature find their explanation in these three words: "in God's image." For, whatever else it means, it at least tells us that man is inescapably self-conscious and inescapably God-conscious. There is something there within man that keeps him struggling with the riddle of his own consciousness—until he acknowledges God.

Recently I led an open-to-all evangelistic Bible study with some university students. When it came time for questions, one student, in all seriousness, asked, "Could someone explain to me why I am here in this room? I have never been interested in these things, yet here I am. What is it that compels me to search? Why can't I be content to live without questioning?"

Man is created in God's image; therefore, he has a natural receptivity to spiritual truth. All evangelism is predicated on this fact.

MAN IS FALLEN.

Three calamities overtook man when he fell: (1) he came to know good and evil; (2) his life became futile; and (3) he died. It is hard to tell which calamity is the most painful to live with.

Man knows good and evil. The serpent said to Eve, "God knows that when you eat of [the tree] your eyes will be opened, and you will be like God, knowing good and evil" (Genesis 3:5). Satan didn't lie when he made this statement. Indeed, the tree was called the tree of the knowledge of good and evil, and when Adam and Eve ate the fruit from it, God said, "The man has now become like one of us, knowing good and evil" (verse 22).

So when man followed the advice of Satan, he gained powers he previously did not possess. What Satan didn't tell him was that he was not equipped to live with this knowledge. Man's first insight from his newly claimed powers was the fact that he was naked. Self-centeredness had been born. Man could no longer look at his mate with the same selfless acceptance he had always had before. Both man and woman, self-conscious in their newborn attitudes toward one another, hastened to cover their bodies.

Self-centeredness gave birth to guilt, and this guilt estranged man from himself, from others, and from God. When God called to Adam and Eve after they had sinned, Adam replied, "I heard you . . . and I was afraid because I was naked; so I hid" (verse 10). Guilt alienates. "I was afraid." Adam was the first neurotic.

As children of Adam, we continue to bear the burden of our knowledge of good and evil. "The requirements of the law are written on their hearts, their consciences also bearing witness . . . accusing . . . defending" (Romans 2:15). Here is another characteristic we can count on being present in the hearts of those to whom we are sent. Because man knows right from wrong, his conscience prods him incessantly with feelings of guilt.

Man experiences futility. Another effect of the fall is man's sense of futility. God said, "Cursed is the ground because of you; through painful toil you will eat of it all the days of your life. It will produce thorns and thistles for you. . . . By the sweat of your brow you will eat your food until you return to the ground" (Genesis 3:17-19). In other words, life is a struggle—a rather pointless struggle. We expend our lives just managing to exist. Then it is back to dust.

The things we plan and look forward to with anticipation never quite measure up to our expectations. They keep coming up "thorns and this-tles." We marry the person of our dreams, then the marriage falls apart. We look forward to having children, then they break our hearts. We sacrifice and study to become established in a profession, then we discover our work to be tedious. So we look forward to retirement. And on and on it goes.

Due to the Fall, life is a struggle against desperation. Probably all of us can identify to some degree with the words of the first existentialist to go on record: "What does a man get for all the toil and anxious striving with which he labors under the sun? All his days his work is pain and grief; even at night his mind does not rest. This too is meaningless" (Ecclesiastes 2:22-23).

Has a person ever lived who has not stopped to ask the existential question, "Why am I doing all this?" only to carry on with the question unanswered and the course of his life unaltered?

This struggle against futility is something God brought upon man. Consequently, it must have a positive function within God's purposes. God expelled man from paradise and plunged him into this struggle, not out of a desire for revenge but out of love. In paradise there is no pain. Those feelings of futility are a gift from God. Without them, who would seek reconciliation? This, too, works toward the progress of the gospel in people's hearts.

Man experiences death. Man's persistence to survive, his perseverance in the face of the absurdity of it all, is another part of the riddle of man. The first clues to this phenomenon are also found in man's fall.

At the Fall, man died. He died in every sense of the word. He died in his relationship to God, in his relationship to his fellow man, and in his relationship to himself. Spiritually, it was sudden death. His physical death was slower. We spend years dying. Guilt eats away at our health. The psalmist laments, "There is no health in my body; my bones have no soundness because of my sin. My guilt has overwhelmed me like a burden too heavy to bear" (Psalm 38:3-4).

Why does man resist death the way he does? Why is he so obsessively fearful of it? The Bible says that Satan holds the power of death and that man is held in slavery by his fear of death (Hebrews 2:14-15). Death is perceived as an enemy that man will do anything to fight off to preserve his futile existence. Why?

I think it is because man instinctively subscribes to his own unique-ness. Although he may consciously disclaim beliefs to this effect, he is normally unwilling to give up on life until he has done his best to live out this uniqueness. He just cannot make peace with the idea that seventy years is all there is.

God has "set eternity in the hearts of men; yet they cannot fathom what God has done from beginning to end" (Ecclesiastes 3:11). So there lies within man a drive for immortality. This drive is often expressed in bizarre ways. The Egyptian Pharaohs devoted their lives to building their own tombs. This drive is another characteristic that people hold in com-mon, a drive that makes them susceptible to spiritual things.

We observed earlier that communication must begin from a common ground—something the communicator and the receiver mutually under-stand. Human beings by nature hold a number of characteristics in com-mon. The individual person knows that he is unique, that he is restless, and that he cannot accept the fact of his own mortality. This is man—as he has always been and as he will always be. Times and cultures cannot eliminate these primal drives.

So there does exist a positive common ground. We *can* communicate spiritual truth. Man *can* understand and respond because God has sown certain things in his heart. I think this is what the Apostle John was describing when he said that Jesus was "the true light that gives light to every man" (John 1:9).

MAN IS INFLUENCED BY HIS SOCIETY.

There is a third major factor that affects the make-up of the people of our times. Rather than unifying, however, this factor differentiates and sepa-rates people into cultures and even generations. It is the factor of *environment.*

The Old Testament warnings to Israel upon entering the land of Canaan attest to the reality of this factor. "You must not do as they do in Egypt, where you used to live, and you must not do as they do in the land of Canaan, where I am bringing you" (Leviticus 18:3).

In the same vein, Paul warns Christians in his letter to the Romans, "Do not conform any longer to the pattern of this world" (Romans 12:2).

Man is highly susceptible to being conditioned by whatever society he happens to be a part of—inescapably so. Countless studies have been made and volumes have been written in the field of psychology on environmental influences. It would be beside the point for us to develop a long discussion on the subject here. Rather, let's begin with the assumption that man is influenced by his environment and that this influence is fundamental to the shaping of a person's ethics, values, and world view.

The clearest illustrations of this assumption are found in the differences that exist between peoples of different cultures. Anthropologist Edward Hall observes, "Any Westerner who was raised outside the Far East and claims he really understands and can communicate with either the Chinese or the Japanese is deluding himself."[5] The differences wrought by environment are real and cannot be ignored if understanding is to exist.

It is intriguing that people are so susceptible to being conditioned by their society. True, most of the process is subliminal, but this tremendous susceptibility raises a question. What is it about man that allows him to blindly embrace the values and characteristics of those that surround him, even when those values are obviously irrational and destructive? Can this not be traced back to man's fallen nature? In Romans 1, we are told that when men cut themselves loose from God to strike out on their own, they lose the ability to reason properly. "Although they knew God, they neither glorified him as God nor gave thanks to him, but their thinking became futile and their foolish hearts were darkened. Although they claimed to be wise, they became fools" (1:21-22).

Man's mind is a good tool for small projects but is often inadequate for large-scale matters. Man is a subjective creature. Consequently, his beliefs and values are, in the main, acquired on the subconscious level.

The important point here is that man tends to unquestioningly embrace the prevailing values of his generation. Although we are inescapably children of our times, often the values of the times are radically different from biblical values. The commonalities that bond us together as human beings are so deeply buried that they are almost invisible.

In 1979, a study was done among teenagers in Sweden, who were asked to respond to the statement, "I think the following could give my life more meaning. . . ." Of those surveyed, eighty-seven percent thought that meaning could be found in a good job, eighty-five percent thought it could be found in a marriage partner, and eighty-four percent thought it could be found in sports and recreation. Only fifteen percent thought that reading the Bible and prayer could help, and another fifteen percent indicated that they thought alcohol could help.

About eighty percent considered the question of the meaning of life important, yet eighty percent considered it unimportant whether Jesus existed as a man on earth or not. Also, eighty-five percent considered it unimportant whether Jesus is the Son of God or not. A full seventy-five percent concluded that the question of God's existence is unimportant.[6]

My experience indicates that this survey is representative of the prevailing values of our times. Because there are similar tendenc throughout Western Europe and many parts of the United States, it appears that this generation is giving up on traditional religious explanations. Although the question of the meaning of life is considered important, people are basically unconcerned about the existence of either God or Jesus. Jesus, whoever He was, is now considered irrelevant. Self-satisfaction and immediate concerns—job, girlfriend or boyfriend, and perhaps skiing—are the important things. Although this tendency is taking place in the mainstream of our society, it is often unobserved by people who are thoroughly immersed in the Christian counterculture without close relationships with people of this generation.

AN EXERCISE IN EMPATHY

Let's imagine for a moment that we have just described you! You, as a child of the times, have given up on looking for religious answers to life. It just doesn't occur to you to think about God or Jesus Christ. You see them as part of the rubble of the crumbled institutions of previous generations. Life is important to you, but you have concluded that there is only seventy years of it and nothing beyond.

The years have gone by. Today is your fortieth birthday. That in itself represents a major crisis. You are no longer "in your thirties"—you are *forty*! Life is important to you. Since seventy years is all you have, you realize that sixty percent of your life is gone. It's time to reevaluate things.

You look in the mirror and, sure enough, you're slipping. The hairline, the extra pounds, the little creases that promise wrinkles to come. Your two children are teenagers who have clearly communicated that they feel parents are an unnecessary complication in their lives. Your career is set. You know you will never be very rich, very famous, or very influential.

Now you have just gotten up in the morning and these are the first thoughts running through your mind. How are you going to react? You'll think, "Life is getting away from me! I've got to make the most of it—enjoy more. That's it!"

But how are you going to do that? How will this resolution make this any different? Within your existential frame of reference, what is important? What is there to look forward to, to give yourself to? Not much. Perhaps a good cup of coffee, a walk in the park, or an extramarital —whatever feels good to the senses. But whatever you do, it will be accompanied by a sense of loss when you realize that another day is gone.

This little scenario highlights the practical difference between the Christian and the nonChristian. The difference is one of *hope*. Ephesians says, "You were separate from Christ . . . without hope and without God in the world."

The Christian and the nonChristian function according to two different value systems. The scope of the life view of the Christian embraces eternity, while the nonChristian lives merely for his seventy years. The enormous distance between these two perspectives results in differences of equal magnitude in the things to which we attach value in our everyday lives.

Projecting yourself one more time into our scenario, one question remains: What do you think it would take to awaken your interest in the Christian message, to induce you to go back and examine it, having already discarded it as an unimportant relic? What would it take for a ray of hope to penetrate the accumulated layers of disenchantment?

NOTES:
1. Arnold Toynbee, *Mankind and Mother Earth* (Paladin, Great Britain: Granada Publishing, 1978), page 2.
2. Toynbee, page 2.
3. Toynbee, page 2.
4. Toynbee, page 3.
5. Edward Hall, *Beyond Culture* (Garden City, N.Y.: Anchor Press, Doubleday, 1976), page 2.
6. Rinus Baljeu, "Evangelism: Secularization and The Navigators" (August 1982), Appendix: Diagrams 6 and 7.

THREE

JESUS AND THE PEOPLE OF HIS GENERATION

Jesus Was the Message

CONTEMPORARY MAN IS remarkably blind, irrational, and highly susceptible to the conditioning of his culture. The institutions of his society are deliberately influencing him to conclude that theistic religious belief is superstition; that liberation and integrity lie in acknowledging the relative nature of truth; that it is somehow noble to live with the ensuing struggle against futility.

How do we as Christians, carrying the truth of the gospel in our hearts, respond to this adverse indoctrination? It is so easy to become intimidated, to feel incompetent in the face of the disparity between the Christian and secular positions. Who, we ask, is competent to mount a counterattack? There may be an unusual person here and there who is equal to the challenge, but we are quite sure that it is not us.

So the temptation to give up, to direct our efforts toward those with whom we feel more comfortable, is almost overwhelming. But we are mistaken. It is not that difficult. It is within the capacity of the average Christian to be effective among the people of this generation. Because we are sent to *every* creature, we can hardly conclude that the mainstream of our society is out of reach!

THERE IS ONLY ONE ISSUE

The Apostle John began his Gospel by describing Jesus as the light of the world. The theme of light and darkness runs throughout the entire book. Such a theme is worthy of our scrutiny because it is the biblical response to

39

the problems of man we have just addressed.

Jesus stated clearly that He is the light that man needs: "I have come into the world as a light, so that no one who believes in me should stay in darkness" (John 12:46).

Now this is good news for darkened minds! And this is *our* message, too. It is the only message we have, because He is the only true light. Our singular objective must be to communicate Jesus Christ.

You may feel that this is a lot easier said than done. Did we not just recognize that those we seek to win don't even care if Jesus existed or if He was who He claimed to be? Since they don't care, how can we expect a response when we approach them with the news that Jesus is the light of the world?

But the fact remains, He *is* the light; there isn't any other. If any ray of hope is to penetrate the thinking of this generation, it is going to be this ray. Impossible? Jesus faced a similar situation. Let's take a close look at the basis of Jesus' communication with the people of His generation.

JESUS, THE UNIVERSAL TRUTH

The people in Jesus' life can be divided into four categories: the multitudes, His enemies, His disciples, and the Twelve. There is one theme that remains constant in His communication with each of these four groups. Because of this consistency and because of the nature of this theme, we can conclude that we are dealing with a universal truth. It is timeless in its significance and in its effectiveness.

This universal truth, when given its proper prominence and offered without adulteration, penetrates to the core, for it appeals to the essential and unchanging nature of man. As it unfolds, even those we regard as the least likely often begin to respond to God's call to enter His Kingdom.

Jesus and His opponents. What was the root issue that put Jesus' adversaries into conflict with Him? Jesus identified it in John 8:23-25: "You are from below; I am from above. You are of this world; I am not of this world. . . . If you do not believe that I am the one I claim to be, you will indeed die in your sins."

"Who are you?" they asked. That is the question! The essential issue of every relationship in Jesus' life dealt with the question of His identity. It is still the foremost question. *Who is Jesus?*

When a mortal man claims he is deity, honest intellectual questions are certainly in order! Jesus clearly claimed to be God, but the fascinating thing about the dialogues between Jesus and His accusers was that the debate never centered on the intellectual tenability of that claim. Almost without exception, the thrust of the dialogue was a focus on the overly subjective nature of their resistance against Him.

Obstacles to faith—Jesus encountered many people who were unwilling to follow Him because of certain areas of resistance in their lives. Those who try to evangelize others still encounter these obstacles to faith.

1. *Public opinion*—On one occasion, Jesus asked the Jews who opposed Him, "How can you believe if you accept praise from one another?" (John 5:44). He was attempting to show them that it was their *concern for their own social status* that was barring the way.

2. *Misinformation*—On another occasion a discussion broke out among the people surrounding Jesus over this issue of His identity (John 7:40-42). "Some of the people said, 'Surely this man is the Prophet.' Others said, 'He is the Christ.' Still others asked, 'How can the Christ come from Galilee? Does not the Scripture say that the Christ will come from David's family and from Bethlehem . . . ?'"

In this case the obstacle was *misinformation*. The things people thought they knew—casually formed, preconceived notions—got in the way of true understanding.

3. *Self-sufficiency*—Later, Jesus was conversing with a man He had just healed who had been blind from birth (John 9:35-41). The subject was the same! "Do you believe in the Son of Man?" Jesus asked.

"Who is he, sir?" asked the blind man. Jesus said, "He is the one speaking with you." Then the man acknowledged his faith in Jesus.

With that, Jesus addressed the crowd: "For judgment I have come into this world, so that the blind will see and those who see will become blind." The Pharisees in the crowd got the point and asked, "What? Are we blind too?" Jesus replied that they were, in fact, blind. Because they insisted that they could see, they were blind to their own spiritual blindness.

In this situation the obstacle was *man's excessive faith in himself*. These presumptuous Pharisees felt they had it within themselves to work their way spiritually through life on their own.

Again, the barrier was not due to lack of knowledge; it was due to an excess of subjectivity.

4. *Concern for position*—Irrationality growing out of a subjectivity apparently knows no limits. The case of Lazarus demonstrates this fact clearly (John 11:1-12:11). As in almost every other situation, Jesus used a crisis to focus on the critical issue of His identity.

Imagine the scene: Lazarus is dead. We spent all night at the wake. Then Jesus appears. By now He is exceedingly famous for His sayings and His miracles. But here is a miracle unlike any other—He raises Lazarus from the dead! How do you react to this? Did the observers conclude that Jesus is God as He claimed?

Amazingly, the reaction of some is, "If we let him go on like this, everyone will believe in him." So what's wrong with that? "Then the Romans will come and take away both our place and our nation" (11:48). *Position, prestige, the status quo—all take priority over truth in the value system of most people.*

So how did those who opposed Jesus handle truth? They tried to eliminate it! The Sanhedrin passed the death sentence on Jesus and, furthermore, "the chief priests made plans to kill Lazarus as well" (12:10). Irrational men! If they can't refute the evidence, they destroy it!

5. *Rebellion*—Finally, it was this issue of Jesus' identity that cost Him His life (Matthew 26:63-68). At His trial, "The high priest said to him, 'I charge you under oath by the living God: Tell us if you are the Christ, the Son of God.' 'Yes, it is as you say,' Jesus replied." With that they declared Him worthy of death.

There is a demanding logic that leads to this irrational rejection of Jesus' claim to deity: To acknowledge that Jesus is God is to acknowledge His authority, and to acknowledge His authority is to acknowledge His right to authority over me. *Rebellion* is the fundamental problem of mankind from the time of the Fall. To concede to His deity without submitting to His authority is to acknowledge that rebellion. This is a very difficult concession for any individual to make. In the final analysis, rebellion is always the real issue.

Jesus and the multitudes. On the surface, the response of the multitudes to Jesus was almost the opposite from that of His religious enemies. The multitudes liked Jesus. They followed Him everywhere He went. They were much like the religious people of our day. To them, it was important to have a faith. It gives structure to life, and, besides, children need to be raised with some solid moral principles. But often their true response was identical to the response of those who were openly opposed to Him.

Two things attracted the multitudes to Jesus: (1) They were amazed at His teaching, "because he taught them as one who had authority, not as the teachers of the law"; and (2) they were amazed at His power: "He even gives orders to evil spirits and they obey him" (Mark 1:22,27). It was exciting to be around Jesus! They enjoyed listening to and watching Him, and they anticipated benefiting from His powers.

Jesus' popularity grew to the extent that on certain occasions "so many gathered that there was no room left, not even outside the door. . . . A crowd gathered, so that he and his disciples were not even able to eat" (Mark 2:2, 3:20-21). Jesus' family became so concerned for Him that they felt compelled "to take charge of him." They thought He had gone out of His mind!

Jesus was famous. He by far eclipsed John the Baptist. Everyone was euphoric about Him—*the multitudes*, who enjoyed everything about Jesus, and *the twelve disciples*, who basked in the reflection of His popularity. But Jesus was not impressed. In fact, He eventually put an end to it all.

On one occasion, Jesus confronted those who were following Him with the fact that He was dissatisfied with their response to Him. He said, "You are looking for me . . . because you ate the loaves and had your fill. Do not work for food that spoils, but for food that endures to eternal life." They asked, "What must we do to do the works God requires?" Jesus answered, "The work of God is this: to believe in the one he has sent" (John 6:26-29).

Again the issue was that of His identity. Jesus was essentially saying, "You are following Me for pragmatic reasons, but that is not good enough. If you are going to follow Me, it must be on My terms—and those terms are to accept Me as God!"

The people understood what He was saying, but they revealed their unbelief with their response, "What miraculous sign then will you give that we may see it and believe you? What will you do?" (6:30).

Unbelievable! They had seen Him cast out demons, heal the sick, and feed the multitudes. They had marveled at His teachings. They could accept Him as a great teacher, as a miracle worker, as a prophet, or as a political leader, but to accept Him as God was just asking too much!

Jesus, knowing this, sent them on their way with a few incisive, difficult statements about Himself: "I am the bread of life. . . . I have come down from heaven. . . . This bread is my flesh. . . . Unless you eat the flesh of the Son of Man and drink his blood, you have no life in you" (John 6:35,38,51,53).

The multitude reacted immediately. The people grumbled among themselves. They argued, they complained, and they were offended. "From this time many of his disciples turned back and no longer followed him" (6:66).

At any given point in this discussion, Jesus could have eased up, but He knew what He was doing. He was deliberately dividing the people with this issue of His identity. In essence, He was saying, "Either believe that I am who I am, accepting all the implications, or go back to your homes! Stop deluding yourselves by following Me around!"

Why was it so hard for the people to accept those conditions? They seemed to be coming along so well! But it was here that they revealed how very similar they were to those who were Jesus' openly avowed enemies. Why is it so hard to acknowledge Jesus' identity? It is because we can't both be in control. There can only be one king! It is so hard to give up our ill-fitting sovereignty.

Jesus and His disciples. This same thread—Jesus' identity—runs through everything He taught His disciples. In fact, Jesus apparently reserved most of His teachings of any significance for those of His followers who committed themselves to the truth of His identity. He spoke in parables and in enigmatic terms to the multitudes. It is clear that they understood very little. Jesus said to His disciples, "The secret of the kingdom of God has been given to you. But to those on the outside everything is said in parables so that, 'they may be ever seeing but never perceiving'" (Mark 4:11-12).

What was happening here? Was Jesus deliberately withholding truth from hungry people? Not at all! The Bible goes on to explain, "With many similar parables Jesus spoke the word to them, *as much as they could understand.* He did not say anything to them [the multitudes] without using a parable. But when he was alone with his own disciples, he explained everything" (Mark 4:33-34, emphasis added).

Jesus taught the multitudes all He could, which wasn't much because they had rejected His divine identity, the very basis of truth. Until we embrace the foremost premise of Jesus' teachings—that He is God—none of the rest is going to make much sense.

Jesus broadened the disciples' understanding of the dimensions of His authority. His authority, too, is rooted in His identity—who He is. Jesus displayed His authority over human authorities (Mark 1:22), over Satan (Mark 1:27), over sin (Mark 2:9), over tradition (Mark 2:27-28), over creation (Mark 4:39), and even over life and death (John 10:18, 19:10-11). In short, His response to His disciples over that question "Who am I?" was essentially "I am authority over everything in heaven and on earth."

A true disciple understands the dimensions of Christ's authority and brings his life step by step under that authority. As he does this, something miraculous takes place. His bondage is replaced by freedom (John 8:31-32). He overcomes the world. This is a critical truth. Jesus says to everyone, "What is your problem? Whatever it is, give it to Me, because I have destroyed the power of that particular problem. I have authority over that one. Leave it with Me. I will resolve it and you can go free."

Making disciples is helping someone else experience and understand the dynamics of Christ's authority so that he, too, can go free. Here again, Jesus' identity is the determinative issue. For Jesus' opponents and for the multitudes who followed Him, the question of His identity determined life and death. For His disciples it determined freedom and bondage. But what about the twelve men who stayed close to Him for three years?

Jesus and the Twelve. In the training of the Twelve, Jesus carried the issue of His identity to its ultimate implications. That this issue was, in fact, central to everything He did with the Twelve is demonstrated in His prayer to the Father in John 17.

He began this prayer by underscoring the centrality of His identity to His entire ministry. "Now this is eternal life: that they [all believers] may know you [the Father], the only true God, and Jesus Christ, whom you have sent" (17:3).

Then He went on to intercede for the Twelve. "I have revealed you to those whom you gave me out of the world. . . . They knew with certainty that I came from you, and they believed that you sent me" (17:6-8). The training of the Twelve consisted of bringing those men into a firsthand acquaintance with God and into a comprehension that Jesus and the Father are one and the same God! Jesus said, "If you really knew me, you would know my Father as well. From now on, you do know him and have seen him. . . . Anyone who has seen me has seen the Father" (John 14:7,9).

Jesus spent most of His short time of ministry communicating this single fact to His small handful of men: He and His Father are one. To grasp the implications of what this unity means is to understand the basis of all spiritual power (John 14:20). As Jesus said, "Apart from me you can do nothing. . . . [But with me you] will do even greater things than [my miracles], because I am going to the Father" (John 15:5, 14:12).

If Jesus had not left behind Him men who were gripped by this understanding of His identity, there would have been no future for the Christian movement. Jesus said, "All authority in heaven and on earth has been given to me. *Therefore* go and make disciples of all nations" (Matthew 28:18-19, emphasis added). A full comprehension and acceptance of Jesus' identity makes us full participants of His power. The Great Commission would have been a fool's errand with anything less.

The continuity of this theme of Jesus' identity as it runs through all His relationships demonstrates that it is an issue of ultimate importance! Every other theme is subordinate to this one. *He* is the gospel. *He* is our message. Everything else we Christians believe and hold dear is an outworking of this one truth. If we are to be effective among the people of this generation, our own understanding of Christ—the implications of His identity, His death and His resurrection—must be dynamic and growing.

FOUR

THE MESSAGE FOR OUR GENERATION

The Issue of His Identity

JESUS MUST BE the substance of our evangelism. Since He considered it vitally important to concentrate on the fact and implications of His Divine identity, we would be well advised to put forth the same emphasis. In this chapter we will look at some of the ways in which we unwittingly blur the focus on Christ.

THE GOSPEL OF POPULAR ISSUES

What is the gospel? This is a question theologians and Christian leaders love to ask. When they pose it, the implication is usually that no one within earshot has the faintest notion of the answer. I usually come away from such dialogues with feelings of frustration.

And yet I've observed something quite significant in these discussions. Almost always when this question of the gospel is posed, the questioner has an ulterior motive. He really wants to make us guess what *his* particular gospel happens to be. It is the gospel—plus his emphasis! For example, one of the big issues today is social justice. So the gospel according to one questioner might be a gospel of social justice. For another, it might be a gospel of prosperity. For another, it might be a gospel of civil rights.

The process is simple. We focus on an issue that so impresses us that it looms in our minds as *the* issue of utmost importance. Then we proceed to make that issue or truth an essential part of our message. When we do that, we create a partisan gospel. We use Jesus to support our private cause. He

47

becomes the Jesus of the poor, or the Jesus of women's rights, or the Jesus of whatever other issue happens to be front page at the moment. But a partisan Jesus cannot also be a universal Jesus.

THE GOSPEL OF OUR PERSONAL EMPHASIS

Most of us emphasize certain doctrines far more than others. We favor certain forms of expressing our faith because they are so natural to us that we can't envision a Christian functioning without them. Often we consider certain behavior to be normative and essential. Our strong feelings prompt us to elevate or emphasize these ideas to the point where they become requirements for anyone we minister to.

This tendency restricts the gospel. We need to be careful of our religious traditions, our forms of worship, our personal doctrinal emphases, or our persuasions concerning Christian conduct—anything that is not in balance with the whole of Scripture. If we are not in balance, then we offer a Jesus who is identified with things that may be important to us but are a stumbling block to those we seek to win. They won't take Him because of the wrappings.

THE GOSPEL AND OUR ECCLESIASTICAL SYSTEMS

Which Jesus Christ are the Swedish youth rejecting? The Christ of the Reformation, of the Free Church, or of the Roman Catholic Church? Almost certainly it is one of these, but probably not the *real* Christ. In the reality of His fullness, Jesus cannot be confined to any system. Did He become a Protestant with the Reformation? Was He ever a Roman Catholic? Rather, He stands above our ecclesiastical structures and our theological systems. He is the gospel focus of all time, for all peoples. When we identify Him with our particular ecclesiastical persuasion, we isolate Him in a limited sphere. In the process, we exclude much of the rest of the world.

I once spent several days teaching the Bible to some Christian friends who were living in Communist bloc countries. These Christian brothers had spent the previous thirty-five years concentrating on survival. Preservation had taken priority over outreach, and understandably so. In this situation the Church moves toward isolationism because it is deemed necessary for survival. Legalism is almost inevitable under such circumstances. Because many Christians in communist countries have begun to realize that this process of excessive narrowness has occurred, they are now taking steps to strike a better balance.

As I read Scriptures concerning the freedom we have in Christ, one woman burst out, "If this is true, then there is hope for my parents! They can be won! Until now I thought they could come to Christ only if they would join the Baptist Church!"

A Baptist Jesus!

THE GOSPEL OF THE CHRISTIAN CONTRACT

Possibly the most common weakness in our contemporary approaches to evangelism is our tendency to focus our message on the Christian contract—how to transact a relationship with God—rather than on the person of Jesus Christ. We become so intent on helping someone understand how to put his faith in Christ that we overlook the very real probability that he is almost devoid of knowledge of Christ.

It is *far wiser to focus on Jesus Christ than on the contract.* Instead of telling people what they need to do, we want to bring them into an understanding of who Jesus is. As this understanding grows, the response—what the person needs to do—becomes self-evident. I have found that, more often than not, when the truth about Christ is fully understood, the response occurs without my help.

This preoccupation with the contract rather than with the person of Christ creates another weakness in our evangelism. We tend to become more interested in responses than in *understanding.* We strive to elicit agreement, and once it is achieved we seek to extract a positive response. We call this "making a decision." This is the forced contract.

Too often this kind of contract is little more than leading a person to verbalize certain phrases that we suggest to him. Once he makes the right sounds, we think he is "saved."

THE GOSPEL OF JESUS CHRIST

The gospel *is* Jesus Christ, who died, was buried, and then rose again and ascended to the Father. He is nonpartisan, standing above our human structures and our secondary issues. If we expect to communicate with the people of this generation, we must allow Jesus His rightful universality. We must offer an unencumbered Christ.

Twenty-five years ago we were beginning our ministry in Brazil. We found ourselves in circumstances that led us to challenge many convictions we had previously embraced without reservation. The students with whom we were working were not responsive to the gospel we were preaching. The barriers were the result of some of the secondary elements we had added to the gospel, plus the fact that we represented something institutional and foreign to them. We weren't presenting an unadorned Jesus.

In this context, we began to understand that our gospel message should be Jesus, and nothing else. We are not sent to defend or promote economic or political systems, religious structures, our own organization, or any of the personal emphases we have described. Our message is that of a Person, and we are not free to represent Him with encumbrances. We realized that we are called to impose no human standards, to honor no traditions. We are called to proclaim Jesus, no strings attached.

When we got that clear, we quickly discovered that we had positive communication with the same kind of people who had previously been keeping us at arm's length. We began to reap a harvest that continues to this day.

This approach to the gospel is so basic and simple. Who is Jesus? Take a look for yourself. If you don't believe, we understand that. But let's go to the Bible with this single question in order to research the answer. You don't accept the Bible? We understand that, too. We begin on this basis— and count on Christ's superiority to accomplish the rest.

TRUST IN THE SUPERIORITY OF CHRIST

Francisco is one of my dearest friends. When we met a few years ago, he was an agnostic emerging from years of Marxism. He had probably never looked inside a Bible, and yet one evening he showed up at a Bible study I was leading.

Francisco is from northeast Brazil, an impoverished area that frequently passes through long periods of drought. Having been raised in poverty, Francisco was motivated to revolt against the system that seems to perpetuate destitution. At eight years of age he declared he would become a medical doctor, and he also decided he would have nothing to do with the Church. For him, God didn't exist. Gifted with unusual intelligence and fortitude, Francisco kept his word.

Years later he was on a surgical team with a Christian friend of mine. God used this friend to awaken Francisco's interest in spiritual things. It was a word spoken here and there, often in a joking manner, often during the course of surgery.

Circumstances of various sorts began to close in on Francisco— family, patients, and others. Francisco decided that my friend was right: He needed to give attention to the spiritual side of life. With typical perseverance he set out to do this. "The spiritual must be related to spiritism," he reasoned. So he enrolled in a year-long orientation course at a spiritist center, and began to study the occult. He kept this fact to himself. Eventually, my friend enticed Francisco to visit our Bible study.

Because Francisco was fascinated by the Bible, he absorbed it avidly.

He brought his wife with him the second week, and from then on they never missed.

Three months went by, during which we were greatly encouraged by Francisco and Danelia's progress toward Christ. Then one day he came to discuss "a special situation" with me. My heart sank as I learned of their involvement with the spiritists. They had been in the course for six months, and he felt he needed to honor his word, following through to the end. He told me that he'd already been offered the position of teacher in a new center but that he hadn't accepted it yet.

As I sat there, my mind raced through the passages in the Old and New Testaments that treat this subject of spiritism. There are enough verses for an overkill, and my first impulse was to use them all. But when you are unsure of a person's exact relationship with Christ, a scriptural deluge can be fatal to the person's further response. I held my tongue.

Finally I said, "Francisco, I'd like to show you something." We turned to 1 John 4 and I asked him to read the first few verses to me: "Dear friends, do not believe every spirit, but test the spirits to see whether they are from God. . . . This is how you can recognize the Spirit of God: Every spirit that acknowledges that Jesus Christ has come in the flesh is from God, but every spirit that does not acknowledge Jesus is not from God."

I went on to explain, "You are receiving information from two different sources, from me and from the spiritist center. Both of us claim to be teaching the truth. Both talk a lot about Jesus. According to this passage, by what criteria will you evaluate and decide who is, in fact, teaching you the truth?"

I continued, "I have a suggestion. When you go to the center, listen very carefully to what they say about Jesus, and then compare that with what the Bible says. Do the same with me. Compare what you hear me say about Jesus with what the Bible says. Then decide who's right on the basis of this passage."

When Francisco left that day, I was very apprehensive. I was aware of the hold spiritism can so easily gain over an individual. And I wasn't even sure Francisco had come far enough to where the Scriptures were authority for him.

But Francisco did what I told him, and it wasn't long before his new birth became evident. The final day of the course at the spiritist center came along. They renewed their offer for him to become a teacher. But he replied, "Thank you very much for the time and attention you invested in me. It has been interesting and informative. But I have also been studying the Bible. I've concluded that the Jesus you present is not the Jesus of the Bible. There is no salvation in your Jesus." And with that he left them. The superiority of Jesus!

OUR ROLE IN EVANGELISM

Our message is the good news about a Person, for the gospel lies in the Person of Jesus. Christianity and Jesus are not the same. People may have Him without embracing the systems that have been built up around Him. Or they can be involved in the system without knowing anything about Him. Whoever receives Him must take Him on His terms. To have Him at all is to take all of Him. Because He is sovereign over all that exists, He is sovereign over my person. This is the gospel in its essence.

Our role in evangelism can be compared with what John the Baptist said about himself. He saw himself as the best man in the wedding. Jesus is the bridegroom. The one who hears and believes is the bride. John's job was to see to it that the marriage occurred successfully, without attracting attention to himself in the process. The bride doesn't take on the best man's name. She belongs to the bridegroom.

When we understand that our intent in presenting the gospel is to bring about a new marriage, even those far away suddenly seem much closer. They are within reach. Of course, some, even after taking an honest look, will turn Jesus down. We cannot prevent that. But we *can* do something about people who reject Him because He comes wrapped in the traditions, dogmas, or moralisms of the messenger. Such potentially damaging influences we can avoid.

We must always remember that evangelism is not merely presenting the terms of a contract. It is introducing the Person of Jesus Christ. It is taking the time to help a person grasp the implications of His identity.

Evangelism is not merely bringing a person to intellectual assent; it goes beyond that. It includes helping a person work his way through his own rebellion and volitional obstacles.

But for many people this whole issue of Jesus' identity is not a concern. They are not asking the question. So how do I get a person to become interested in searching for an answer to a question to which he is indifferent? It will take the rest of this book to answer that one!

FIVE

THE FACT OF ISOLATION
Overcoming the Barrier of Mutual Fear

BECOME BLAMELESS AND pure, children of God . . . in a crooked and depraved generation, in which you shine like stars . . . as you hold out the word of life. (Philippians 2:15-16)

LIGHT IS MEANT FOR DARK PLACES

This theme—that light is meant for dark places—runs throughout the entire Bible. The idea that Christians are to be actively involved in the world creates tension for many of us. Apparently, this has been the case throughout the history of the Church. The pendulum has swung back and forth between isolation and compromise from the start. On the one extreme are those who attempt to isolate themselves from the rest of humanity. On the other extreme, we have Christians who absorb the values and behavior of their business and social environments to the point that they are indistinguishable from the rest of the world.

This is a tension not easily resolved, caused by the fact that God calls on the Church to exercise two seemingly incompatible functions simultaneously: the edification of the saved and the discipling of the unreconciled. How do we do both?

Once we have a nucleus of Christians, the temptation is almost irresistible to take them off to some safe corner to edify them. The problem is that when we do this, we remove people so far from their peers that further outreach among them is virtually impossible. The edification of the saved must be carried on in the midst of the world, with all its hazards.

53

This process of isolation I've just described is so common today that few Christians have meaningful relationships with nonbelievers. It has been observed that the average Christian has no nonChristian friends after he's been a believer for two years. Our contact with the world is then limited to casual acquaintances. We need to relearn how to build relationships with people outside our normal circle of Christian involvement.

In an article entitled "Old Time Religion" on the front page of *The Wall Street Journal* on July 11, 1980, Martin Marty, divinity professor at the University of Chicago, describes this isolation as follows. "If you're part of the evangelical sub-culture, it's your whole life. . . . You go to church, you buy the religious books, you watch the television programs. But if you're not part of the sub-culture, you never know it exists."

This article emphasized the degree to which evangelical Christians are isolated from the world around them. The subtitles reveal the reporter's conclusions:

An Evangelical Revival Is Sweeping the Nation but with Little Effect
Shunning the Sinful World
Effect Has Been Small
Shying From Involvement

The Journal's staff reporter, Jonathan Kauffman, writes: "The current evangelical revival has so far sowed little except curiosity among non-believers . . . the movement has affected American society far less than the Great Awakening of the mid-1700s." He also notes the "historical tendency for evangelicals to shy away from involvement in the secular, sinful world."

The distance between the church and the world was brought to my attention by some early experiences in Brazil. Osvaldo was the first Brazilian student who became a Christian. We invited him to move into our home, and he lived with us for three years. While we taught him all we could about following God and obeying the Scriptures, he taught us all he could about Brazil's language and culture. The benefits were mutual.

As Osvaldo grew in his love for God, the relationship between the two of us also grew. He soon became a faithful friend. As I observed this progress, I decided it was time to begin taking him to church with us. It was Osvaldo's first exposure to Protestantism. Everything seemed to go fine. He never discussed his reactions, but he always went with us. I began to observe, however, that he was struggling.

One Sunday as we were walking home, I said, "Osvaldo, you don't really enjoy going to church, do you?" That opened the door. Out came the questions: "Why do they express themselves so strangely?" "Why do they sing like that?" "Why do they change their voices when they pray?" And on and on. His questions were very sincere; he was just looking for honest answers. But they irritated me. My attempts to answer them also irritated me, because I didn't do very well.

The incident passed, but Osvaldo's questions stuck. Because of them, I began to see those services through the eyes of an outsider. I had to concede that almost insurmountable communication problems existed on both sides. The outsider would never feel at home until he submitted himself to a series of modifications in his customs and lifestyle. And the congregation was not willing to extend their fellowship to him until it was evident these changes were taking place.

Sometimes it is possible for a new Christian to accept this process and submit to the changes. It's not hard to find illustrations to support this. But even successful transitions are dubious victories because they are often at the price of severed communication with the new Christian's former peer group.

This is hard to admit, but the secularized person who comes to Christ often has no place to go. He and many of our existing churches are worlds apart culturally. This is even more true of those unreached people of the world who live in totally different cultures.

Apparently, I'm not alone in this conclusion. In *Let the Earth Hear His Voice*, Ralph Winter asks, "Are we in America . . . prepared for the fact that most non-Christians yet to be won to Christ (even in our country) will not fit readily into the kinds of churches we now have?"[1]

There are several reasons why this distance between the Church and the world exists. It would be beside the point to go into all of them here. Some of the reasons are positive, others are negative. What does concern us here is the fact that Jesus Christ has sent the Church into the world, and for this reason we cannot dare lose touch with those who live in the world.

As Jesus related His ambitions for the Church to His Father just before His death, He said, "I will remain in the world no longer, but they are still in the world . . . they are not of the world any more than I am of the world. My prayer is not that you take them out of the world but that you protect them from the evil one. . . . As you sent me into the world, I have sent them into the world" (John 17:11,14-15,18).

To a large degree, our purpose for remaining in the world is for *its* sake, not just our own.

But even as Jesus expressed His will for us, He recognized the dilemma He was thrusting upon us: being *in* the world but not *of* it. How can a Christian obey the call to "come out from them and be separate" (2 Corinthians 6:17) and at the same time be "sent . . . into the world" (John 17:18)?

The Christian's relationship to the world has been a point of tension throughout Church history. Over the centuries, as Christians have sought to strike a balance between these two seemingly contradictory commands, we have swung from one extreme to the other—from hermit-like isolation to conformity to the world. But either extreme defeats God's purpose. Conformity to the world obscures the glory of God. Isolation renders the Christian model useless. The value of the congruence between our lives and our faith will be lost to the world if separation becomes isolation. "Neither do people light a lamp and put it under a bowl" (Matthew 5:15).

THE PULL TOWARD ISOLATION IS UNDERSTANDABLE

The world is a hazardous place! "Be self-controlled and alert. Your enemy . . . prowls . . . looking for someone to devour" (1 Peter 5:8).

Compatibility with nonChristians is limited. "What fellowship can light have with darkness? . . . What does a believer have in common with an unbeliever? . . . We are the temple of the living God. . . . Therefore come out from them and be separate" (2 Corinthians 6:14-17).

Certain activities don't fit comfortably any longer. "For you have spent enough time in the past doing what pagans choose to do. . . . They think it strange that you do not plunge with them into the same flood of dissipation" (1 Peter 4:3-4).

All things considered, the prudent thing to do seems to be to retreat to a "safe distance." The question is, what constitutes a safe distance?

A few years ago, I attended a seminar where the lecturer said, "As a Christian takes his stand, he forces his nonChristian friends and acquaintances to choose. They will either be drawn into the Christian life or they will withdraw. Withdrawal also means loss of friendship. Consequently, there will come a time when the maturing Christian has no real friendships among nonChristians." Another teacher said, "As we become more and more mature, we become less and less effective with the world."

Is this what we mean by a safe distance—to think it is a Christian virtue to have no real friendships with unbelievers? If we do, that is tragic, because such isolation has a destructive effect on a local body of Christians, as well as destroying our communication with the lost. Christians who keep to themselves, who do not experience a continuing influx of people just arriving from the dominion of darkness, soon isolate themselves within their own subculture. Receiving no feedback from people fresh from the world, they forget what it's like out there. Peculiar language codes, behavioral patterns, and communication techniques emerge that have meaning only for the insiders. As such, a local body becomes increasingly ingrown. It also becomes stranger and stranger to outsiders. Eventually, communication with the man on the street is impossible.

So what is a safe distance? Jesus answered this question with an intriguing statement in John 17:17. He asked His Father (in the context of sending His disciples into the world) to "sanctify [set apart for sacred use or make holy] them by the truth; your word is truth." Fundamentally, sanctification is not a matter of geography (where we are), but of the heart (*who* owns it). A safe distance is maintained as we are constantly transformed by the renewing of our minds through the truth of God's Word. This requires time alone with Him, when we are actively submitting our minds to the truth. If this practice is not a part of our lives, or if it is not effective, we are ill-prepared for encounters with nonChristians in the world. In such a case, perhaps isolation would be best after all!

MUTUAL FEAR
A Barrier to Honest Relationships

The Christian fears the influence of the ungodly. On one hand, this is legitimate. "Bad company corrupts good character" (1 Corinthians 15:33). On the other hand, it is not, because the Christian has been given adequate resources to stand while living *in* the world.

But whether fears are real or unnecessary, they constitute a formidable blockade against the communication of the gospel. Think for a moment. If you were absolutely free from any fear, what kind of witness would you be?

Even the intrepid Apostle Paul had to deal with fear. He told the Corinthian Christians that he came to them "in weakness and fear, and with much trembling" (1 Corinthians 2:3). He asked the Ephesians for prayer that he would "fearlessly make known the mystery of the gospel" (Ephesians 6:19). Paul's fears were based on past experiences with ships, prisons, and stones. Our fears are usually based on more abstract dangers, but are no less valid.

It is also true that the nonChristian fears the Christian, and his fear is also predictable. "For we are to God the aroma of Christ among those who are being saved and those who are perishing. To the one we are the smell of death; to the other, the fragrance of life" (2 Corinthians 2:15-16). The presence of the Christian is a reminder of God's impending judgment. Some of the nonChristian's fears are real, some are groundless.

The nonChristian fears in part because we are a reminder to him of facts he prefers not to think about: sin, death, and judgment. But some of his fears are due to the censure we transmit to him. This is unnecessary, because we are not his judge.

Overcoming the nonChristian's fears. The Christian tends to measure the nonChristian against a rather ad hoc list of acceptable and unacceptable behavior. The list is a mixture of clear-cut commands from the Word of

God, such as "do not commit adultery," along with relative issues which come from our traditions, such as total abstinence from alcohol.

The nonChristian picks up the vibrations and feels he is judged. He sometimes even apologizes for his unacceptable habits, indicating that he feels he has fallen into the hands of someone bent on reforming him. Where there are such judgments, communication is hopeless.

But how do we avoid this? How do we relate to someone who is destroying himself and those around him through sin? Do we close our eyes when we are with someone who may be brutalizing his family by his infidelities? Can we hide the censure we feel toward him? What is the solution?

Look at Jesus. Jesus managed to accept the worst of us. How? It was because He was a realist. He knew man's capacity for evil, so that was all He expected from him. He also knew man's worst actions are only symptoms of something deeper and uglier: rebellion against God. It is rebellion, not ignorance, that keeps man from God. And this rebellion is the source of all man's problems. Jesus didn't spend much time treating symptoms. He went for the cure.

This ability to see beyond the surface symptom to the true need is the key to establishing honest relationships with nonChristians. We do not have to condone their behavior to accept and love them.

I have a friend who, when I met him, lived in what was then described as the counterculture. He worked very little and was on drugs. He was not married to the girl he was living with. We began studying the Bible together, but since time was limited for me, I invited him to join a study group with several others. These, too, were on their way toward Christ, but the others were a bit more straight, and some were more philosophical than my friend. Consequently, much of what we discussed went right past him.

Finally, during one study, he exploded. "You don't know where I'm coming from! What goes on here doesn't speak to me!"

I agreed. I did not understand him. In response, with a challenging attitude, he invited me to visit his world. We set a date for the next week to spend the evening where his friends gathered. I was in for an education!

We were the first to arrive. Gradually, the place filled up. Each individual was a lesson in himself. Finally the leader strode in. He was fastidiously unkempt, he had very long hair and a beard, and his front teeth were missing. As he sat down he announced, "I quit my job today." By the response of the others, I realized he had just performed the most prestigious action within their structure: quitting one's job. It meant keeping loose, avoiding enduring commitments, letting society pick up the tab.

As his story unfolded I discovered how he had earned the number one ranking among his peers. A university graduate with a military career, he had suddenly left his wife and a job at the Pentagon just to follow his whims. He pushed drugs to sustain an undemanding lifestyle. All he owned was a black pickup truck, a pair of skis, and two large dogs. It was a lifestyle that avoided any serious thinking and reflection, preferring what felt good at the moment.

Instructed by the experience, I took my friend out of the Bible study group with the others, and together we studied the Bible in his apartment. His friends, knowing what was happening, would drop around. Occasionally they would take his Bible and read it for themselves. His girlfriend became interested, sat in, and did not miss a word!

But what about dealing with their sin? After they came to Christ, we began to work on clearing up its symptoms. The first problem we dealt with was his lack of commitment to his girlfriend.

Thankfully, the laws of God are rational. They are not mindless or arbitrary. I believe that if someone possessed all wisdom, and were to provide guidelines to assure the survival of a society and a value system that would cause it to thrive, the answer would be the Ten Commandments.

What the Bible says about adultery and marriage is not unreasonable. So one day when my friend and I were together, I casually described what I imagined the relationship between the two of them was like—that they really liked each other, that neither wanted to lose the other, but that both knew that no commitments existed on either side. Consequently, they would pretend to a harmony they really didn't feel.

Then I made a projection about the future of their relationship. I told him that eventually the relationship would become a charade as they continued to feign loving responses to each other. Therefore, their relationship was destined to disintegrate under its first real crisis. When the blowup came, both parties would go their way—both very hurt. I then went on to explain how God intends to join man and woman in an inseparable union (Matthew 19:6). This is because any human relationship, if it is to survive, must be based on a mutual commitment.

My friend didn't say a word, but two weeks later we received a wedding invitation. Today they are walking with Christ.

We need to accept the nonChristian as he is, go for the cure, and *then* help him pick his way through the things that are destroying him. Whenever we get this sequence turned around, we become reformers rather than offerers of true healing.

Dealing with our own fears. It's our move. If we are going to break the deadlock of isolation, it is obviously up to us. Jesus gave us some simple things to do to help us avoid isolation and be light where it will do the most good—right in the middle of this world's darkness.

In Matthew 5:43-48, He said we should be like our Father, who causes the sun to rise on the evil and on the good. Basically He said, "Don't just love those who love you back. Even tax collectors do that. Don't just greet your brothers. Everyone does that. Take the initiative in being friendly, and in observing what is happening among those around you. That isn't very difficult, is it?"

Jesus provides another simple and practical step for getting started. In Luke 14:12-13, Jesus suggests that when we give a dinner, we shouldn't invite just our friends and relatives. You know how that goes. This time it's our turn, next time it's theirs. In the end, everyone breaks even. It hasn't cost anyone anything. Rather, He says, invite the poor, the crippled, the lame, and the blind who cannot repay you—until the day of resurrection when they will be there to salute your faithfulness to them.

In other words, be hospitable. Deliberately break out of your daily routine of people and places for the gospel's sake. I know of no more effective environment for initiating evangelism than a dinner at home or in a quiet restaurant.

That's not too hard either, is it? We must go into the world to establish the rapport needed to draw people into our lives.

NOTE:
1. Ralph Winter, "The Highest Priority: Cross-Cultural Evangelism," in *Let the Earth Hear His Voice* (Minneapolis: World Wide Publications, 1975), page 221.

SIX

FROM ISOLATION TO COMMUNICATION

Dynamics of the Process

ONCE WE UNDERSTAND the fears of our listeners and learn to deal with our own, we can turn our attention to the dynamics of communication. I have learned that talking is not always communicating and that telling is not teaching. The test of communication is not to be found in the words of the communicator but in the understanding of the listener. Telling is a one-person function. Communicating is a two-way street.

Osvaldo was one of the first Brazilians I talked to about Christ. He was working as an industrial chemist when I looked him up. We knew each other through his brother, with whom I had studied the Scriptures while I was in language study. Osvaldo was curious about what was going on because he couldn't imagine his brother becoming involved in anything religious. His brother just wasn't that kind of person. So, when I invited Osvaldo to dinner in our home, he eagerly accepted.

The conversation began with Osvaldo asking questions about our motives for being in Brazil and about what was happening between his brother and me. The best way I could think of to answer his questions was to explain the gospel to him. I got a piece of chalk and a Bible and used the wooden floor as a chalkboard. I spent the next two hours showing him a favorite diagram I often used to explain the message. I was quite satisfied with my performance, and when I finally finished, I leaned back to observe his reaction, certain that he would be on the verge of repentance.

Instead, he gazed at my illustration, then at me. He was puzzled. "Do you mean to tell me that this is why you came all the way to Brazil—to tell people *that?*"

THE DISCOVERY
Evangelism Is a Process

To Osvaldo, what I had said seemed insignificant and irrelevant. I recognized at that moment that I was facing a communication problem I had never been aware of before. In my mind I had always equated evangelism with reaping. But here before me was an empty field. Planting, watering, and cultivation would have to occur before I could hope to reap.

I invited Osvaldo to begin reading the Scriptures with me. For the next three months, we met several times a week to read and discuss the Gospel of John together. His movement from a free-thinker's humanistic philosophy towards accepting the truth of Christ was plainly visible, and the process resulted in his submission to Christ.

The method of using such a sustained exposure to the Scriptures became a pattern. I soon found I was bringing people to Christ in Brazil that I would have passed up as indifferent or out of reach in the United States. I also found that these new Christians, born after a longer period of gestation, had fewer spiritual problems. Spiritual casualties were rare. "Good soil . . . produced a crop, multiplying thirty, sixty, or even a hundred times" (Mark 4:8).

I had learned some much-needed lessons about the dynamics of communication and had expanded my understanding of evangelism to include planting, watering, and cultivating as well as reaping. I learned that *evangelism is a process.*

When we bring someone to a decision to trust in Christ in the course of a conversation or two, we can be sure of one thing: considerable preparation and laboring has already occurred in that life before we arrived on the scene. I think this is what Jesus was saying to the Twelve in John 4:36-38: "Even now the reaper draws his wages, even now he harvests the crop for eternal life, so that the sower and the reaper may be glad together. Thus the saying, 'One sows and another reaps' is true. I sent you to reap what you have not worked for. Others have done the hard work, and you have reaped the benefits of their labor."

God uses many influences to accomplish the necessary preparation: people, circumstances, and events.

Some of the essential steps along the way only He can accomplish. The God-consciousness planted in the heart of every man is one of these (see Romans 1:20). God has also written His law in men's hearts, accompanying it with a conscience and a sense of guilt (see Romans 2:14-15).

Sometimes He uses political situations. Josiah found a dusty copy of the Scriptures in the temple and through reading it led his nation to revival. Economic uncertainties, political upheavals, revolutions that disrupt the routines and values of normal life—all of these events can serve to move people along the continuum, away from the dominion of darkness and toward the kingdom of light.

Even chance comments can be significant. An ex-Buddhist friend, describing his conversion to Christ, pointed back to a comment by his mother while they were in the Buddhist temple as being the trigger that started his search that led him to Christ. She wondered aloud why the "true God" was positioned last, not first, on the shelf of idols in the temple. He never forgot his mother's question. Her comment prepared him to respond to the Christian gospel.

God uses an endless variety of ways and means to sow the seed of the gospel message and move us along from ignorance and rebellion toward faith. The most obvious means, and by far the most effective, is a strong Christian family—growing up where the truth of Christianity is practiced and taught in the home and church. After such an education, often the sole remaining need is reaping. People with a Christian heritage still exist in significant numbers in many places. In those situations, reaping by itself produces encouraging results. But this can mislead us into thinking the whole world is at the same level of preparedness. It can make us forget that evangelism is, in fact, a process.

CONTRAST WITH PREVIOUS UNDERSTANDING

My own first efforts at influencing people for Christ reflected the common misconception that evangelism is an activity, an event. As a young Christian, I had acquired the habit of spending considerable amounts of time studying and meditating on the Scriptures. The positive effects this had on me were numerous, and I was excited about what was happening to me. But I also grew restless because I knew witnessing was expected of any Christian who was serious about obedience. The thought of talking to others about Christ paralyzed me with fear, however, and I couldn't bring myself to open my mouth.

I had a mental caricature of what a "good witness" was like. In part, this image was derived from my concept of the Apostle Paul: preaching to the philosophers on Mars Hill, speaking in the crowded marketplace, or conversing with the praetorian guard. Projected into contemporary society, I imagined a good witness was like a good salesman—unabashed, aggressive, fearless of strangers. But my world was full of strangers, and I *was* afraid of them. I concluded I didn't "have the gift" and tried to put evangelism out of my mind.

That didn't work either. Inner tension continued to build. I *wanted* to evangelize. On several occasions I would drop whatever I was doing, get into my car and drive to the Student Union at the University of Minnesota where I was studying, determined to witness to someone. I made several clandestine trips, but never talked to a soul. Finally, I revealed my frustration to a mature Christian who I knew was a fruitful witness. In response, he took me with him to a university campus where I watched him spend the afternoon initiating conversations that led into opportunities to present the gospel. Terror gave way to enthusiasm as I discovered personal witnessing wasn't impossible. The experience was a breakthrough.

Over the next months I witnessed to all of my friends. Some became Christians, others did not. As I pressed each person to decide, my relationships with those who refused became strained. Soon I had polarized all my friendships. But that was fine with me because I had overcome my frustration. I even thought the polarization reflected my spiritual integrity!

With no friends left to witness to, I began to visit student dormitories, going from door to door. I tried fraternity meetings and visited military bases. Some people became Christians as a result of my efforts, but the casualty rate was almost as high as the birth rate. I simply explained away my poor results with the parable of the sower: poor soil—it was their fault, not mine. It was with this mistaken mentality that I found myself in Brazil talking to Osvaldo.

DOES OUR AUDIENCE UNDERSTAND US?

I have seen these same misconceptions about communication and the nature of evangelism played out in so many situations that I believe the problem is general.

In the middle 1970s, three North American couples joined together as a team and moved to Caracas, Venezuela, to work as missionaries. All three couples were experienced, having spent several years in grassroots evangelism and discipling on university campuses and in communities.

Their initial target in Caracas was the university student. They spent their days on the campuses, explaining the gospel to anyone who would listen, initiating relationships, conducting Bible studies, and attempting by every possible means to establish a nucleus of new Christians who would eventually join them in their efforts.

In several ways, Caracas is unique. It is oil rich, and public works abound. The currency is strong and jobs are relatively plentiful. Job seekers have flowed there from Europe and North as well as South America. Money comes easily to everyone but the poor. The city has become a crowded cosmopolis with nowhere left to grow, since it is wedged among the Andes Mountains. Historically, Caracas has resisted the Christianizing attempts of both the Roman Catholic and Protestant churches. This all adds up to a basically pagan society with little else but materialism to live for.

After a full year of hard work with very little fruit, one of the missionaries wrote me: "We all agree we are learning to do evangelism all over again. Or perhaps it's that we're learning to truly evangelize for the first time. In the States, more often than not, when doing cold evangelism, a person's head will drop as soon as you mention God, the Bible, or spiritual things. That never happens here! More often than not, their response is more like, 'What a pity!'" In other words, the Caracas students were sorry to see these otherwise normal people involved in such folly.

The letter continued, "We don't see much evidence of conviction of sin nor of any sense of need. . . . There is absolutely no interest in the Bible or in what it has to say."

What was happening? Why were those couples not seeing the same response in Caracas that they would in a typical North American city? Two variables, the audience and the communicators, were worlds apart. This problem is not one just missionaries face. The same difficulty will be faced by individuals sharing the gospel anywhere.

THE AUDIENCE

There is a significant difference between the spiritual heritage of the average nonChristian in Caracas and the average North American who is not a Christian. Not all the people in the world are equally predisposed to respond to the gospel.

The Apostle Paul made some fascinating observations about this in his Mars Hill discourse. He declared it was God's idea to compartmentalize the world into races, languages, cultures, and nations.

Paul said, "He himself gives all men life and breath and everything else. From one man he made every nation of men, that they should inhabit the whole earth; and he determined the times [periods of history] set for them and the exact places [geographical locations] where they should live. God did this so that men would seek him and find him, though he is not far from each one of us" (Acts 17:25-27).

Having spent a good part of my life struggling with cultural and linguistic barriers, I tended to view them as something this world could easily do without. So it was a surprise to discover that the existing arrangement was God's idea and that He did it this way with the reconciliation of the world in mind! Apparently, these barriers serve as a preservative, limiting the influence of the decadent or burned-out cultures on the others (see Genesis 11:1-9).

For this discussion, the important thing to recognize is that not every nation or people is at the same point of preparedness. This is certainly going to affect the kind of communication that must take place and the degree of response one receives as one moves from a typical American city to a foreign and secularized one like Caracas.

This comes into focus quite easily when we compare a Bible-belt city in America with an unreached city like Caracas. Yet it is just as true, though perhaps more obscure, that similar distances exist between Christians and nonChristians even within our American cities!

THE COMMUNICATORS

What happens when a communicator attempts to carry on a conversation with someone who does not share the same presuppositions or the same emotional conditionings?

Recently, I observed a conversation between a young missionary and a nonChristian Latin American student. The missionary was experiencing the excruciating frustration of unwittingly turning his nonChristian acquaintances away every time he attempted to discuss the gospel.

On this occasion, he made an appointment with a friend with whom he had played soccer for several months. Hoping that an observer could help him understand what was going wrong, the missionary invited me along.

He began well. He explained that the purpose for his moving to that country was his involvement in a Christian student movement. He was there with the intent of finding people who were interested in examining the Scriptures to see if they held the answers for life's questions. Then he went on to explain that in order for him to do this effectively, he first needed to understand the mentality of those he was trying to influence. So far, so good.

He then proceeded to ask certain questions of his friend. These, too, were well-received, but he soon ran into difficulty.

The questions ranged over the basic Christian beliefs: What was his concept of God? Who was Jesus Christ? What was his concept of salvation? All these his friend answered readily, but with answers straight out of the catechism!

Accepting these answers at face value, my friend assumed he was dealing with a person who shared many of his own presuppositions. That was his first mistake. His second soon followed.

The student asked my friend how he would answer those same questions. He probably shouldn't have answered at all at this point, but he mistook the question as an opportunity and seized it. His reply was, in his own eyes, a clear synthesis of the Christian message. Jesus was God. He died for our sins. We can be reconciled to God by grace through faith, and so on.

I watched the student as my friend talked. Disappointment was written on his face. He did not really accept the catechism he had just quoted. In fact, he had long since given up on religion. His answers had been a trial balloon. He liked this American and *hoped that what he had to offer would somehow be different.* But the differences between his catechism and what he was hearing from the American were too subtle for the student to grasp. Both the speaker and the listener were unwittingly communicating in separate languages. They used identical terminology, but never realized that the message each received and the ways they interpreted the meanings of the words they used differed greatly. The student interpreted what was said as a reinforcement of his rejected religion.

My friend had unknowingly, but irreversibly, pigeonholed himself! Instead of sharing his beliefs immediately, he should have asked additional questions until he was sure he understood what the other thought and believed. He should have spoken only when his friend was truly ready to listen, measuring his content according to the hearer's ability to absorb.

Estrangement is often the result when people differ in their starting points, as these two did. Further attempts to communicate often leave us farther apart rather than closer together. The differences may go unperceived by both parties, resulting perhaps in an illusion of understanding. We think we are transmitting truth, but our communication is being reprocessed by the hearer. Our words are interpreted according to his existing frame of reference. The result is that, instead of having an impact and producing change, our gospel is simply being synthesized into the listener's personal philosophy. In reality, he hasn't heard at all.

So we could say the primary communication task the team in Latin America faces is to successfully close the gap between themselves as communicators and their audience. This requires two things: an understanding of the hearers' thought patterns, and the translation of the gospel message into their everyday language. The missionaries' message needs to be translated out of North American Protestant terminology and communication forms and into patterns which will be understood by Latin American students.

This problem in communication is not limited to situations in which we are crossing major cultural frontiers. It occurs any time we are communicating outside our own subculture, with people who do not share our presuppositions and are not familiar with our terminology. The problem can be as close as your next door neighbor.

At this point you may be asking, "How does all this compare with what went on in the New Testament? How do we reconcile this with the phenomenal responses enjoyed by the early church in Acts?" This is what we will now consider in the next section.

PART TWO

TWO ASPECTS OF EVANGELISM

SEVEN

PROCLAMATION
Biblical, Essential, and Effective

AS STATED EARLIER, there are two broad aspects to the process of evangelism in the New Testament. The first is the *proclamation* of the gospel. This is an *action* through which the nonChristian receives a clear statement of the essential message. It is something that happens at a certain point in time—for example, during an evangelistic crusade. Another example would be a personal presentation of the gospel message to an individual. When someone declares the terms of man's reconciliation to God, the gospel has been proclaimed.

The Bible commands us to proclaim the gospel to the entire world, so whether we should engage in this is beyond discussion. Proclamation, however, must be used wisely if we expect to communicate the message to all kinds of people. Proclamation is mainly effective among a certain kind—the prepared.

The other aspect of evangelism is necessary if we expect to reach significant numbers of the great majority of the world who do not possess a religious heritage. I call this second mode the *affirmation* of the gospel.

What is the affirmation of the gospel? It is a *process* of incarnating and demonstrating the Christian message. This is effective among the unprepared—that is, people without a Christian heritage, or those for whom Christianity does not constitute a credible basis for their lives. They are depending upon some "ism"—humanism, materialism, existentialism, socialism, or capitalism—to give coherence to life. With rare exceptions, drawing such individuals into the Kingdom of God requires more than a summary statement of the gospel.

71

Both aspects of evangelism—proclamation and affirmation—are essential if we are to evangelize people from a nonChristian environment as well as those who have a religious heritage. One cannot be judged better or more important than the other. Both are essential and both are limited. The New Testament pattern seems to be that both should work together all the time. What is important for us to know is when to do what! To insist on using affirmation while proclamation would suffice is an unnecessary effort. But to persist in proclaiming where more is required to get through is ineffective. By the same token, when proclamation is effective, affirmation has already occurred. And when affirmation is effective, proclamation is always an essential component.

PROCLAIMING THE GOSPEL

Proclamation—the Greek word *kerusso* means to announce, to proclaim, to herald. This is the function of our daily newspaper and newscast. They announce what is happening. In the Roman context, the word described the action of the announcer at the public games. But it would not be accurate to limit the meaning of proclamation to public preaching. It can take many forms, including individual, person-to-person persuasion.

In all four of the Gospels we are commanded to proclaim. In Matthew 24:14 Jesus said, "This gospel of the kingdom will be preached [*kerusso*] in the whole world." There are not just certain places in the world where it works to proclaim. We are to do it in *all* the world. Mark 13:10 is identical. The gospel must be preached (*kerusso*) to all nations. Mark 16:15 is even more specific: "Go into all the world and preach [*kerusso*] the good news to all creation." In Luke 24:47 the same word is used, and Luke tells us what the content of our proclamation should be. Jesus said we should proclaim "repentance and forgiveness of sins . . . to all nations."

Stop and think for a moment about what we expect to happen when we proclaim. Let's say we approach a twenty-four-year-old person with the intent of proclaiming the gospel to him. He has spent twenty-four years doing what he wanted to do, establishing habits, and developing his own value system. Almost everything he has fed into his mind is contrary to the Word of God. Let's say we spend an hour with him, during which we clearly explain the Christian faith. Now what do we expect to happen? We expect him to conclude that the direction he is taking in life is wrong. We expect him to say, "For twenty-four years I have been mistaken. In one hour you have shown me how to make an about-face in everything I have done until now."

Aren't we expecting the impossible? Yes, we are. But many times a day, all over the world, this conversation actually occurs. It is often effective. Why? There are several reasons.

In Acts 11:21, Luke reported that there were results when the gospel was proclaimed because "*the Lord's hand was with them.*" This is important. This is what makes proclamation possible. If the Lord's hand is not with us, then we are, in fact, wasting our time. But the Bible says there are other reasons we can expect results from proclamation.

Acts 11:24 gives a second reason. It is because the proclaimer (Barnabas) "*was a good man, full of the Holy Spirit and faith.*" That's a powerful trio: a good life, the Holy Spirit, and faith. There were results because of the quality of the message bearer.

In Acts 13:48, once again the gospel was being proclaimed, and as Luke wrote, the Holy Spirit explained why there were results: "*All who were appointed for eternal life believed.*" I understand this to mean that God has prepared certain people, who at the point of our encounter with them are ready to respond. We can expect to find at least some people like this almost everywhere we go.

But there are yet other reasons why we can expect results from proclamation. In Acts 14:1 Luke wrote, "*They spoke so effectively that a great number of Jews and Gentiles believed.*" Then in Acts 16:14 we find still another reason. Referring to Lydia, Luke wrote, "*The Lord opened her heart* to respond to Paul's message" (emphasis added).

So we have a number of reasons to expect results from the proclamation of the gospel. We can expect the Lord's hand to be with us if we are men and women of faith and purity. We can expect to encounter some prepared people everywhere we go. We can learn how to share effectively. And we can expect the Lord to open people's hearts to respond.

THE HERITAGE FACTOR
Prerequisite for Effective Proclamation

Perhaps the predominant reason why people respond to proclamation is their previous preparation.

There were two kinds of people who responded to the proclamation of the gospel, according to the account in Acts. The first were the Jews, who in New Testament times had sixteen centuries of religious heritage. God had given them the Scriptures—the Law and the Prophets. Until they were conquered, their system of government and their religion were one and the same.

The Jews were well-prepared. The celebration on the day of Pentecost brought "*God-fearing Jews from every nation*" to Jerusalem (Acts 2:5).

The second kind were converts or near-converts who joined in the Jewish worship. They were known as "proselytes" and "God-fearers."

When God made His first move to spread the gospel to the Gentiles, he began with Cornelius, a Roman soldier whom Luke described as "devout and God-fearing" (Acts 10:2).

The next step was the beginning of the missionary movement. Paul was serving in Antioch as one of five leaders in the church. Barnabas was another. The Holy Spirit separated Paul and Barnabas to be sent off as missionaries.

They followed a certain tactic everywhere they went. First they visited the synagogue. Obviously, almost everyone found in a synagogue would have some spiritual interest. Although these people had not heard about Christ, they were seeking after God according to their traditional patterns. They had the benefit of a religious heritage. The result was that many of them believed when Paul and Barnabas preached the gospel. Both Jews and proselyte Gentiles became Christians.

An unusual thing happened when they arrived in Philippi. There was no synagogue in that city. Apparently, Paul and Barnabas heard there was a place by the river where people regularly met for prayer. They went there and discovered Lydia. But, again, she was a person who was "a worshiper of God" (Acts 16:14). In this case as well, they were taking the gospel to those who were prepared.

In Athens it was a different story (see Acts 17:16-34). Paul "was greatly distressed to see that the city was full of idols. So he reasoned in the synagogue with Jews and the God-fearing Greeks, as well as in the market-place day by day with those who happened to be there" (Acts 17:16-17). He even argued with the Epicurean and Stoic philosophers.

The philosophers were intrigued by his new teaching and took him to the Areopagus so he could give a discourse. This is the only recorded message given by Paul to a pagan crowd (people who did not have a religious heritage). Notice the difference in the content of his message. He did not appeal to the Old Testament; he was more philosophical. He even quoted the Greek poets. He started witnessing in a different way—he began with the Person of God. Then he spoke about Jesus and the resurrection. The results were meager. "A few men became followers of Paul and believed" (Acts 17:34).

Compare the results of Paul's message with the results of Peter's address on Pentecost (2:37-41). What was the difference? Was Peter more Spirit-filled? Was Peter a better communicator? No. The difference was the Jews' religious heritage, which prepared them to respond eagerly to the gospel.

Getting substantial results from proclamation presupposes some advance preparation of the hearers (planting and watering). Yet we are commanded to proclaim throughout the entire world. Why? Because we must assume God is at work preparing some in every place. *But He never intended us to limit our witnessing to efforts that include only proclamation.*

THE SCOPE OF PROCLAMATION
Its Limited Effectiveness

Proclamation is commanded. It is globally effective, but it is limited. It is limited as to the audiences it can reach as well as in its purpose.

Paul recognized this and consequently restricted himself to working within certain guidelines. This approach was essential to his success. He didn't try to do everything. He was primarily a proclaimer. He ranged his world proclaiming the gospel until he could make the amazing statement in his letter to the Romans: "So from Jerusalem all the way around to Illyricum, I have fully proclaimed the gospel of Christ. . . . But now that there is no more place for me to work in these regions, and since I have been longing for many years to see you, I plan to do so when I go to Spain" (Romans 15:19,23-24).

What did Paul mean when he said he had finished his work? Did he mean he had evangelized every living person from Jerusalem to Illyricum? He couldn't have. His tactic was to go to a city, reap those who were prepared, establish them, and then move on. What percentage of the population of a city like Corinth, the sin capital of the Roman Empire, had ever seen the inside of a Jewish synagogue? Only a fraction of the citizens had. But in many cities Paul's evangelistic outreach did not reach beyond the synagogue. On what basis could Paul claim he had finished his job in those places?

Paul wrote the Corinthians, "We, however, will not boast beyond proper limits, but will confine our boasting to the field God has assigned to us, a field that reaches even to you. . . . Neither do we go beyond our limits by boasting of work done by others. Our hope is that, as your faith continues to grow, our area of activity among you will greatly expand" (2 Corinthians 10:13-15). Paul was saying his sphere of ministry was to establish beachheads of new believers. He didn't do everything; he just established beachheads. Then he counted on the continued growth of his offspring to enlarge that sphere. The entire success of Paul's effort depended on the continued growth and subsequent expansion of the gospel through his spiritual children.

Often it was persecution that kept Paul moving, but even when he wasn't forced on, he didn't settle down for long. He would move on (Ephesus, where he stayed three years, was one exception) when the prepared were reaped and had received the basics of the faith.

In our contemporary evangelistic efforts we tend to want to emulate

Paul, but we fail to complete the picture. We labor as if the gospel, once proclaimed to the world, has had a full opportunity to work. If we could just get the gospel to every person once in this generation, we think our job would be done. But we must recognize that even if we did achieve that goal, we would have only begun the job of evangelizing the world. Beachheads would be established, but the larger challenge would still be before us. We would have to admit that we were then only in a position from which to *begin* thoroughly evangelizing the world!

Our environments illustrate my meaning. Think for a minute. What percentage of your friends and acquaintances are reasonably close to the Kingdom? How many would readily submit their lives to Christ if someone explained the gospel to them? What about the others? Are they beyond hope? If not, how could they be reached? Who will do it?

We live in a world that we are scarcely influencing with the gospel. In part, the problem is our limited view of evangelism. We see it only as the activity of proclamation. Not everyone is reapable by proclamation. Once we recognize that there is more to evangelism than proclamation, we are free to communicate the gospel in a way all can understand, and many more become reachable.

Viewing evangelism as only proclamation restricts the mobility of the gospel in two ways. It is limited as to whom it will reach—only those with prior preparation. And it is limited as to who can do the proclaiming. Few middle-aged businessmen or housewives find themselves in an environment where proclamation can be a daily way of life. Sustained proclamation implies constant access to new groups of people. Jesus sent the Twelve out two-by-two, but neither they nor their offspring spent their lives organizing similar expeditions.

Can our understanding of evangelism be complete if it does not realistically allow for the average Christian to enjoy a lifetime of personal involvement and fruitfulness? This is made difficult if proclamation and reaping are perceived to be the sum total of evangelism. The result is frustration and disillusionment for many Christians.

THE REAPING MENTALITY
Are We Too Anxious for the Harvest?

Several years ago, a close friend visited us in Curitiba, Brazil. He was a missionary with ten years' experience in organizing city-wide evangelistic crusades. He and his team would enter a city, unite the pastors, and spend three to six months training counselors, organizing follow-up, and making other necessary preparations.

We were sitting in his Volkswagen bus, parked in front of the post office, when he said, "I'm going to try it one more time. I've been at this for ten years and I've yet to see any permanent results for my efforts. We organize a crusade and there are scores of decisions. Local pastors give glowing testimonials to the effect that their churches have been transformed. But then it's all over. When we return three months later there is not a trace to show we were there at all. If things aren't different after this attempt, I'll give up, return to the United States, and go into business."

And that's what he did! Such frustration and disillusionment are the fruits of attempting to reap where there has been little previous labor. Let me give some examples of the limitations of the reaping approach to evangelism.

The idea of "saturation evangelism" was born some years ago. In his book *Frontiers in Missionary Strategy*, Peter Wagner wrote that the aim of this form of evangelism was "to present the gospel in spoken and written form to every people of the land, to every stratum of society, to every home and individual. . . . Saturation evangelism seeks to mobilize and train every believer available to become an active and effective evangelizer for Christ."[1]

These are stirring objectives. I could easily give my life to seeing them accomplished—if only they were realistic!

Saturation evangelism crusades have been carried out on numerous occasions in Latin America and in other countries. But studies done on their effectiveness by various missiologists show little or no lasting effect. Wagner quotes Dr. George Peters of Dallas Theological Seminary who concluded, "From the records and statistics available there is no appreciable, immediate, and measurable acceleration in church growth evident in most churches . . . in the years following the campaigns."

In fact, Wagner shows that the church was actually growing better *before* the "in-depth" effort. Citing an example in Bolivia, he says, "The percentage of annual growth of the seven cooperating denominations . . . was greater during the year just before Evangelism-in-Depth than it was either during the year of effort or during the two following years."[2]

In country after country, mobilization has successfully occurred during the Evangelism-in-Depth year, but at the end of the effort it has fallen off. Why is this? "For one thing," Wagner explains, "the majority of people who participate suffer from sheer exhaustion. The pressure of the program saps the energy from all involved. Some discontinue their regular activities . . . and afterwards they find themselves with a huge backlog of work. Some postpone their vacations and then feel that they deserve a double one. . . . Some leaders came out with a bad case of. . . 'evangelistic indigestion,' from which it took them a full year to recover."[3]

Dr. Win Arn, president of the Institute for American Church Growth, examined statistics from a recent large-scale evangelistic campaign in an article in *Church Growth: America* magazine.

A typical report follows: 140 leaders trained; 7,200 telephone calls made; material shared with 1,987; 525 decisions; 72 interested enough to enroll in Bible study (with 20 of these becoming new church members, of which 16 had previous church affiliation).[4]

This report was from a North American, midwest "Bible-belt" city. I would expect even less to be reported from areas with fewer prepared people. Of course, church membership is not the exclusive measurement for evaluation, and I do not question the validity of the efforts. There was some fruit.

These kinds of evangelistic programs are gigantic efforts, requiring overwhelming organization—but they produce disappointing results! This will be the predictable outcome wherever we try to maintain a reaping mentality while evangelizing among unprepared peoples.

The overall evangelistic thrust of most local churches is producing disappointing results as far as reaching out to society. One very successful church in Minneapolis recently employed a marketing-analysis firm to do research among the 200,000 people within ten minutes' drive of the church. Eighty-six percent were totally unaware of the church's existence, even though it is quite prominent and located on a main thoroughfare. Only seven percent thought there was any possibility that they would ever visit the church.

Another Minneapolis pastor shared these results of his six-year ministry in an evangelical church of 350 members: Of 159 new members during this time, 117 came by transfer from other churches. Thirty-six were children of church members, leaving six that could have been converts from the community.

The same problem is also observable in much of the evangelism conducted on a smaller scale and even on the individual level. I could fill this book with accounts of my own efforts and those of others I've observed where reliance on proclamation produced meager fruit, some of which was not permanent.

I do not intend this as criticism. We should give thanks whenever the gospel is communicated in any form. The point is that we must change our tactics if we hope to effectively evangelize the unreached segments of our population.

RESTRICTING COMMUNICATION

Dr. Ralph Winter, director of the United States Center for World Mission, has observed, "Nominal Christians emerge automatically in the second generation and seem everywhere eventually to ring the Christian church around like a soft doughnut, which then in turn prevents the committed Christians from even getting out beyond that doughnut to the non-Christian world."[5] In other words, he asserts that we are exhausting our evangelistic energies on ourselves—on the nominal Christians who surround us. Can this be so?

Several years ago I became suspicious about the effectiveness of our communication with the lost. I tried to answer the question, "Just who are we reaching in our evangelistic efforts?" I soon discovered that information such as this is hard to find. For one thing, we are not accustomed to thinking in these categories. For another, it is difficult to find accurate data on the state of Christianity in the United States. So I devised a simple test that would at least reveal how my circle of co-laborers were faring in this area.

I have estimated that up to half of the American population does not view Christianity as the basis for their personal philosophy. They might, if pressed for religious preference, opt for Christianity. But for practical purposes, it is meaningless. It seemed to me that if we were effectively reaching the unreached half of our population, those converts would have to show up somewhere in the Body of Christ. So I formulated a question and have posed it to Christian audiences at every opportunity for several years.

I have asked this question in churches, seminaries, conferences, and in university campus groups. I have been especially interested in the campus groups because these are usually "grassroots" situations. My own organization, The Navigators, holds to a philosophy of "growing our own disciples" by evangelizing the lost and training converts in discipleship. Consequently, the starting point for any local Navigator ministry is evangelism. For obvious reasons, I would be anxious to survey such gatherings because they usually include many new Christians won through personal evangelism. I wanted to discover where they came from. Did they have a church background, or were they from the world? Were any of them won to Christ in a secularized context?

The question I ask is, "How many of you do not have a Christian heritage? That is, how many of you did not attend church with some regularity at some point in your youth?"

My rationale: Their responses would quickly divide the audience into two categories, those with religious background and those without. By comparing this response against my estimate of the national profile (one-half the population with a religious heritage), we would arrive at some notion as to our effectiveness among the two groups.

With a few notable exceptions, I discovered that roughly ninety percent of those in our Christian structures have a religious heritage. Rarely have I found a group where more than one in ten came from another background. In other words, approximately ninety percent of the active Christians on campuses have come from that half of the population that has had extensive previous religious exposure, while only about ten percent comes from the other half.

EVANGELISTIC CRUSADES

Several years ago, I had the opportunity to discuss this subject with Charlie Riggs of the Billy Graham Team. Mr. Riggs had been with the Graham team for more than thirty years at that time and had been responsible for follow-up.

I asked him what kind of people were coming to Christ through the Graham Crusades in the early years. Where did they come from? Then I asked where the people were coming from who are responding today. He explained that earlier, those making decisions were generally from the "liberal churches where they were not hearing the gospel." But now, he said, more than ninety percent of those making decisions are from "our evangelical churches."

I asked him when this transition occurred and how he interpreted it. He replied that the shift took place in the middle 1960s. He thinks "the tree has been shaken." In other words, the bulk of the unreached who would respond to a proclamation of the gospel have done so!

The accomplishment of reaching those who have responded to the gospel should not be minimized. But we cannot allow ourselves to think the gospel has been fully communicated in North America. Communication implies a minimum of two: a teller and a listener. People are highly selective in what they hear and pay attention to. Therefore, those of us who communicate the gospel must improve the ways we communicate.

DEDUCTIONS

I readily admit my approach is anything but scientific, and that my conclusions are subject to many exceptions. But I will have to leave a precise study for someone more disposed to pursuing this kind of research. Since my figures are more impressionistic than precise, you may want to test them yourself as they relate to your situation. It should be a simple thing to do. Simply compare the religious profile of your city or suburb against that of your own local fellowship. How does your fellowship rate in reaching out into society?

What does all of this tell us? If ninety percent of our fruit is coming from the half of the population who have at some point already been among us, we have a communication problem with the other half. It means we have yet to cross the frontiers of different mentalities and reach those from nonChristian backgrounds with the gospel.

We cannot deceive ourselves into thinking we are already effectively discharging our trust to share the gospel. Nor can we think that if we keep doing what we have been doing—and even redouble our efforts—we are going to reach our world. It will take more than that. Our patterns of evangelism must change.

As the Billy Graham Association was making preparations for a Congress on Evangelism in the early 1970s, they issued a statement summarizing the intended thrust of the Congress. *Church Growth Bulletin* published the statement under the title: "Billy Graham's New Vision."[6] The article noted plans were being made that

> will, for the first time, tackle a startling problem, formerly overlooked: most (at least one billion) of the unreached peoples of the world are not within the normal evangelistic range of any church anywhere. This fact is surprising since we know that there are now Christian churches in every country of the world. The problem is that ordinary evangelistic efforts simply do not carry effectively across the high barriers constituted by ethnic, cultural, and social differences. It is an embarrassing fact that the churches in the United States and around the world, which are geographically closest to these unevangelized peoples, or ethnic groups, are often the farthest away from them culturally and emotionally . . . This amazing new element smashed the illusion many Christians have had that the world can be won if only the world-wide Church will evangelize the people with whom it is normally in contact.

For me, the most disturbing thing in connection with this statement is the amazement of the reporter!

CONCLUSION

Our limited ability to communicate has a direct bearing also on the effectiveness of our world missions. In a recent worldwide survey of one Christian mission organization working in more than thirty countries, it was discovered that eighty-seven percent of the people it had reached already had a Protestant heritage!

Perhaps we are going to have to learn to communicate effectively with the secularized and other people within our own culture in order to be truly effective outside of it. Are we sending people who are limited to working only among those who share our own evangelical presuppositions? Where are the apostles to the Gentiles in this generation?

NOTES:
1. C. Peter Wagner, *Frontiers in Missionary Strategy* (Chicago: Moody Press, 1971), page 135.
2. Wagner, page 143.
3. Wagner, pages 159-160.
4. Win Arn, "A Church Growth Look at 'Here's Life America,'" *Church Growth: America* (January-February 1977), page 7.
5. Ralph Winter, "Who Are the Three Billion? Part II," *Church Growth Bulletin* (July 1977), pages 139-144.
6. "Billy Graham's New Vision," *Church Growth Bulletin* (November 1972), page 278.

EIGHT

AFFIRMATION

The Often Missing Factor

THE PUZZLING EPISTLES
Where Are the Exhortations to Witness?

Before reading this chapter, read the New Testament letters and note every exhortation about witnessing.

Earlier we observed how Paul limited his sphere of ministry to establishing beachheads of believers, usually in key centers. But his vision did not stop there. His work did, but his vision did not. He depended upon the ongoing growth of those little bodies of Christians for the preservation of his labors and the continued expansion of the gospel in the world. In fact, he maintained that if this did not occur, his labor would ultimately prove to have been for nothing (see Philippians 2:16).

This being the case—with so much resting on the performance of those little churches—one would expect Paul's letters to them to abound with exhortations to witness, to get out and continue what he had begun, proclaiming the gospel to every person. But no such exhortations are there! Why not? Perhaps it's because Paul realized that *merely more of the same would be counter-productive.* He had come in and reaped. Winning the remainder of those pagan societies required more than words. Before there could be a new harvest, more planting and cultivating needed to occur.

This is supported by what Paul did say in his letters about winning the lost. For example, he told Titus to "teach the older women to be reverent in the way they live . . . they can train the younger women to love their husbands and children, to be self-controlled and pure, to be busy at home,

83

to be kind, and to be subject to their husbands, *so that no one will malign the word of God*" (Titus 2:3-5, emphasis added).

He urged him to "encourage the young men to be self-controlled. . . . In your teaching show integrity, seriousness and soundness of speech . . . *so that those who oppose you may be ashamed because they have nothing bad to say about us*" (Titus 2:6-8, emphasis added).

These cause-and-effect statements reveal Paul's clear recognition of the importance of the people of God *modeling* the character of God before sharing the gospel. Almost without fail, when he discussed the problem of the lost world, he focused on our "being" as the fundamental solution.

"Whatever happens, *conduct yourselves in a manner worthy of the gospel* of Christ. Then . . . I will know that you stand firm in one spirit, contending as one man for the faith of the gospel" (Philippians 1:27, emphasis added).

THE EXAMPLE OF SERGIO

Sergio was among the first generation of Christians who came from our university ministry in Brazil. He belonged to a family of industrialists who had established a reputation for lack of concern about honesty and integrity. Sergio was studying law and economics, preparing to assume the responsibility for the legal needs of his family's various business ventures.

Sergio had polio when he was four years old. He walked with a full-body brace and crutches. He possessed an incredibly strong will, the result of his years of battling against the confines of his paralyzed body.

When we first met, he was a cold, hard person. We would meet once or twice weekly and drive to a favorite spot overlooking the city where we would study the Scriptures together. As Sergio moved from his agnosticism to Jesus Christ, he began to change. By the time he was finishing his studies, he was a mature Christian, and the changes in his personality were obvious to all who knew him.

But there was a problem. What was he going to do about his future? His family was putting him through school with the understanding that he was being prepared to work with them. But how could he do this without compromising his integrity? After all, wasn't it a lawyer's function to help the businessman get away with as much illegal activity as possible? I could see Sergio was disturbed about this, but I didn't know how to help him.

The year Sergio was to graduate from the university, Brazil went through a financial crisis that drove many businesses into bankruptcy. The industries belonging to Sergio's family were among these. Suddenly he was free from his obligations to work for his family. He was on his own.

The week he graduated, he came to me and announced he had made two decisions. He had decided to put God first, and to be honest. With that he moved back to his hometown, rented an office, and opened his own law practice.

A few months later, one of the local farmers was on the verge of losing his farm because of unpaid back taxes. The farm went up for public auction, and Sergio bought it. A murmur ran through the town, for the purchase appeared to be typical of the opportunism that characterized the rest of Sergio's family. But what Sergio did next stopped the town in its tracks. He went to the farmer and gave him back the deed to his property, instructing him to repay the debt as he was able!

Sergio didn't have to do this. It was his legal right to keep the farm. But he acted with grace, not merely with justice—just as God does with us.

Sergio probably has another thirty-five years in business ahead of him. If he continues the way he has begun, the sheer influence of his life will go a long way toward breaking up the spiritual soil in that valley where he lives.

I learned a lot as I watched Sergio work out his discipleship in the context of his business. His foundational decisions to "put God first and to be honest" were strategic! Without that he would have neither a platform to witness from, nor a message backed by a Christian lifestyle. He could only look forward to living out his life with little hope of being used by God in others' lives.

Jesus said, "You will receive power when the Holy Spirit comes on you; and you will be my witnesses" (Acts 1:8). It seems to me this statement summarizes what we're saying in this chapter. The command is not to *do* witnessing, but to *be* Christ's witnesses. Evangelism is not merely an activity; it is a way of living. When we lose sight of this, if all we do is proclaim, the people we win will not learn how to reproduce themselves spiritually. We must obey Christ's command to make disciples by "teaching them to obey everything I have commanded you" (Matthew 28:20), or those we win will never go on and bear fruit themselves, and there will be no second crop. The harvest will be limited to that first cutting. But where *being* is in focus, the crop is perennial.

In the light of this, I hope you will take the time to review the New Testament epistles again and note all that they do say about our witness to the world.

AFFIRMATION IN ISRAEL
God's Chosen People

There is one underlying purpose entwined in everything God is doing in relation to man. It can be summarized in one word: reconciliation. "God was reconciling the world to himself in Christ" (2 Corinthians 5:19). He committed the "message of reconciliation" to men. We've observed that God even divided the world into cultures and nations with reconciliation in mind.

The people of God have always been essential to the accomplishment of His purposes. Until we grasp this, we will never have an adequate understanding of evangelism—or of the Christian life.

Israel: the least likely. As a nation, Israel got off to an improbable start—it was the nation least likely to succeed. It all began with one man and a promise. Abraham was seventy-five years old and Sarah was sixty-six when they left Haran to seek the fulfillment of God's promise. After eleven years of desert life, when Abraham was eighty-six and Sarah seventy-seven, they lost their patience. The result was Ishmael. But he didn't count, and they were worse off than before.

They waited another fourteen years for Isaac, the son of the promise, to be born. By now Abraham was a hundred years old, and Sarah was ninety-one. Forty years later Isaac married Rebekah. By then his mother had already died. Isaac and Rebekah waited twenty years for their twin sons, Jacob and Esau, to be born. But only one of the twins, Jacob, was to share the promise. So after eighty-five years, from God's calling of Abraham to Haran to the birth of Jacob, the nation of Israel still consisted of only three people: Jacob and his parents.

Neither Jacob nor his mother were exactly models of integrity. Jacob deceived his father, swindled his brother, and fought with his uncle. His wives were idolaters. But Jacob's family swelled into a clan of seventy people, a band of nomads with doubtful moral standards.

So after 225 years (during which they wandered from Haran to Egypt), the nation only consisted of one family of seventy people.

Next came 430 years of slavery in Egypt. They were years of silence on God's part: no miracles, no signs, no renewed promises. Not a sound from God. Over those centuries, all Israel had to go on were the aging stories passed from father to son about a seemingly distant God who had occasionally visited their ancestors Abraham, Isaac, and Jacob. And now Israel was in slavery—hardly an environment conducive to cultural development.

Finally, under Moses' leadership, Israel fled Egypt as a nation numbering a million men. While wandering in the desert, Israel acquired a culture that was so sophisticated and comprehensive that it leaped centuries, leaving the neighboring nations behind in stark contrast. God gave Israel guidelines for medicine, hygiene, economics, agriculture, ethics, politics, law, and religion.

There were 655 years between the departure for Haran and the

Exodus. That's a long time! If he were superimposed on our calendar, Abraham would be like a figure out of the Middle Ages. Why did God do it this way? The book of Deuteronomy gives us some clues. God was after more than Israel. He wanted the world.

Moses challenged the nation to think of this greater purpose when he told the people, "I have taught you decrees and laws . . . so that you may follow them in the land you are entering. . . . Observe them carefully, for this will show your wisdom and understanding to the nations, who will hear about all these decrees and say, 'Surely this great nation is a wise and understanding people.' What other nation is so great as to have their gods near them the way the LORD our God is near us whenever we pray to him? And what other nation is so great as to have such righteous decrees and laws as this body of laws I am setting before you today?" (Deuteronomy 4:5-8).

God chose Israel, not because they were the best or the greatest, but because they were so unlikely. It was obvious that if anything ever came of them, it would have to be God's doing. "Understand, then, that it is not because of your righteousness that the LORD your God is giving you this good land to possess, for you are a stiff-necked people. . . . You provoked the LORD your God to anger. . . . From the day you left Egypt until you arrived here, you have been rebellious against the LORD" (Deuteronomy 9:6-7).

Israel was God's mouthpiece to the world. Judging from their history, the world would have to recognize that the living God had, in fact, taken up with this nation. That was precisely the point. It worked. By the time of King Solomon, he "was greater in riches and wisdom than all the other kings of the earth. The whole world sought audience with Solomon to hear the wisdom God had put in his heart" (1 Kings 10:23-24).

God made an alliance with Israel. He so identified Himself with her that He was known in the world as "the God of Israel." How Israel prospered through this relationship! She became beautiful because she reflected the personality of God Himself. The world beat a path to her door.

All went well as long as the people of Israel were obedient to God's commandments. But God made Himself vulnerable through this alliance. Israel possessed the power to mislead the entire world! All she had to do was disobey God or embrace her neighbors' gods and she would garble God's image before the world. The world would begin to draw wrong conclusions about Him. And that's what happened.

This explains why God was so intolerant of her idolatry and why He withdrew His name and His presence from her as dramatically as He gave them. Moses taught the Israelites that if they rebelled and experienced God's judgment, then "all the nations will ask: 'Why has the LORD done this to this land? Why this fierce, burning anger?' And the answer will be: 'It is because this people abandoned the covenant of the LORD'" (Deuteronomy 29:24-25).

God had to make it clear to the world that He was not a party to Israel's injustices or perversions. Through Ezekiel the prophet, God said, "They will know that I am the LORD, when I disperse them among the nations and scatter them through the countries. But I will spare a few of them from the sword, famine and plague, so that in the nations where they go they may acknowledge all their detestable practices. Then they will know that I am the LORD" (Ezekiel 12:15-16).

In her obedience, Israel glorified God. That is, she served to reflect the nature of God to the world. God's attributes were incarnated by His people. Israel was a flesh-and-blood phenomenon for all to see. Because the nation of Israel existed, the world could no longer plead ignorance of God and His ways.

AFFIRMATION IN THE CHURCH
A Unique People

"You, though a wild olive shoot, have been grafted in among the others and now share in the nourishing sap from the olive root" (Romans 11:17). This is the Church, the new people of God, but rooted in the same promises and fulfilling the same purposes as ancient Israel once did.

Israel collapsed and no longer functioned as a positive voice in the world. As she decayed, most of her people moved in one of two directions. Some, using the beauty and wealth with which God endowed the nation, fed their appetites to the extent that perversion, injustice, and corruption became the predominant national characteristics (see Ezekiel 16).

Others, the devout, were horrified by this abandonment of the old values, and purposed to be the heroic remnant—the preservers of the faith. They expanded on Moses' five books with a seventy-volume commentary and kept the administrative structure of seventy elders which he had set up intact (see Exodus 18). Bent on maintaining the old standards, they fell into the trap of dead works (see Malachi 1-2). The sect of the Pharisees was born.

It is amazing how anything as beautiful as Israel once was could become so ugly. It was a toss-up as to which extreme was more disgusting—the irreverent or the legalists. Both had an adverse impact on the world (see Romans 2:24).

But God's plan did not change. Through His own Son, He generated a new people, grafting them into the same rich root from which Israel had grown.

The beginnings were parallel: twelve sons of Jacob, twelve apostles. But the pace was different. What took 225 years with Israel, Christ accomplished in a little over three years. Jacob left a clan of seventy in Egypt, while Jesus left a body of 120 in a room in Jerusalem. Just as God distinguished Israel with a unique culture, so Jesus did with the Church. But here we observe a marked contrast. While Israel's culture was sociopolitical in nature, the sphere of this new people was fundamentally spiritual.

The Church: the outpost of the Kingdom of God. Jesus came preaching the Kingdom of God. It was the first thing He talked about and the last. Even though He made the Kingdom His primary theme, few, if any, clearly grasped its significance. We can hardly blame them, as His words still seem obscure and often enigmatic.

He described the Kingdom as being present, yet future; revealed, yet a mystery; among us, yet not of this world; like a small seed, yet pervading everything. He compared it to a net full of fish, twenty virgins, a treasure hidden in a field, and a pearl merchant.

The apostles betrayed their lack of insight about the Kingdom in their very last conversation with Jesus, just before He ascended. They asked if He wasn't about to fulfill their expectations by restoring Israel's political order. They failed to grasp the true scope of the Kingdom. They failed to realize that Jesus, in His teachings, was introducing a truly radical order. He was introducing a new lifestyle with new values, new attitudes, new relationships—in short, a new culture: the Kingdom culture!

It is in understanding what Jesus teaches us about citizenship in God's Kingdom that the radical uniqueness of the Christian life dawns on us. His words are to us what the book of Leviticus was to Israel. Jesus intends for His people, the Church, to model "life in the Kingdom."

E. Stanley Jones observed that the Kingdom of God is really a totalitarian order, and not like human systems that must content themselves with outward conformity. The Kingdom of God reaches to our inmost thoughts. One cannot think a thought without the approval or disapproval of the Kingdom. The Kingdom also ranges to the outermost rim of our relationships. This sounds like bondage! But the effect is just the reverse of man's authoritarian systems. Rather than enslaving people, entering the Kingdom culture and practicing a Kingdom lifestyle liberates them.

Perhaps Jesus' words seem so obscure because they oppose the world's value system. We read His teachings, and we understand the sentences, but we conclude that somehow He couldn't really have meant what He said.

For now, the important thing to recognize is that just as God raised up

Israel to amplify His voice throughout the world, He has assigned us the same function. Peter's words repeated what the Israelites had been taught centuries earlier: "You are a chosen people, a royal priesthood, a holy nation, a people belonging to God, that you may declare the praises of him who called you out of darkness into his wonderful light. . . . Live such good lives among the pagans that . . . they may see your good deeds and glorify God on the day he visits us" (1 Peter 2:9,12).

SUMMARY

Paul's emphasis on our *being* is supported by the sweep of Scripture. The existence of a unique people, whose lives are marked by God Himself, has always been fundamental to His program of reconciling the world to Himself. His people incarnate His character; they audio-visualize the nature of His eternal reign.

How this works out in practice has been, and is, one of the most difficult issues the Church struggles with. The pendulum has steadily swung back and forth for 2,000 years between the extremes of isolation and compromise.

Neither extreme is acceptable. Where there is compromise, the gospel and its power get lost. Where there is isolation, whatever light that is shed is lost to those who need it the most.

PART THREE

THE MESSENGER AFFIRMS THE MESSAGE

LIGHTING UP THE DARKNESS

The Essence of Light

WE ARE THE first account of the gospel most people will ever read. Either they will desire more, having read us, or they will decide that there is nothing there for them.

The first two chapters of this book describe the nature of the shifting spiritual climate in parts of the Western world and the effects of this shift on the individual. We concluded chapter 2 with two questions: What does it take to awaken interest, to induce a person to go back and seriously examine the Christian message after he has already discarded it as an unimportant relic? What ray of hope could penetrate the accumulated layers of disenchantment?

In chapter 3, we examined how Jesus related to the people of His generation. We saw how He consistently communicated a single theme: His identity. That man, who for a very short period in human history walked the streets among us, was also God the Creator. As such, He re-illuminated a world that had suffered a power failure, where the lights had gone out. He said, "I am the light of the world. Whoever follows me will never walk in darkness, but will have the light of life" (John 8:12). People who believe in Jesus do not spend their lives in the dark. On the contrary, they are able to see where they are going.

Jesus passed the torch to His spiritual offspring. He said, "You are the light of the world. . . . Let your light shine before men" (Matthew 5:14-16). This statement places a very large responsibility on us. He moved on; we stepped in. Just as His manner of life and His speech illuminated the way out of darkness into a relationship with His Father, so we, by our manner of

93

life and our speech, are to bridge this same distance for those who continue in darkness.

"You were once darkness, but now you are the light in the Lord" (Ephesians 5:8). Light catches the eye. Advertisers vie with one another for attention by creatively illuminating their slogans. The reflection from a single mirror in a forest will be seen immediately. If we are light, we will be noticed.

FAITH, HOPE, AND LOVE

What is it that makes the Christian stand out? Unfortunately, some of us stand out for all the wrong reasons. Our distinction as Christians frequently degenerates into an adherence to our own peculiar set of behavioral scruples. But some really do stand out for the right reasons.

Once I participated in a conference in Africa with people from several black African countries. Among them was a young man who had lost his eldest brother a few months earlier. The brother had been witnessing to some Muslim friends. Then one day he was found strangled in his room. The slain brother was the eldest of eight children. The father had died, so he had assumed the headship of the family. The grief and sense of loss was obviously still very strong in the brother who was attending the conference.

There is a significant percentage of Muslims in many of the black African countries. For this reason, Fouad Accad, a Lebanese Christian who has devoted most of his life to understanding Muslim thought, was invited to present a series of lectures at the conference. One does not have to be around this man for long to perceive that he has a singular obsession and love: the one billion Muslims in the world. He exudes love for the Muslim. To hear him talk, Muslims are the most wonderful people on earth.

As Fouad Accad delivered his lectures, the young African who had just lost his brother struggled with what was being said, thinking, "It is easy for those who have never suffered to talk." Fouad Accad, recognizing the struggle, recounted some of his own losses. He told of how the Muslims had sacked his home, carrying off his wife's trousseau and a lifetime of accumulated memories. He told of how his two most faithful protégés had been murdered. These accounts helped not only the young African—they served as a message to all of us. Fouad Accad lives life on a different value system. Because he does, he is able to love those he would otherwise hate. This is what it means to be light.

In everyday terms, the difference between the Christian and the nonChristian lies in the fact that the two operate on different value systems. Paul wrote, "These three remain: faith, hope and love" (1 Corinthians 13:13). These three qualities are the foundation stones of the Christian's value system. To the degree that our lives are, in fact, constructed on these three foundations, we are light.

You may be thinking, "This is not exactly the story of *my* life! Where and how does one acquire this faith, hope, and love?" Interestingly, all three have their origins in a single source: Jesus Christ.

Faith. The New Testament states again and again that the foundation of our faith is in the (person), Jesus Christ. "Let us fix our eyes on Jesus, the author and perfecter of our faith" (Hebrews 12:2). We "live by faith in the Son of God" (Galatians 2:20). Our faith is based on the conviction that Jesus is what He said He was, and that He will keep His promises.

Hope. Our hope is rooted in three facts about Jesus Christ. First, there is the fact that *He was resurrected* from the dead. God "has given us new birth into a living hope through the resurrection of Jesus Christ from the dead" (1 Peter 1:3). Second, there is the fact that *He ascended* to the Father where He constantly defends our case. "We who have fled to take hold of the hope offered to us may be greatly encouraged. We have this hope as an anchor for the soul, firm and secure. It enters the inner sanctuary. . . where Jesus, who went before us, has entered on our behalf" (Hebrews 6:18-20). Third, there is the hope that *He will return.* "We wait for the blessed hope—the glorious appearing of our great God and Savior, Jesus Christ" (Titus 2:13).

Love. "This is how we know what love is: Jesus Christ laid down his life for us" (1 John 3:16). "This is love: not that we loved God, but that he loved us and sent his Son as an atoning sacrifice" (1 John 4:10). Hence, Christian love has the death of Jesus Christ as its source.

Certainly all of us feel woefully weak in these areas of faith, hope, and love. How to grow is the question. The most practical advice I can think of is to suggest that you make it a lifetime daily habit to contemplate the significance of what God has done for us in Jesus Christ. Anyone who is truly gripped by these great truths will become transformed by them (2 Corinthians 3:18).

The outworking of faith, hope, and love is very distinct. Each will produce its own fruit in your life. For example, faith will produce both freedom (Romans 14:2) and obedience (Romans 1:5). Love will make you a servant (Galatians 5:13) and will give you patience (Ephesians 4:2).

Hope, too, will bear its fruit. Apparently, hope causes the most readily observable changes in a person. According to Ephesians 2:12, the fundamental difference between the Christian and the nonChristian is this factor of hope: "You were . . . without hope and without God in the world." Peter advised people, "Always be prepared to give an answer to everyone who asks you to give the reason for the *hope* that you have" (1 Peter 3:15, emphasis added).

Hope is attractive. It produces joy and peace (Romans 15:13), purity (1 John 3:2-3), self-control (Titus 2:11-13), and endurance (1 Thessalonians 1:3). We could go on expanding this list.

Stop and think: What is everybody looking for? Ask anyone. People say they want happiness, peace, freedom, a clear conscience, stability, security. But everything they want out of life is to be found in the hope that comes from Christ. The Christian who appears on the scene with even a minimum of these qualities *will* stand out as a light in the darkness (Ephesians 5:8).

So people are attracted by our *hope.* As they come in closer for a better look, our *love* disarms them, removing the would-be barriers and judgments. Bearing all things, believing all things, and enduring all things, it makes a bonafide relationship possible. In this context, as we explain our hope and exercise our love from Christ, people are led into *faith.*

Years ago I heard Dr. Bob Smith, a godly and beloved professor at Bethel College in St. Paul, Minnesota, make a casual comment that has made a permanent mark on me. He had just returned from two years of teaching in the Middle East and his mind was filled with fresh experiences of involvement with Muslims. He described how the people grasped at whatever display of personal interest or friendliness he would show them. Then he said, "You know, ninety percent of evangelism is love."

I didn't know that! In fact, at the time, as a hungry young Christian bent on achieving, I saw evangelism simply as an activity I engaged in. The people involved were more like objects needing saving rather than real persons. I was after results, with no time to waste on loving anybody.

But Dr. Smith was right. The Apostle Paul said, "Christ's love compels us, because we are convinced that one died for all" (2 Corinthians 5:14). Notice the origin of this love that motivated Paul. It was Christ's love. Christ's love, in turn, reflected the Father's love. God started it. "We love because he first loved us" (1 John 4:19). This is the witness of a life.

I have to admit I never saw much enduring fruit in evangelism until I began to understand the importance of this truth and began to put it into practice.

Jesus "became flesh and made his dwelling among us. We have seen his glory . . . full of grace and truth" (John 1:14). We Christians are called upon to be like Christ, to be concerned about grace and truth (Ephesians 4:15). This means being redemptive in our relationships, just as He was. This is being *light.*

TEN

THE CONGRUENCE OF LIFE AND BELIEF

Modeling God's Grace

WE HAVE SEEN that a person with a good testimony is one who, because his life is characterized by faith, hope, and love, is redemptive in his relationships. Wherever he goes, he sows life and hope rather than despair, conflict, or death. Such a person is the most significant figure in our society. Jesus called him the salt of the earth, the light of the world, and the good seed. He is a singular exception in a disoriented world.

About the time the Watergate scandal was being revealed, I was on a plane going to Washington, D.C. I was engrossed in a book on politics, quite oblivious to the person seated next to me. Evidently what I was reading stirred his interest because he initiated a conversation with me about the book. I soon learned that he was an attorney assigned to negotiating labor disputes. Our conversation drifted to Watergate, and I asked him what he thought its root causes were. He replied that it reflected "incompetence in leadership, and isolation from reality at the top."

I said I felt at least one other factor had to be included, and that was the absence of moral absolutes. He didn't understand what I was saying, so I illustrated it with the story of a California lawsuit.

In the early sixties, several restaurant owners in California began employing topless waitresses. The local citizens filed suit against the owners, charging them with immoral conduct. When the citizens won their case in the state courts, the restaurant owners appealed the decision to the U.S. Supreme Court. There they got a reversal on the state court's decision and were given the legal right to continue operating with topless waitresses.

97

I pointed out to my companion that the disturbing thing about this case was the basis upon which it was won by the restaurant operators. The decision (along with a few other contemporary cases) set a precedent in American law that continues to undermine the entire system. The restaurant owners won their case with this argument: Our topless restaurants are frequented by some of the leading citizens in the community; therefore, what takes place reflects the community's moral standards. Since the citizens of a community are the ones who should determine its moral standards, what is going on in those restaurants is *right.*

I explained that once we concede the assumption that it is the citizens who determine what is right and wrong, we have cut ourselves adrift in a sea of relativism. To dramatize the fallacy, using the same argument those leading citizens could decide they don't like Spanish-speaking people or any other group and justify killing them.

(If this sounds extreme, think for a moment of what the leading citizens of Russia decided in the 1920s, Germany in the '30s, or Argentina in the last decade. Tens of millions of innocents have suffered unnatural deaths on the basis of precisely this rationale. Paul Johnson, the modern historian, describes how leaders, in the name of "class," "race," or "national security," discarded the idea of any absolute morality. He refers to "an unguided world adrift in a relativistic universe.")

Returning to the Watergate case, I reminded my companion of the repeated explanation by the defendants that they were just doing what they felt would accomplish their goal—keeping President Richard Nixon in office. I explained that once "right" becomes whatever contributes to the prevailing goals, the ultimate result is disintegration. He saw my point and agreed. So the two of us sat there for a few moments contemplating the unfortunate fact that since absolutes no longer exist in our society, our survival is compromised.

Finally, inevitably, he asked, "What absolutes would you suggest?"

I said, "I'm a Christian."

He couldn't see what this had to do with it, so I went on to explain. "Let's suppose for a moment that both you and I are Christians. That would mean we both believe in God. If we could accept that, He would be an absolute, wouldn't He?"

My companion agreed.

I continued, "But even if God exists, it wouldn't do us any good unless we had some word from Him as to what life is all about, would it?"

Again he agreed.

I went on, "That's exactly what the Bible is—a word from God as to what life is about. So as Christians, you and I would have two absolutes: God and His Word. That would be an adequate basis of truth for us to operate on, don't you think?" This launched us into a dynamic discussion about Jesus Christ.

It is true that collectively man cannot thrive without moral absolutes. It is just as true, though perhaps less apparent, on the individual level.

A few years ago, our family moved into a new neighborhood during a temporary stay in the United States. One of our first friendships was with a young couple who lived down the block and across the street from us. While we were out for dinner together one evening, my wife and I told them we were thinking of inviting some of our neighbors to discuss common problems in marriage, the family, and other human relationships, using the Bible as our basis. They reacted enthusiastically. The husband said, "I think we could get everyone on the block to come. We don't know of a single couple in this neighborhood who could be called happy."

Ours is, in fact, a neurotic society. Problems and tensions in society are widespread, while on the individual level man is asking survival questions. "How do I cope with feelings of futility and insecurity?" "How do I get along with this woman?" "What should we do with our children?"

Answers to questions such as these will not be forthcoming from either our social scientists or our philosophers. France's "new philosophers," mirroring our times, say all ideologies are dangerous delusions. They, and others, have concluded that there really are no answers to man's basic questions. With this conclusion, they are probably closer to the truth now than secular man has ever been!

God has predicted the end result of man's attempt to light his own way. In Isaiah 50:11, God says, "All you who light fires and provide yourselves with flaming torches, go, walk in the light of your fires and of the torches you have set ablaze. This is what you shall receive from my hand: You will lie down in torment."

When Jesus said, "I am the truth," it was good news indeed. He is our reference point, allowing the Christian to walk through the ruins of man-made philosophies on a true course. As he walks in the light, in the truth that is Christ Himself, the Christian is a statement from God to the world that there is another option.

THE CHRISTIAN VALUE SYSTEM

"You were once darkness, but now you are light in the Lord. Live as children of light" (Ephesians 5:8). Being light presupposes congruence: harmony between God's ways and our own. One thing that disrupts this harmony is the constant, subtle, often subliminal influences our society exerts on us.

Jesus was speaking about this danger in His comments on leaven (yeast). He warned His disciples to "beware of the leaven of the Pharisees and Sadducees" (Matthew 16:6, RSV) "and the leaven of Herod" (Mark 8:15, RSV). Leaven symbolizes human imperfection (see Exodus 12:15-20, 13:3-8; Leviticus 2:11; 1 Corinthians 5:6-8). Jesus was warning against mixing imperfect human ideas with God's truth. The Pharisees had mixed their own religious traditions with the teaching of the Scriptures; the Sadducees were the philosophers of Jewish society; and Herod represented the world system. These three influences—tradition, philosophy, and society—seem inevitably to work their way into and become part of the value system of any Christian community to such an extent that it is possible to be a Christian, but live almost entirely within a pagan value system, and *not even perceive it.*

This possibility began to dawn on me when we moved to Brazil and changed cultures. Culture is hardly perceived as long as we do not leave the only one we really know. A fish doesn't perceive the water in which it swims, and neither are we aware of our culture, or the influence it exerts on our thoughts and actions. Often we must step outside of it to understand it—and to understand ourselves!

I have since learned that this experience is common to those who cross cultural lines. One acquaintance, Bob Malcolm, who spent many years as a missionary in the Philippines, observed, "I spent most of my time in the Philippines trying to sort out which of my beliefs were American, which beliefs were Filipino, and which were Christian. I came to the conclusion that much of what I believed belonged to the first two categories."

As we moved into the Brazilian culture, we gradually became aware of the origins of our value system. I was chagrined to discover that much of my "biblical Christianity" did not really come from the Bible at all. My attitude toward work and material things came out of cultural distortions of the Puritan work ethic. My thinking processes and my approach to problem solving were marked by the computer revolution. Marketing and consumerism had influenced my definition and evaluation of progress. Madison Avenue and television had helped to set my living standard. I found I had a greater disposition for violence than the people we were ministering to—a result of our American history. My philosophy of child raising was affected by humanism. Even women's liberation and the Beatles had affected me. What a shock to realize the collage my supposedly biblical Christianity really was. I was a sub-Christian Christian!

As this dawned on me, I asked myself, "Is this the message I'm going to pass on to my Brazilian friends?" I thought I needed to "Brazilianize" my Christianity. But I soon realized that also would be sub-Christian because all human systems are marred.

It was at this point in my thinking that the phrase "Kingdom of God" began to get my attention. For me the Kingdom had always been one of those things to skip over in the Bible. It seemed distant, among the more impractical Bible truths. But now, for some reason, I began to mark the word *Kingdom* with ink every time I ran across it in my Bible. I was still at it two years later, but didn't know why. Whenever I would attempt to tell others what I was learning on the subject, I'd go blank—a sure sign I hadn't put the pieces together. I asked God for help to clear it up for me, because by then the Kingdom seemed to be standing out on every page. *Surely such a predominant theme was significant!*

Then I realized this was the third option! Not an Americanized Christianity, nor a Brazilianized Christianity, but a Christianity growing out of the culture of the Kingdom—*the Kingdom culture!* Not a provincial, flawed, human order, but God's untarnished, universal domain—a whole new way of living. There it was, beautifully laid out by God for His people. When the unique Kingdom culture comes into focus, the incongruities in one's life, the areas that had previously escaped the redemptive process, are called into account. No other biblical truths call our attention to the radical uniqueness of the Christian life as do the teachings on the Kingdom.

It was in the context of Jesus' words about the Kingdom that He spoke about the dangers of leaven. Where does leaven come from? Jesus described the leavening sequence in Mark 7:6-13. He pointed out that the process begins with a good idea. It is so good, in fact, we agree it should become a norm, a rule. Consequently, a man's idea gains equal weight with the Word of God.

The next step is neglecting the Word of God while still adhering to that good idea. By now the idea has become a tradition. We soon find the tradition more to our liking than the Word of God, so we set His Word aside. Finally, the tradition comes full circle. Jesus said, "You nullify the word of God by your tradition" (Mark 7:13). This happens when our practice actually works against doing the will of God.

To illustrate, let's take one of the most successful forms that exists in our churches today—the Sunday school. The Sunday school was a good idea.

Originally the Sunday school was brought into being as a means of teaching children who did not have Christian parents; children who would have had little opportunity to receive the gospel apart from it. In those early days, no self-respecting Christian parent sent his child to Sunday school, as it would have been an admission of failure on his part. He would have been considered negligent of his responsibility to teach his own

children, as we are instructed in Deuteronomy 6:6-7: "These commandments . . . are to be upon your hearts. Impress them on your children. Talk
about them when you sit at home and when you walk along the road, when
you lie down and when you get up."

Apparently, the benefits of the Sunday school were so evident that the
attitude of the Christian parents changed. Soon no self-respecting Christian parent would neglect sending his children to Sunday school.

The next step is predictable. Dad neglects his scriptural responsibility
for instructing his children in God's Word and turns it over to the church—
a responsibility the church simply cannot fulfill. The church cannot fulfill
it because it is a parental responsibility. The Sunday school can contribute,
but it can't assume what only Dad can do.

This sequence illustrates Jesus' description in Mark 7. When Dad lets
go of his responsibility, disaster very often strikes *him!* His felt need for
maintaining a godly life, for developing his mastery of the Scriptures, and
his ability to teach them drops off. When he delegates responsibility for his
family, he's free to wander.

If there's any one thing that prods me into maintaining mental and
spiritual discipline, it's the realization that my children and their children
will inherit the fruit of my thought life. Holiness seems very sensible when
seen from this angle (see Deuteronomy 4:39-40).

So how does it happen that incongruities leaven our Christianity? To
summarize, "The good news is converted into behavior and behavior into
habit. The habit can become mere custom and quite irrelevant. Similarly
faith tends to become *creed* and creed ends up as a mere recitation."[1]

Now what does this matter of congruence—that is, harmony with
God's ways—have to do with reaching the unreachable? It has a great deal
to do with it. A congruent life is the secret of naturalness in communication. And naturalness is the secret of attracting rather than repelling with
our witness. On the other hand, where there are incongruities in our lives,
we usually have to resort to devices or gimmicks to get our message across.

We must ask ourselves, where did I get my opinions on everything:
finances, success, marriage, child-raising, business, time-use, sex, people,
pleasure, education, progress, society, sports, politics, organization, and
religion? Did any of my beliefs come, in fact, from God's Word? It is not
acceptable for the Christian to borrow from the world's value system. As
J.B. Phillips translated Romans 12:2, "Don't let the world around you
squeeze you into its own mold, but let God remake you so that your whole
attitude of mind is changed."

If we can trace our value system in these areas back to the Word of
God, communicating our faith becomes infinitely easier. Any subject, if
explored far enough, will lead us into a discussion of the good news. We

must always be prepared to explain why we are the way we are (see 1 Peter 3:15).

In my early Christian life, when I first began witnessing to my friends, the great hurdle was always getting started. I never seemed to know what to say. I began keeping a page of "openers" in a notebook. These were questions I would ask to get me into the subject. They included, "Was there ever a time in your life when you seriously considered becoming a Christian?" "What did you think of the sermon?" "Are you interested in spiritual things?"

Such questions can help, but they often backfired on me. I could never seem to get the timing right. I would "casually" throw these questions out in the midst of an otherwise normal conversation. At that point everything became abnormal. My quarry would tense up and become almost as nervous as I was. Then, awkwardly, I would go into my presentation. This approach was just as alien as the opening question. It consisted of heavy offers of eternal life and vague references to happiness now. Where there is incongruence, that's about all we have to offer. What we represent is not substantially any different from what the receiver already has. Even eternal life is not particularly attractive to him. He's already ambivalent about the life he does have—both hating and loving it—but not loving it enough to want it to go on forever.

A few years ago, I had been away from home for many weeks on a long trip and had been with people constantly. I was desperate to get away from people for awhile. So when I got on the plane, I sat in an aisle seat. The middle seat was vacant and the window seat was occupied by a young woman. As I waited for the plane to take off, I retreated as deeply as possible into a book I was carrying. It was purely an anti-social maneuver. But the young lady wanted to talk. She asked, "What are you reading?"

"A book," I replied.

"What is the name of it?" she persisted.

"*Psycho-Cybernetics* by Maxwell Maltz," I said.

"Do you study psychology?"

"No."

Everything was monosyllabic. By then the engines were running and we were beginning to taxi down the runway. She kept at it. I had a head cold and could hardly hear. Finally, I closed the book and moved to the vacant seat between us, and we began to converse.

I soon realized what she really had in mind was to pick up a man. Going straight to the point, I said, "I travel a lot and many times I am lonely. I often encounter temptations to be unfaithful to my wife. But I've decided it's not worth it. I know I could deceive her, but the basis of our relationship is our mutual love and confidence. She trusts me, and I trust her.

"I've lived long enough to realize that meaning in life is not found in seeing what I can get away with, or in bigger achievements, or in a position, or in how my leisure time is spent. I've learned that meaning is found in relationships. Consequently, I don't intend to destroy the best relationship I have. If I came home having been unfaithful to my wife, even though she might not perceive it, and even though I could keep it from her, I'd know. She would come to me with her blind confidence and I'd have to somehow create a distance between us. We'd be pulled apart and she would never know why. Soon we would be strangers living together under the same roof.

"The ones who would pay most heavily would be my wife and children. That strikes me as the height of selfishness."

She was dumbfounded!

Then she began to open up. She said, "I'm twenty-four years old. I ought to be getting married, but all my married friends have affairs and if that's the way it is, I don't want it. When my friends go away for a weekend, their husbands are soon knocking at my door. They are like little boys. I just don't think I could handle it if my husband were like that."

Then she added, "I've never heard ideas like yours. Where do they come from?"

"You'd laugh if I told you."

"No, I wouldn't," she said.

"I got them from the Bible," I said. I went on to explain to her what the Christian message is and how it changes a person so he can get his life in order. By then we were about to land. What frustration! We were in the middle of my explanation. She was intensely interested in every word, but we had to quit.

As the passengers moved into the aisle, I let her go on ahead. When I came off a bit later and walked up the concourse, I passed her standing with a circle of about ten of her friends who had come to meet her. They were the ones she had told me about on the plane. She stopped me and made the round of introductions. I stood there for at least ten minutes while she related our conversation to them. That just added to my frustration. I thought, *If only I had a few days with these people. Perhaps I could help change their darkness into light.* I felt indispensable, but I had to go on my way.

But God was preparing me for one more big lesson. God is the one who orchestrates the reconciliation of people to Himself, not us. Just one year later I was back in that same city. It was a Sunday morning, and I was seated in a church. In walked the same woman I had talked to on the airplane. She sat down directly in front of me. When the service was over, I stood up to introduce myself. It was unnecessary. Her reply was, "Of course, I remember. I'll never forget that conversation. What a difference it has made!"

This story illustrates how having values rooted in the Scriptures will enable us to turn almost any conversation into a discussion of the gospel.

But, I must confess, I still have apprehensions when I see a new neighbor move in, when we move to another city, or when I meet a stranger. My first reaction is often anxious. How will I ever get to that person? He doesn't look like the type. At these times, I have to remind myself there is no barrier that making his acquaintance won't resolve. Eventually, a conversation over dinner or some leisure time together will lead us to a spiritual discussion there. We'll have to talk about *something*. And all conversations eventually lead to Jesus Christ.

Melker, a first-century priest, described the ideal. "The kingdom of God is to begin with us, in the inner life, and rule there, and from the inner nature all outward actions are to flow in conformity with revealed and written teachings and commands of God. . . . Until the outward is like the inward; and thus advancing on from individuals to nations."[2]

A GOOD TESTIMONY
Often Just Legalistic Caricature

When he was thirteen years old, my son Todd asked, "Dad, how can I be a good testimony? I'm not as good a Christian as Michelle (his older sister). She's talking to her friends about Christ."

My mind flashed back to the time I was thirteen. I remembered how I had been caught between two unreconcilable desires. I wanted to measure up to what I imagined my parents expected of me so far as having a Christian testimony among my friends. But at the same time I had to meet my needs for approval among my peers. I remembered the guilt and tension this conflict caused me. Now, how could I help my son avoid the same problem?

Finally I said, "Todd, don't worry about words. Just concern yourself with one thing. Be a peacemaker." I explained that if he would be genuinely considerate of the other person, and if he would take the initiative in resolving the conflicts that arose, he would be doing what God wants of him. This was something my thirteen-year-old could handle.

A few weeks later, Todd had an argument with Eduardo, our neighbor's boy, and their friendship broke up. When Todd and I talked about this incident, we reviewed our discussion on being a peacemaker and read Romans 12:17-18 together. "Do not repay anyone evil for evil. Be careful to do what is right in the eyes of everybody. If it is possible, as far as it depends on you, live at peace with everyone." Todd decided to take the initiative, visited Eduardo, and restored their friendship.

Soon after that, Eduardo's mother invited my wife over to her home to talk. She explained that her family had observed Todd's friendship with Eduardo and concluded, "We think you have what we need." A thirteen-year-old's life opened the door to another family.

The witness of a life! It is a truth rooted in God's purposes for Israel and in the teachings of the apostles. "Our gospel came to you not simply with words, but also with power, with the Holy Spirit and with deep conviction. You know how we lived among you for your sake" (1 Thessalonians 1:5).

This great truth has been reduced to the phrase "having a good testimony." But the phrase doesn't fit. In fact, this truth is sometimes further restricted in practice to mean merely reinforcing the caricature that both Christians and nonChristians share of what a "good Christian" should look like. This caricature consists of those extrabiblical scruples that always seem to grow up around Christian groups. We are afraid that if we do not live up to the expected image, we will offend those in the group as well as nonChristians. This fear maintains the caricature. The observant nonChristian picks up the cue—and holds the Christian accountable for living up to his own criteria.

This is enough to virtually canonize that caricature of what it means to be a Christian. As a result, the sad truth is that we effectively bar access to the gospel for many otherwise interested people.

"What must I forsake?" a young man asked.

"Colored clothes for one thing. Get rid of everything in your wardrobe that is not white. Stop sleeping on a soft pillow. Sell your musical instruments and don't eat any more white bread. You cannot, if you are sincere about obeying Christ, take warm baths or shave your beard. To shave is to lie against him who created us, to attempt to improve on his work."[3]

Quaint, isn't it—this example of extrabiblical scruples? And perhaps amusing. The list has constantly shifted over the 1,800 years since this one was actually recorded. It has even changed in my generation. It also varies according to who and where you are in the world. But in spite of the relative nature of our standards for Christian conduct, we always tend to take them very seriously.

It seems that moralisms (human standards imposed as norms) inevitably emerge to threaten the dynamic in every expression of the Body of Christ. There are a number of reasons for this, but we will not concern ourselves with them here. Our concern is the effect moralisms have on the gospel's mobility in the world. Jesus maintained that the Pharisees "shut the kingdom of heaven in men's faces" with their teachings (Matthew

23:13). Whenever the emphasis is on what Christians *do* rather than what they *are*, this will be the effect to a greater or lesser degree.

Jesus spoke about this in the Sermon on the Mount. He said, "Let your light shine before men, that they may see your good deeds and praise your Father in heaven" (Matthew 5:16). Later in this discourse, He seemed to contradict Himself when He said, "Be careful not to do your 'acts of righteousness' before men, to be seen by them" (6:1). What was the difference between these two statements? Their contexts set them apart.

Jesus' first statement introduced the thought that we should live in such a way that people see God in us. Here His emphasis is on our *uniqueness in relating to people and situations.*

The context of the second statement has to do with activities: giving, praying, and fasting. Jesus did not say, "Don't do these things." He commanded us to do all three. What he said was, "Don't let anyone catch you at it!" Why not? The answer relates to the motives of the heart. If my Christian activities are the most visible element of my faith, I'm probably guilty of glorifying myself. Consequently, I'm bound to misrepresent God. Outsiders will never want to come in once this begins to happen. Who wants to quit eating, give his money away, and spend all his time on his knees just to go to a heaven he's not even sure he will like?

We do the gospel considerable injustice when we attempt to promote our faith by publicizing our scruples, promoting our church activities, or describing our devotional lives. If, after all this, someone still found the idea appealing, they would probably think, *Perhaps I should be a Christian too, but how would I ever find the time?*

BEING FULL OF GRACE AND TRUTH

What then is a good testimony? An individual with a good testimony is one who models the character of God. "We have seen his glory . . . full of grace and truth" (John 1:14). What a beautiful, irresistible figure! Not that of a legalistic caricature, but the reflection of the very Person of God. I believe that is what it means to glorify God. It is to reveal His Person.

Grace and truth, mercy and justice—these are the inseparable marks of God's Person. In Ephesians 4:15 (emphasis added) we are told to "speak the *truth* in *love*," a similar couplet. Truth without love destroys. Love without truth deceives.

BEHAVING AS SONS OF THE TRUTH

Even Jesus' enemies acknowledged His commitment to truth. On one occasion, in a preface to a trap question, they made this observation:

"Teacher . . . we know you are a man of integrity and that you teach the way of God in accordance with the truth. You aren't swayed by men, because you pay no attention to who they are" (Matthew 22:16). As members of His Body, we are called upon to imitate Christ by being honest. As Peter wrote about Jesus, "No deceit was found in his mouth" (1 Peter 2:22).

What does truth have to do with being a good testimony? For one thing, almost all of our world's social problems, from broken marriages to poverty, have their roots in selfishness and greed. The problems begin in the heart of man, so the solutions must also begin there. The opposite of selfishness is doing what is right even when it is to your disadvantage (see Psalm 15). That is integrity. One of the most fundamental needs in this world is for men and women of integrity. And if integrity isn't found among the people of God, where will it be found?

When the Christian models integrity, he affirms to the world that there is a better way of doing things.

GRACE

We can exercise the grace of God only in our relationships with others. Have you ever noticed how much emphasis Jesus gave to the quality of our relationships? When asked to identify the greatest of God's commands, He replied that all of the Law can be summed up with two statements, each involving a relationship: "Love the Lord your God with all your heart and with all your soul and with all your mind . . . and love your neighbor as yourself" (Matthew 22:37-39).

Much of what Jesus has to say in His Sermon on the Mount consists of a call for us to be redemptive in our relationships. Consider this paraphrase of Matthew 5:21-48:

"You have heard it said, 'Do not murder.' I say, don't be angry with your brother.

"You have heard it said, 'Don't be contemptuous of others.' I say, don't even belittle another.

"Be reconciled to your brother even before you stop to commune with God.

"Settle matters quickly with your adversary, and out of court.

"Anyone who looks at a woman lustfully has already committed adultery with her in his heart.

"You have heard it said, 'Eye for eye and tooth for tooth.' But I tell you, do not resist an evil person.

"Give to the one who asks you, and do not turn away from the one who wants to borrow from you.

"You have heard that it was said, 'Love your neighbor and hate your enemy.' But I tell you, love your enemies and pray for those who persecute you, that you may be sons of your Father . . . perfect, therefore, as your heavenly Father is perfect."

These are difficult statements to cope with. They seem impossible to put into practice. But that's the way the grace of God always appears—impossible, just the opposite of what we instinctively "know" to be right, whether it is on the level of faith versus works for salvation, or unfairness versus justice in the day-by-day affairs of life.

Grace, by nature, is what a person least deserves. That's how God relates to us, and that's how He wants us, in turn, to respond to others. Insight into this truth of the grace of God—as we receive it and as we exercise it—could be called the starting point of all spiritual progress. As Paul wrote, "This gospel is bearing fruit and growing . . . among you since the day you heard it and understood God's grace in all its truth" (Colossians 1:6).

All our natural inclinations run contrary to this great truth. Paul Tournier, the Swiss psychiatrist and author, observed that our tendency is to be lenient or indulgent toward our own weaknesses (I'm overweight because it runs in my family) while bringing others to account (why doesn't he discipline his eating?).[4] There needs to be a reversal in our attitudes here.

Perhaps in part, the word *conversion* implies turning this around. To do this means to seek to understand *why* another individual is the way he is, and to make allowances accordingly, while holding ourselves responsible for our own behavior. This is the message of the "forgiveness chapter," Matthew 18. "Shouldn't you have had mercy on your fellow servant just as I had on you?" (verse 33). The chapter ends on a sobering note: "In anger his master turned him over to the jailers to be tortured until he should pay back all he owed. This is how my heavenly Father will treat each of you unless you forgive your brother from your heart" (verses 34-35).

Unforgiving words on forgiveness! How can that be? I wonder if Jesus isn't saying, "If you do not forgive or exercise grace in your dealings with people, it is a sure sign you never understood the Cross!"

To be treated with grace is to taste redemption. Have you ever found yourself being accepted and understood when you expected and deserved just the opposite? It's overwhelming. But to act graciously toward someone else is even better.

So we may conclude that a "good testimony" is a person whose quality of life identifies him as a child of his heavenly Father, full of grace and truth. Like his Father, he is redemptive in his relationships, from the inner circle within his own family to the outer fringes where his enemies stand.

NOTES:
1. The source for this quote is unknown.
2. Letter of Melker, first-century priest of the synagogue of Bethlehem to the higher Sanhedrin of the Jews at Jerusalem, translated by Dr. McIntosh and Dr. Twyman, *The Archko Volume* (New Canaan, Conn.: Keats Publishing Inc., 1975), pages 71-72.
3. Elisabeth Elliot, *The Liberty of Obedience* (Waco, Tex.: Word Books, 1968), pages 45-46.
4. Paul Tournier, *The Person Reborn* (New York: Harper & Row, 1966), pages 128-129.

ELEVEN

DON'T OBSCURE THE MESSAGE

Truth Eclipsed by Tradition

PEOPLE DO NOT "light a lamp and put it under a bowl" (Matthew 5:15). With this statement Jesus warns us of the very real possibility of our obscuring the work He has done in us, thereby frustrating the purposes He intends to accomplish through us.

Probably the first thought that comes to mind when we talk about blotting out the light is the factor of sin. "If we claim to have fellowship with [God] yet walk in the darkness, we lie" (1 John 1:6). It is certainly true that a Christian who continues to walk in sin is not giving off much light. But there are several even more subtle ways of burying your light under a bowl. These can easily happen without our perception. Our light can be obscured by such things as our associations, our expectations, our expressions, or our actions.

Our associations. How am I perceived by those I am seeking to win? Usually, when two people meet for the first time, the search for identity is immediately on for both parties. Both are busy searching for the appropriate pigeonhole, the proper classification to identify the other. It's not fair, but we all do it.

"What do you do?" I ask you. (The answer to that one gives me a lot of clues. I can now begin to speculate on your social status, your financial situation, and your educational background.)

"Where do you live?" (That's another question equally rich with misleading information. The city or the part of town helps me modify and embellish the image I'm creating.)

"Where did you go to school?"

"What did you study?"

"Oh, do you know James? How did you come to know him?" (Pay dirt! I've identified a mutual acquaintance. And since I already have a pigeonhole for James, my research is nearly completed. After all, people are known by the company they keep.)

When we approach people with the gospel, the same procedure occurs. *What church is he from?* they think. *Is he with some sect? What is he trying to get me into?*

This factor of identifying someone by association is a very difficult one to deal with. As we discuss the gospel with people, one of the implications is, "If you accept this message, you'll become like me." And if our Christianity is integrally and exclusively identified with a particular denomination, church, or organization, then we will be rejected by others before we know what has happened. The secularized person especially is just not looking for something to join. He quickly rejects unnecessary identity changes.

A few years ago, some friends of mine organized an evangelistic thrust aimed at university students in their country. They worked out an approach, had materials printed, and then proceeded to systematically interview students in their residences. Their objective was to generate interest and participation in some evangelistic Bible studies.

My friends interviewed 800 students, but they were defeated before they began. They just didn't realize it. At the top of the materials they distributed was the heading, "[the name of their organization] Invites You. . . ." They thought they were inviting the students to look at Christ. But the students saw them as people who were inviting them to join their organization. Only three of the 800 showed any response, and the entire effort yielded no permanent fruit. Organizational appeals and calling programs inviting people to church rarely stir secularized people to a response.

Obviously, no Christian would consciously allow his own name or identity to compete with the name and identity of Christ. We would be shocked and chagrined to discover such a turnabout. The problem, then, is not with how we view ourselves but with how we are perceived by others. A good question to constantly ask ourselves is, How am I perceived by those I'm seeking to win?

Our expectations. This second "bowl" under which we sometimes hide our light is related to the first. An exaggerated commitment to our religious identity often goes hand in hand with an equal concern for that group's growth and success. The success of a church is customarily measured in terms of people. Numbers of people participating at various levels in church programs are studied and reported as a part of our process of evaluation. Because of this focus on church growth and programs, the temptation becomes almost irresistible, as we reach out to the nonChristian, to approach him with his entire agenda already worked out ahead of time. We scarcely consider whether or not he is ready for what we have for him—or whether or not that will truly fit him.

Our expectation is that new Christians will like what we have for them and that they will conform. We expect them to fit into our structures, respond to our forms, participate in our activities, and embrace our patterns of conduct. It is unbelievable how quickly a person who is considering Christ will pick up on all this. Sometimes he accepts the new patterns and fits in. But more often he reacts negatively. I can look back on my own ministry and give you the names of people I alienated with this kind of manipulation. They just disappeared. They never explained why, but in retrospect it is obvious what went wrong.

Thus, we can eclipse the light by our expectations. When we mix our own desires for personal or corporate success into our evangelism, we compromise its true purpose.

Our expressions. One common characteristic of every sub-group is that each has its own terminology. In Brazil, where I lived for twenty-three years, it takes only a few minutes of conversation on spiritual issues to identify a Catholic from a Protestant, and one kind of Protestant from another kind of Protestant, on the basis of the choice of words alone. There is no problem with this, as long as each sub-group person is among his own kind. But our primary interest is precisely to go to those who are not of our own kind. I've seen our use of religious terminology put people off again and again. Consequently it, too, can be another "bowl" that obstructs the light.

As our Bible study group was just beginning to expand among our neighbors, several nonChristians who had no Christian background began to participate. Most of the participants worked together in the same hospital, so soon the word about our Bible study began to get around.

One day one of the participants told me he had a colleague who was interested in attending. I agreed that it would be good to invite him. So Marcos showed up at our next study. He turned out to be a beautiful, mature Christian man. No wonder his Bible was tattered—he seemed to know it by heart.

But as I led the group in our discussion, I quickly realized I was in trouble. As soon as I would ask a question, before anyone else had time to think, Marcos would give the answer. Now I wasn't looking for answers to my questions. I already had those. I was trying to get the group to think. To complicate matters even further, his answers were always right—unintelligible to the rest of the group, but right. They left nothing else to be said.

So I tried another tactic. I asked a question and then gave a cross-reference passage where the answer could be found. That didn't work either. Before the others discovered whether the passage was located in the Old or New Testament, Marcos had found it, read it, and commented on it—all of it, of course, in the Portuguese equivalent of King James. The recourse for me was to lapse into lecturing, which is the least effective means of communication.

One evening, at the end of a study, one of the wives commented to me, "I know I can't say things the way Marcos does, but I need the chance to express myself, even if what I say isn't very profound. But just when I open my mouth, Marcos has already said it." I knew she was right. The next day I invited Marcos over to my home. I explained the situation and we agreed it would be better for him not to continue with us. That was a difficult day for me.

Any biblical term that is not a part of our everyday language needs translation. Some of these are very common words for us: grace, sin, faith, justification, reconciliation, regeneration, walking in the Spirit, etc. Technical theological terms are also confusing. When we talk about dispensations, ecclesiology, or eschatology, we will certainly mystify many people. Then there are the in-house terms. An individual is referred to as "brother" or "sister." We talk about "receiving Christ," "going to the throne of grace," and so on.

Our prayers, too, have certain patterns. Many Christians seem to have a special voice, with certain intonations they reserve for religious occasions.

We need to try to hear ourselves with the ears of those we are seeking to reach.

Our actions. We often obscure the gospel by our scruples. For some unfortunate reason, we Christians are generally known for what we abstain from. If our reputation was one of abstaining from immorality, injustice, and dishonesty, it would be wonderful. But the list is not that noble. It consists primarily of how Christians are to behave, especially in areas where the Bible does not give specific instructions. We impose these norms for behavior even though the Scriptures specifically instruct us to refrain from passing laws on doubtful issues. Colossians 2:20-21 says, "Since you died with Christ to the basic principles of this world, why . . . do you submit to its rules: 'Do not handle! Do not taste! Do not touch!'?"

A few years ago, a young couple came to Christ while spending a few months in Mexico. Soon afterward, they returned to their home country. We didn't have much hope that they would grow spiritually because they were so new and because they would probably be cut off from further help. But when they arrived in their home city, they immediately began to teach the little they knew to their friends. Soon there was a nucleus of seven couples looking to these new Christians for help in their spiritual growth.

Being nominally Roman Catholic, the couple turned to the local priest for help. That didn't work out, so they located a Protestant missionary. After a few months of involvement with this missionary, the couple became alarmed at the effects. At great personal expense, they traveled back to visit the person who had first helped them understand the gospel and asked him to promise to bring help to them. Their explanation was, "We did not step out of one set of traditions just to enter another. What we need is someone who will teach us the Bible only."

This young couple precisely identified the problems that our norms of Christian conduct create. These norms introduce a second authority into our Christian fellowship: tradition. The effect of these contrived external norms presents a false concept of what the Christian life really consists of. This in turn puts off those who would otherwise be responsive.

Our associations, expectations, expressions, and actions all add up to the image we project. We need to be careful that this image does not obscure the message!

TWELVE

WHO ADAPTS TO WHOM?

Making the Other Person Comfortable

CLOSING THE COMMUNICATION gap between ourselves and the non-believer in our society must become a primary concern if we are to go beyond evangelizing our own kind. In the previous chapters we have examined several factors that are necessary to accomplish this. We saw how congruence of faith and practice are a part, and we discussed ways in which people can be put off by our associations, expectations, expressions, or actions.

These things in themselves, however, do not resolve the problem of distance. More is required. There remains the need on our part to adapt to those we seek to win. Without this adaptation, even the most exemplary life will go unobserved by those who need it most. Without adaptation on our part, there will not be the prolonged exposure that makes observation possible.

The Apostle Paul dealt with this matter of adaptation in 1 Corinthians 9. The subject of this passage was clearly evangelism. Paul wrote,

> Though I am free and belong to no man, I make myself a slave to everyone, to win as many as possible. To the Jews I became like a Jew, to win the Jews. To those under the law I became like one under the law (though I myself am not under the law), so as to win those under the law. To those not having the law I became like one not having the law . . . so as to win those not having the law. To the weak I became weak, to win the weak. I have become all things to all men so that by all possible means I might save some.

117

I do all this for the sake of the gospel, that I may share in its blessings. (1 Corinthians 9:19-23)

Paul was saying that as a witness he recognized it was up to him to adapt to the unevangelized. *The witness adjusts to those he seeks to win,* not vice versa. Paul defended his freedom to be all things to all men because he knew that freedom was necessary to the correct balance between being "in the world" and being "separate" from it. To be in the world one has to be free to participate in the lives of those around him. Being separate means we do this without compromising the sovereign rule of God in our heart—without sinning, in other words.

What does being "all things to all men" mean in practice? What did it mean for Paul to live like a Jew while among Jews, and then change and live like one without the law when he was among the Gentiles? It meant he would respect the scruples and traditions of whomever he was with, and have the flexibility to set one group's practices aside as he entered the world of persons with different customs.

This struck many as a scandalous thought, but Paul was willing to pay the price for his position. He was a controversial figure among Christians and nonChristians until the day he died. It takes maturity and courage to "go to the Gentiles."

As we discussed why a team of missionaries in his country was having difficulty establishing a solid ministry, a South American said, "Their sanctification is American. I get the impression they are afraid to adapt to the culture because in so doing they would become soiled by the world. They fear they would be 'going pagan.'"

Change *is* hard to face, especially in areas of behavior. Going into the world requires change. It implies participation in people's lives. It means to think, to feel, to understand, and to take seriously the values of those we seek to win.

The incarnation is our prototype. Jesus set his glory aside, "made himself nothing . . . in human likeness . . . he humbled himself" (Philippians 2:7-8). Consequently, "we have one who has been tempted in every way, just as we are—yet was without sin" (Hebrews 4:15). He came into the world, lived life in our presence, and participated with us in life as we live it. He drew the line only at sin. To what degree could we identify with God if there had been no incarnation?

Paul followed the same principle. He went to nonChristians in order to bring them to God, but he knew their route to God had to pass through his own life. "You are witnesses," he reminded the Thessalonians, "of how holy, righteous and blameless we were among you" (1 Thessalonians 2:10).

For better or for worse, the life a Christian lives in the presence of those he seeks to win is a preview of what the nonChristian's life will become if he accepts what he is hearing. Generally, he will decide either to accept or reject Christianity according to what he has seen. I stumbled onto this rather unnerving truth unwittingly.

A Brazilian friend, Mario, and I studied the Bible for four years together before he became a Christian. As an intellectual who had read almost all of the leading Western thinkers from Rousseau to Kafka, he had blended together his own personal philosophy that was fundamentally Marxist—with Bertrand Russell as his patron saint. Mario was a political activist, a leader in many Marxist activities. Why he kept studying the Bible with me for four years, or why I stuck with him so long, neither of us can explain today. But there we were.

Since he lived life on the philosophical plane, our Bible studies were often pitched in that direction. One day, a couple of years after Mario had become a Christian, he and I were reminiscing. He asked me, "Do you know what it really was that made me decide to become a Christian?" Of course, I immediately thought of our countless hours of Bible study, but I responded, "No, what?"

His reply took me completely by surprise. He said, "Remember that first time I stopped by your house? We were on our way someplace together and I had a bowl of soup with you and your family. As I sat there observing you, your wife, your children, and how you related to each other, I asked myself, 'When will I have a relationship like this with my fiancee?' When I realized that the answer was 'never,' I concluded I had to become a Christian for the sake of my own survival."

I remembered the occasion well enough to recall that our children were not particularly well-behaved that evening. In fact, I remembered I had felt frustrated when I corrected them in Mario's presence.

Mario saw that relationships with Christ bind a family together. The last verse in the Old Testament promises the turning of "the hearts of the fathers to their children, and the hearts of the children to their fathers" (Malachi 4:6).

Our family was unaware of its influence on Mario. God had done this work through our family without our knowing it. Most Christians are probably unaware of the changes God accomplishes in us in the sanctification process.

We tend to see the weaknesses and incongruities in our lives, and our reaction is to recoil at the thought of letting outsiders get close enough to see us as we really are. Even if our assessment is accurate, it is my observation that any Christian who is sincerely seeking to walk with God, in spite of all his flaws, reflects something of Christ.

It is not enough, then, to occasionally drop into another individual's world, preach to him, and go on our way. Somehow, he needs to be brought into our world as well. If he isn't, the view he gets of us is so fragmented he could miss the total picture. He doesn't see the effects the grace of God has had in our day-to-day lives.

But this two-way interaction will never happen unless we Christians learn how to become "all things to all men," and apply this adaptation in a way that will lead to friendships and genuine relationships with nonChristians.

ENHANCING THE MESSAGE IN FRIENDSHIP

In affirmation evangelism, the message is inextricably linked with the messenger. The matter of image *is* important because "we have this treasure [the gospel] in jars of clay" (2 Corinthians 4:7). The first response of the unbeliever will be related to what he sees in us. So each of us needs to ask, "When a nonChristian looks at me, who does he see? Is my lifestyle attractive to him?"

As you can see, this kind of evangelism can hardly be called an activity in which one engages on certain occasions. It is *life.* Living itself becomes evangelistic. We draw nonChristians into our lives and step into theirs. As the relationships expand, so does the gospel. As Joe Aldrich puts it, "Evangelism is a way of living beautifully and then opening up those webs of relationship to the nonChristian."[1]

The process begins with the development of a friendship, which tends to follow a predictable pattern. For a friendship to develop between two individuals, one usually starts it off by taking the initiative. He makes some attempt to communicate with the other person. If this overture is accepted, rapport begins to be established between the two. This rapport is reinforced by acts of friendship. Friendship is the context in which good relationships are built.

Let's take a closer look at those four stages of building friendship, listing some possible aspects of each phase.

1. *Taking the Initiative.*
   - Being the first to say hello.
   - Being friendly.
   - Making small talk.
   - Remembering the other person's name and using it often.
   - Being genuinely interested in him.
2. *Establishing Rapport.* Rapport is an attitude of mutual acceptance.
   - Thinking in your heart, "I accept you as you are."

- Listening with interest to what the other person says.
- Expressing approval; giving compliments where they are due.
- Being sensitive to specific needs and opportunities where you could serve.
- Looking for an occasion to invite the other person to join you in some activity.

3. *Being a Friend.* Friendship has a price tag: time. It means putting other people first.

- Listening; being attentive to thoughts and feelings.
- Affirming the other person; expressing what you like about him.
- Being transparent; openly expressing your own feelings.
- Allowing your friend to serve you and also to do you favors.
- Accepting him as he is, without trying to reform him.

4. *Building a Relationship.*

- Letting the other person know what you're thinking; allowing him to see inside.
- Seeking his counsel.
- Sharing your personal resources: money, abilities, etc.
- Making time for him.
- Not overdoing it; not trying to control him or be possessive.

By no means do I want to suggest that the above list is a prerequisite to evangelizing someone. Evangelism can occur at any point and is often effective in the very early stages. As we proceed through the following chapters we will see how this works out in practice.

NOTE:
1. Joseph Aldrich, from a lecture, "Developing Vision for Disciplemaking."

THIRTEEN

THE WITNESS OF THE BODY

Supplementing Each Other's Abilities

IN THE SECTION on proclamation, we talked about the necessity of the verbal witness. In the section on affirmation, we talked about the witness of the life. It is certainly true that the body of believers may be involved in each of these aspects of evangelism. But it is also true that the very existence of a group of Christians with unique relationships to one another is in itself a witness. We have seen that from the beginning, one of God's primary means of revealing Himself to the world has been through a people. First, there was Israel, the nation that moved from slavery to incomparable beauty in a few generations. Then God raised up the Church, turning a bewildered group of 120 disciples cloistered in a Jerusalem room into a unique people whose very existence placed the world in check.

God has always used a people to amplify His voice in the world—and He always will. This fact has major significance for both our concept of evangelism and how we witness.

In practical terms, what *does* this mean? There are two major implications. First, there is the corporate testimony; second, there is the body principle.

THE CORPORATE TESTIMONY

In his book, *The Church at the End of the Twentieth Century*, Francis Schaeffer observes, "The church is to be a loving church in a dying culture. How then is the dying culture going to consider us? Jesus said, 'By this shall

all men know that ye are my disciples, if ye have love one to another.' In the midst of the world, in the midst of our present dying culture, Jesus is giving a right to the world. Upon his authority, he gives the world the right to judge whether you and I are born-again Christians on the basis of our observable love toward all Christians."[1]

Jesus prayed, "that all of them may be one, Father. . . so that the world may believe that you have sent me" (John 17:21). In commenting on this verse, Schaeffer writes, "Here Jesus is stating . . . we cannot expect the world to believe that the Father sent the Son, that Jesus' claims are true, and that Christianity is true, unless the world sees some reality of the oneness of true Christians."[2]

The Christian who seeks to win the lost while operating alone or separated from other believers is deprived of a critical resource. Even though he may clearly demonstrate the fruit of the Spirit, those he seeks to win often do not feel the full impact of his witness, just because he is alone. It's so easy to discount or explain away an isolated individual: "He has an unusual background," or, "he's different." But when faced with a body of believers, the common denominator—the Holy Spirit—quickly stands out. Then their corporate testimony is irrefutable.

Sometimes working alone is unavoidable. For example, working alone, or as a small team, is inherent in the work of an apostle who goes to places or peoples where no Christian community exists. Paul said, "It has always been my ambition to preach the gospel where Christ was not known, so that I would not be building on someone else's foundation" (Romans 15:20).

This apostolic or missionary function is still an essential element in the church because the world is still full of peoples and subcultures which do not have a Christian base. I have spent most of my life in such a culture.

It is an excruciating experience to start from scratch. Those first contacts are usually hard to come by. Finally there are a few, scattered here and there about town. They may not even know one another, and have no sense of unity. But soon they begin to demonstrate a desire to see their friends and families come to know Christ. Often this desire is present from the very first days of their spiritual life. I wonder if this isn't something God plants early in the heart of a new Christian to make him aware of his dependence on others. As a new Christian begins sharing the good news with others, he becomes aware of his need to learn more effective ways of presenting the message. The desire to meet this felt need is one of the major gravitational pulls that draws new Christians together into relationships with more mature believers.

This was another of those discoveries I stumbled onto through experience, only later to discover its biblical origins.

Several years ago, a co-laborer and I found ourselves in a nucleus of new Christians who needed and wanted to learn how to communicate the gospel to their peers. But they were in no way equipped to do this themselves. Most of them had never even picked up a Bible before we met them. How could we help them to influence their friends effectively?

Often, when faced with such a situation, the Christian worker takes it on himself to go and talk to the friend. This is generally an opportunity lost, for when it happens, the new Christian quickly draws an erroneous conclusion: evangelism is for the professionals only. When the Christian worker goes out to make such a visit, the new Christian heads for the sidelines where he often sits for the remainder of his Christian life.

We had to avoid that! But how could we lead a group of new Christians who knew so little into effective evangelism?

In seeking an answer, we came up with what we called "the open study." The open study is a series of six weekly or fortnightly studies geared for nonChristians. It is conducted in a neutral, personal environment, usually in someone's home. There is an informal atmosphere—in the Brazilian culture it was samba music and coffee. A short, provocative presentation on some facet of the Christian message is given, such as "Who is Jesus Christ?" or "What is man?" This is followed by a free-for-all discussion where *any* question is welcomed. To keep it alive, we made sure that at least half the group were not Christians.

To get the most out of the open studies as a training experience, we would coach one of our new Christians and help him prepare to lead the discussion. Christians who attended were instructed to avoid giving those suffocating pat answers of which Christians are so capable.

The open study was a success—such a success that one day Osvaldo came to me and said, "I've decided not to bring any more of my friends to those open studies. Everyone who comes ends up becoming a Christian. I feel the studies are becoming a crutch for me. I'm not learning to evangelize a person on my own."

I didn't know how to respond to Osvaldo, but I began to observe more closely what was happening. What made the open study so effective? It couldn't have been content, for often the presentations were quite weak. And it wasn't the discussions. My colleague and I had resolved to keep mostly silent. Many times that was painful as we watched the nonChristians massacre our offspring. But I began to hear one comment over and over again from the guests: "I've never seen people like this before—they are different from any I've ever been with." Finally, after frequent repetition, the message got through. People were responding in the open studies not primarily to what they were *hearing,* but to what they were *seeing.* They had never seen a group or a nucleus of Christians before.

Then some more thoughts began to fall into place. Where did Osvaldo get the idea that he should be able to carry on the evangelization of his friends single-handedly? Undoubtedly, from me! And where did I get that idea?

God never intended evangelism to be an individualistic effort. The biblical pattern is for the individual's witness to be carried on within the setting of a corporate effort. The corporate witness says, "Look at all of us. This is what you too can become. There's hope." It's possible to discount or explain away an isolated individual, but it's impossible to refute the corporate testimony. The Apostle John observed, "No one has ever seen God; but if we love one another, God lives in us and his love is made complete in us" (1 John 4:12).

THE BODY PRINCIPLE

Evangelism tends to assume one of two forms: either mass proclamation or personal witness. Both of these are good, but they represent only a fraction of what really should be taking place. Both approaches tend to exclude most Christians. Mass proclamation can easily deprive the individual of his responsibility to develop as a witness, while on the other hand, when it comes to personal evangelism, the Christian is usually left to learn by himself. And many Christians do not feel gifted for personal witnessing.

When it comes to winning the lost, more often than not, we distribute a few tools, occasionally conduct a short-lived evangelistic assault, exhort, and generally leave everyone with a guilty conscience. Isn't there some way for the average Christian to be involved in evangelism in a more enduring, more realistic manner?

The one overriding truth in the New Testament regarding the Church is the fact that it is a Body, a living organism whose members must exist in a constant state of interdependence. (See Romans 12, 1 Corinthians 12, and Ephesians 4.) If this truth needs to be applied anywhere, it is in this matter of evangelism.

Much has been written and taught about discovering and exercising one's spiritual gifts. Generally the question, "What is my gift?" is a difficult one. On what basis do we answer? It is better to ask, "What can I *do*?" Everyone can answer that. It is in doing what we are able to do that we can answer the first question. We will discover our gifts in action!

How often have you heard someone say, "Evangelism isn't my gift"? Technically, there is no such thing. No one possesses the gift of evangelism. Some, however, possess gifts that make them especially effective in evangelism. First Corinthians 12:4-6 describes different kinds of services *and* different kinds of gifts.

When we begin to look at evangelism as a corporate ministry, we soon discover that virtually any spiritual gift that builds up the Body also has its place in winning the lost. That is because we cannot separate winning the lost from edifying the Body. One cannot exist without the other. Evangelism as a function of the Body takes place when a handful of disciples band together, and pool their abilities and resources for the sake of reaching into the world with their message. Under these circumstances, whatever gifts are represented can be put to good use. Whatever comes naturally for you—hospitality, the ability to organize, gregariousness, the ability to pray, cooking, Bible knowledge, teaching—whatever you can do, can be useful in evangelism. Your gift—your abilities, strengths, and interests—can build up the Body and also build bridges of communication to nonChristians. Start with what you have. As you go along, you will acquire abilities you do not now possess.

A few years ago, five engineers graduated in the same class from the University of Curitiba in Brazil. All were young Christians of varying degrees of maturity. Together they decided to move to the city of Sao Paulo for the sake of the Kingdom of God.

Sao Paulo is a city of fourteen million with a minimal Christian presence. It is one of the neediest cities on earth. None of the five had found jobs when they moved into an apartment together. They pooled their money; it ran out. Finally, as they were beginning literally to go hungry, one of them found a job. He was the youngest Christian of them all. Six weeks had gone by. The five began living off his salary. Eleven months later, the last of the five, Evilasio, found employment. He was the most mature Christian of them all—the one whose faith had spearheaded the venture.

None of these men knew much about evangelism. None was an experienced leader or Bible teacher. But the little they had learned, when pooled together, was enough. They planted the gospel among their new acquaintances and colleagues. A new body of believers was born.

Ephesians 4:11-12 clearly indicates that the function of the leaders (the apostles, prophets, evangelists, pastors, and teachers) is to prepare God's people for the ministry. We need to understand that the ministry is every Christian's responsibility. There are to be no spectators because whatever gifts one has are important when used jointly with other gifts. Then we begin to see things happen that are otherwise impossible. Evangelism is not limited to those who specialize in the proclamation of the gospel. We accomplish together things we can never hope for when operating alone.

Probably the most simple, reproducible application of what we've been talking about is the neighborhood Bible study. What's required? It calls for being an observant, thoughtful neighbor. It means making a home available. It involves inviting people and knowing their interests and needs. It means being willing to lead a Bible discussion. Someone needs to feel responsible for holding such a group together and keeping it moving. When it gets too big, someone needs to realize it is time to divide and start a new outreach group. And that's about it! Imagine what would happen if all of us were involved in an effort of this sort.

What we just described is close to the basic form available to the Church for the first three hundred years of its history. Persecuted, the Christians could not operate openly. There were no church buildings. They depended on homes and other structures (see Romans 15-16). I wonder if the Church didn't lose something essential to its nature when we extracted it from our living rooms and shops and began to house it in specially-designed buildings. Gone was the insatiable demand for leadership development that those networks of cells produced. As routines became more established, the pressure of responsibility was lifted from the average Christian. But we need those pressures. The Church is intended to be more like a guerrilla force than a fixed fortification.

CONCLUSION

We are individually responsible before God to use whatever abilities and resources we have to win the lost. But this does not mean evangelism is to be an individual exercise. Evangelism is a group effort. Few of us can fulfill our part in this ministry unless we band together, pooling our resources with a few kindred spirits to accomplish the common objective: to witness as a body of believers by actively participating in the lives of some nonChristian friends.

NOTES:
1. Francis Schaeffer, *The Church at the End of the Twentieth Century* (Downers Grove, Ill.: InterVarsity Press, 1970), pages 136-137.
2. Schaeffer, pages 138-139.

FOURTEEN

THREE SIMULTANEOUS INFLUENCES

Life, Body, and Verbal Witness

IN DESCRIBING AFFIRMATION evangelism we have emphasized three things:

THE WITNESS OF THE LIFE

This requires congruence of life and belief, not in a demonstration of perfection but as a recipient of God's grace. The result is the incarnation of the gospel, enabling us to be redemptive in our relationships.

THE WITNESS OF THE BODY

We have also considered the collective impact a nucleus of Christians can have on the nonChristian. The simple fact that the group exists, with its unique ability to love one another, is in itself a powerful statement to the world. It is a testimony to the reality of our message: we are a transformed people; Jesus was truly sent by the Father; and there is hope for anybody.

But if we expect this testimony to be heard and heeded, the members of the Body of Christ need to see themselves as being *in* the world, *for the sake of the world.* This is the witness of the Body.

THE VERBAL WITNESS

If our witness should end with the first two, however, it would be incomplete. "How can they believe in the one of whom they have not heard? And

129

how can they hear without someone preaching to them? . . . 'How beautiful are the feet of those who bring good news!'" (Romans 10:14-15).

What people see must be verbally interpreted before the communication circle is closed. "How can I [understand] . . . unless someone explains it to me?" the Ethiopian asked Philip (Acts 8:31). We must talk about our faith.

DOING THREE THINGS AT ONCE

It would be easy to get the impression that I am suggesting a sequence—that it's necessary to devote a period of time to establishing a personal friendship, so that eventually the person can be brought around to meet our Christian friends, so that finally we can say something to him. If I left you with this impression, I would lead you into a non-productive trap.

We can expect God to use us in all three ways *at the same time.* These three influences—our lives, the band of kindred spirits of which we are a part, and our words—should all be *sustained* until the person we are seeking to reach encounters Christ and moves into discipleship.

Any one of these influences, by itself, is incomplete. The defects of a silent witness are obvious, but an exclusively verbal witness is also seriously defective. An exclusively verbal witness is impersonal, even when carried on at an individual level. In 1 Thessalonians 2:8, Paul wrote, "We loved you so much that we were delighted to share with you not only the gospel of God but our lives as well, because you had become so dear to us."

So all three influences work together. Which comes first varies with the situation, but it has been my experience that I need to talk about my faith early in a relationship. I've found that the longer I wait, the more difficult it becomes. Patterns develop in the friendship that are hard to break out of later. We don't have to say much at the outset; often just enough to "get the flag up" will suffice.

When the verbal witness comes first, the other two influences need to be brought in as soon as possible.

Larry was a secularized individual, a fringe counterculture existentialist. We had just moved to a different city in the United States, and I made his acquaintance at a party we attended soon after arriving.

As we chatted together, I explained that I was new in town and, therefore, had few acquaintances. I told him I customarily met with a few friends to examine the Bible, and since I was not yet doing that, it was something I missed. I said he would be doing me a favor by joining me. He replied that he didn't believe in God and knew nothing about the Bible, but if he could help me, he would be happy to try. He was my favorite kind of person, and I told him so. We set a time to meet again.

We started out as strangers studying the Bible together, but soon we developed a close yet informal social relationship as we played tennis, skied, and ate meals together. Meanwhile, I had gathered together a few more friends and acquaintances who joined us.

Larry struggled with the content and claims of the gospel. He had many honest intellectual problems, as well as the customary battles with the will. It is when these inner battles begin that the importance of love in a relationship becomes crucial. The natural reaction for the nonChristian at this point is to flee the message—to go anywhere but near that Bible again! But mutual love and friendship within a small circle of friends hold him. The Holy Spirit uses these influences to sustain the nonChristian's exposure to the Scriptures.

This is what happened to Larry. These three influences—the witness of a life, the witness of the Body, and a verbal witness—worked together until it became apparent he had become a Christian. In his case, the initial point of contact was a verbal witness.

In the following and final section of the book we will discuss the practical aspects of affirmation evangelism.

PART FOUR

PRACTICAL
GUIDANCE IN
LIFESTYLE EVANGELISM

INTRODUCTION: METHODS SECONDARY TO MIND-SET

BY FAR THE most frequent question that arises regarding evangelism has to do with how to awaken interest. How do we approach evangelism among people in the mainstream? The subject of religion is not at all included among the concerns of secularized people. Thus, how to awaken interest among the uninterested is the first question in evangelism!

Then, as we actually become involved in the lives of our nonChristian friends, a myriad of other how-to questions quickly surface. We discover that methods and explanations that were once effective simply no longer communicate. So there is a perpetual need for new methods and approaches that correspond to the changing mentality of society.

It is vitally important to have right methods, for they serve as our tools. But it would be misleading to give the impression that fruitfulness is simply a matter of right tactics. There are two other factors that are even more fundamental: (1) We need an accompanying change of mind-set and (2) We need to be dependent on spiritual resources, not on techniques.

CHANGING OUR MIND-SET

Cultural shifts produce deep changes in world views and values. For this reason, we need to learn to be cross-cultural missionaries right on our own block! Communication depends on our understanding of the people we go to. This understanding is accomplished as we put ourselves in the other's shoes for the sake of seeing life from his perspective. This is what it means to change one's mind-set. It involves undergoing a change in our own thinking. Thus we come to understand and empathize with the other's value system. This cultural insight becomes the footing for the bridge that will span the distance between them and Jesus Christ.

RELYING ON SPIRITUAL RESOURCES

Probably the most dangerous thing about methods is that when they work, we begin to rely on them. We experiment with something. It works. We do it again, and again it works. As we become successful, we slip into thinking that continued success is a matter of just keeping that activity going. We feel that if we just repeat it long enough and hard enough, we will accomplish our goals. But when we transfer our confidence to such success-formula approaches, we are also resorting to carnal weaponry.

Our primary spiritual resources are the Spirit of God and the Word of God. Any true progress, any real spiritual victory, is gained through the power of these two forces.

THE METAMORPHOSIS FROM SAUL TO PAUL

Paul's experience of shedding his past to become the first apostle to the Gentiles is an illustration of learning to rely on spiritual resources. Paul had to undergo a metamorphosis of his mind-set, relinquishing his confidence in himself and relying instead on the Spirit of God and the Word of God.

Paul began his ministry immediately after his conversion. He had all the qualifications for success. After all, he was a ranking Pharisee, schooled under Gamaliel. If anybody had the potential to be effective among the Jews, Paul did. In Damascus where he was converted, he immediately began to unleash his impressive powers on the Jewish community. "Saul grew more and more powerful and baffled the Jews living in Damascus by proving that Jesus is the Christ" (Acts 9:22).

Paul seemed to win every argument. But rather than inspiring belief, he inspired his hearers to hatred. They wanted to kill him! He escaped Damascus in a basket.

In Jerusalem, Paul again showed himself to be an invincible debater, but with similar results. So "the brothers . . . took him down to Caesarea and sent him off to Tarsus. Then the church throughout Judea, Galilee and Samaria enjoyed a time of peace" (Acts 9:30-31). Perhaps there was a connection between Paul's departure and the ensuing peace!

As Paul departed for Tarsus, he might have considered his encounters in Damascus and Jerusalem as a double failure. But according to him, those failures were some of the most significant experiences of his action-packed life (2 Corinthians 11:30-33). Failure is usually a very effective teacher, especially when under the guidance of God.

In the following years, alone with God, the Scriptures, and his own thoughts, Paul underwent a transformation. When he returned, he was a different man with apparently a different kind of approach. Laying aside all carnal resources, the transformed apostle resolved to approach the ministry with exclusively spiritual weaponry (see 2 Corinthians 10:3-4).

Here is how Paul described his way of presenting the gospel after the change: "I did not come with *eloquence* or *superior wisdom*. . . . For I resolved to know nothing while I was with you except Jesus Christ and him crucified. . . . My message and my preaching were not with *wise and persuasive words* . . . so that your faith might not rest on men's wisdom" (1 Corinthians 2:1-5, emphasis added).

What constituted carnal weapons for Paul? Eloquence, superior wisdom, and wise and persuasive words! Although he was a natural at using all three, laying them aside was a deliberate decision, something he "resolved" to do. In contrast, we often tend to appeal to our lack of eloquence, wisdom, or persuasive abilities to justify our non-involvement in evangelism.

Apparently, during that time when Paul was alone with his thoughts, God impressed upon him the fact that the knowledge he possessed and the prestige he enjoyed were not what people needed from him. He would have felt more secure had he continued to operate from his own natural strengths and advantages. But he set them aside, and, instead, with fear and trembling he came in at the hearer's level of need.

THE BEST METHODS ARE YOUR OWN

Methods in and of themselves have inherent limitations. A method is normally born in an attempt to meet a local need within a given set of circumstances. Then the word gets around and others begin to use that proven method. But as its use is extended to other situations, its effectiveness is limited to the degree of similarity between the two environments. Therefore, I do not intend to set forth "a method" on the following pages. Rather, my purpose is to offer principles and examples that will stimulate new ideas. Creativity involves the ability to see new combinations between things that are already familiar.

You will need methods. If you take any methods from these pages, be sure to adapt them to your own situation. The result should be uniquely your own.

FIFTEEN

EVANGELISM IS A TEAM EFFORT

Balance of Gifts Within the Body

YOU WANT TO be involved in evangelism. You would hardly be reading this page in this book at this moment if that weren't the case. Let's say you are sufficiently motivated to be willing to commit yourself to action. What should your very first step be? I would suggest that it be to find at least one kindred spirit, one other individual who shares that same desire, and commit yourselves to working together.

Surprising? Perhaps, but it shouldn't be because we really weren't made for going it alone. On more than one occasion, Jesus sent His followers out two by two. The Apostle Paul, undoubtedly one of the most eminently qualified Christians in history, almost always worked with a team. He was very selective regarding his co-laborers. Certain qualities were required of those who traveled with Paul. John Mark fell short; consequently, Paul and Barnabas split up over Paul's refusal to keep Mark on the team (Acts 15:36-41).

COMBINING RESOURCES

There are several very important reasons for teaming up. To begin with, none of us has all the gifts. Alone, we have a limited range of abilities and limited time. Stop for a minute and take stock of yourself. What are your strengths? What are you able to do? How much time do you have in your week for involvement in the lives of other people? What are your limitations, your fears?

If you are like the rest of us, your answers to these questions may

139

discourage you. You may be tempted to give up on having a significant ministry of evangelism before you ever get started, never even getting beyond the stage of wishful thinking. But you probably also know enough about the Scriptures to realize that to be uninvolved is not an acceptable option. Passages like Ephesians 4:11-16 make it clear that there are no bleachers for those who would rather just sit and watch. God's people are to be prepared for "works of service." The Body will grow only "as each part does its work." Every Christian is to be a laborer, involved on whatever level of maturity and gifts he finds himself as he helps to win the lost and build up the saved. So in either direction there is tension! Upon assessing our personal resources, most of us conclude that we don't have the necessary equipment to take the message into our own worlds. But staying on the sidelines is also not acceptable. How do we resolve this dilemma?

Among the most basic truths concerning the Church is the fact that it is a Body, an organism. This means God never intended for individual members to function in isolation from one another. True, we are individually accountable to God, but the Christian life and ministry is not to be individualistic. We can't do it by ourselves.

I find it interesting that God has refrained from giving all His gifts to a single individual. Of course He could have done so. At first glance, it might appear that He would get a lot more work done today if He would simply give each individual all he needs to carry on a ministry by himself. But instead God has made us all specialists. He has given us gifts in some areas and withheld them in others. We need our limitations as much as we need our strengths. Without our limitations, we could go it alone. With them, we become interdependent. Our limitations serve as the cement that binds us to one another. The end result is greater strength.

So we need to team up. Once you have prayerfully chosen one or more kindred spirits, the next steps are (1) to commit yourselves to co-laboring and (2) to take stock of your assets, putting them to work. This little team of two or more persons will serve as your vehicle for evangelism.

A COMMITMENT TO CO-LABORING

Most of us have three enemies to conquer before we can be free to become truly involved with people. These enemies are busy-ness, inertia, and procrastination.

Busy-ness tends to creep up on us. We begin to participate in an activity in one situation, we accept a responsibility in another, and before we know it every night of the week is committed. We never really intended to let it happen, but suddenly we find ourselves under the tyranny of an endless cycle of commitments.

At this point the second enemy, inertia, moves in on us. *Inertia* is the force that maintains, or gives continuation to, the status quo. We are too busy. We know it. We complain about it. We even know way down in our hearts that we're occupying our lives with the wrong things. But, nonetheless, our lives go on unaltered week after week, year after year. It is hard to break out of our stagnation.

Procrastination is the third enemy. We realize that we are being carried along by a cycle of activities that have a momentum of their own. We know that we are exhausting our lives on matters of secondary importance. We know that the real purposes God has in mind for us are being neglected. We know that we must stop, reevaluate, and regain control over our lives, but we don't. We keep putting it off. We procrastinate.

Jesus said, "Enter through the narrow gate" (Matthew 7:13-14). He was probably referring to a person's choice between salvation and judgment here. But we can take counsel from this analogy of the two gates throughout our lives. Select the narrow gate. Make the harder choice. Don't let life carry you along. "For wide is the gate and broad is the road that leads to destruction, and many enter through it." Following God involves a lifetime of choosing the narrow gates. Paul points out that some of us are going to appear before God like survivors of a hotel fire—with nothing to show for our lives but the pajamas on our backs because we dedicated our lives to perishable pursuits (1 Corinthians 3:15).

Most of us need help to defeat the enemies of busy-ness, inertia, and procrastination.

One of the great life-revolutionizing benefits of becoming accountable to a few kindred spirits is the ensuing restructuring of priorities and commitments. "As iron sharpens iron, so one man sharpens another" (Proverbs 27:17). People who are working together as a team need to allot time to pray together, to open up their lives with one another, and to unite their hearts together on the basis of God's commands and promises. This is the commitment of co-laboring.

OVERCOMING FEARS AND DISCOURAGEMENT

Another benefit gained from teaming up with others is the support it provides for overcoming the fears that always seem to accompany our efforts in evangelism. Often fear is the true cause of our procrastination—at least that has been my experience.

It is strange how fear sets in. To this day, I often experience fear when I begin to discuss the gospel message with an individual for the first time. Often I'll feel anxiety all day long as I anticipate the conversation we have scheduled for that evening.

But we fearful souls are in good company. Earlier we observed that Paul also "came . . . in weakness and fear, and with much trembling" (1 Corinthians 2:3). The only personal prayer request he left with his brothers in Ephesus was that he would be able to overcome his fears (Ephesians 6:19-20). The first recorded prayer of the early Church was for boldness (Acts 4:29).

What are these strange fears that perturb us? In some cases there is good cause to fear physical harm. Paul knew all about flogging, stoning, and imprisonment. Believers in much of today's world live under threat of physical harm because of their faith. But remove the physical dangers, and the fears still remain! What do we fear? Rejection? Failure? Embarrassment? Probably all of these.

We might as well make peace with the fact that our fears will always be with us. About all we can do about them is confess them to one another, and then together take them to God. Fear in itself is not sin. But when I let my *fears* influence my *actions*, I am acting in unbelief (Mark 4:40). I suspect that this matter of fear was one of the primary reasons Jesus sent the Twelve out two by two. The person who is alone with his fears is the one who will be overcome by them.

"Two are better than one, because they have a good return for their work: If one falls down, his friend can help him up. But pity the man who falls and has no one to help him up!" (Ecclesiastes 4:9-10).

Inevitably, you are going to experience some failures. You will make plans, you will pray over them, you will set out to do what you planned— and nothing will happen. Then what? A very normal response would be to give up the whole idea of having an outreach. Failure is always discouraging. Any new effort is an experiment, and inherent in experiments is the probability of failure. At such times, it will take the objectivity of the person or persons you have teamed up with to regroup and keep moving.

TAKE STOCK OF YOUR ASSETS AND PUT THEM TO WORK

A few years ago, we moved our family to a new city in central Brazil. My responsibilities required that I travel close to half the time, so we chose the city primarily for its schools for the children and because of its airport. Once we were settled, I began to think about a personal ministry. The fact that I spent most of my time traveling, teaching, evangelizing, and helping others in their ministries did not satisfy my personal needs for ongoing involvement with nonChristians and spiritual babes. Of course, my wife and family shared these same needs.

The following months were sheer frustration. I would manage to make a few acquaintances and then get them interested in looking over the Bible with us. Inevitably, at that point my schedule would require a four-to-five-week trip. When I would return home, those acquaintances would have all but forgotten my name, and I'd have to start over. This pattern occurred again and again until I was totally frustrated. I thought, "Maybe it's just not possible for someone with a travel schedule like mine to do what I'm attempting to do." But I knew that if I were helping a business executive who had to travel, I would not let him get by with such an excuse.

As my wife and I prayed over this situation, it occurred to us that my ministry team was my own family, and that our ministry would have to begin within the family's sphere of relationships. Who were our children playing with? Did we know their parents? So my wife and I began to pray for the parents of our children's friends. A friendship began to grow with one couple in particular. We did them favors and they returned them. Since both the husband and wife were professional people who traveled quite a bit themselves, we felt they would understand our situation.

One day my wife and I simply explained our intentions to them. We told them that we were accustomed to studying the Bible with our friends, that we needed this interaction because we wanted to orient our lives around biblical principles. We told them of our frustration because of my schedule. Then I said, "Marge and I have talked it over and we would like to invite you to join us in studying the Bible." They felt honored and we began immediately.

When my next trip took me away, my wife and family were there to sustain the relationships. When I returned, we resumed our studies. This went on for eighteen months, until both the husband and wife understood the grace of God and were growing in Christ. Our team had doubled.

After reevaluating our assets, we decided it was time to reach out again. So we invited two more nonChristian couples to join us. We went back to John 1 and started all over again. But this was familiar ground for the first couple, so in my absences the husband led the discussions. My travel schedule had begun to work in our favor. It was forcing others to assume leadership.

Such were the beginnings of the outreach in which I participated for several years. This outreach continues to grow dynamically to the degree that every participant, even if he has not yet come to faith, does his part. Some participate with hospitality. Others maintain communications among the participants. Others constantly sow among their network of relationships, stirring up new interest. Still others are strongly involved in prayer. Two or three teach. Others keep things organized and moving.

It is important in a group to utilize whatever abilities are found in the group members. If people do what they can do today, tomorrow they will be doing what they couldn't do yesterday. The converse is also true. If we let our abilities go unused we eventually lose them.

We could visualize this basic idea with the following diagram:

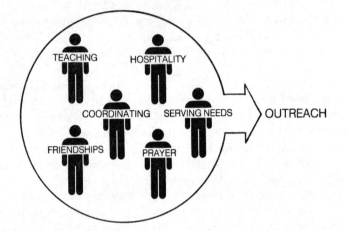

An outreach such as this will constantly have to think in terms of dividing if it is to remain dynamic. This creates a healthy demand for new leadership and increased participation by everybody. Divisions should respect the lines of affinity within the group.

WHAT WILL MY CHURCH SAY?

Very likely a question is growing in your mind as you are thinking, "Won't this put me in conflict with my other commitments? What about my church? Won't I be in conflict with the vision and programs of my local church?"

The answer depends on how your particular fellowship defines itself. If your organized church can envision itself as a base of operations out of which the living Church (that is, the people) operates, then its vision will be broad. If, on the other hand, it envisions itself as a fortress that sends out occasional patrols to gather a few more into its security, then its vision will be narrow. In such cases, there could well be tension over a conflict of purposes.

If we, the Church of this generation, hope to touch the lost of this generation, our vision must be sufficiently broad. We must include involvement in the kind of outreach I have just described as an integral and essential part of the Church. Perhaps we need a new definition of the Church, one that draws a large enough circle to include its calling to go into the neighborhoods and the marketplace. But that is a subject for another occasion.

All that is really needed for now is support from your church, permitting you to restructure your priorities and granting you the freedom to adapt your lifestyle to accommodate your ministry.

There are signs of such beginnings. There are churches that are moving in this direction. I heard Gene Getz tell his congregation that one visit to the church building in a week is enough. More than that would rob them of prime time with their nonChristian friends. The rest of their activities should take place in homes.

Joe Aldrich says, "We need men and women that are being urged to go out and mix it up at the front lines . . . with the nonChristian community." He also talks about "deploying Christians into the world."[1]

The kind of evangelistic approach we're talking about can hardly be organized as one more facet of the church program. How do we organize the casual and unstructured hours required for meaningful relationships with nonChristians? This is the Church fulfilling its mission. It is the Church (the Body of Christians) where it belongs—in the world. If we are going to engage the people of this generation, it will only happen on their turf. They will not come to us.

NOTE:
1. Joseph Aldrich, from a lecture, "Developing Vision for Disciplemaking."

SIXTEEN

TAKING THE FIRST STEPS

Conversion Occurs a Step at a Time

RECENTLY IN MY hometown, I conducted a workshop on evangelism. An old friend was in the audience. Twenty-five years earlier, he and I had spent many hours together. Because he was a new Christian then, I had tried to pass on to him the things I had been learning about discipleship.

During that initial time together, I showed him how to explain the gospel to another person. Then he accompanied me as I witnessed in several situations. Next I had him make up a list of his friends and business associates. After he showed me the list, we prayed together over those names for several weeks. Then I encouraged my friend to invite his acquaintances out for lunch, one at a time, to share the gospel with them.

After the workshop, this friend came up to me and said, "You sure have changed." "Yes," I replied. "I have." He reminded me of the process I had taken him through twenty-five years earlier and of how he had presented the gospel to each of his friends. "I did that," he told me, "until all my friends were gone!"

I had thought I was teaching my friend to evangelize. But in reality, I was contributing to his isolation from the very people he most wanted to win for Christ. I had made the mistake of encouraging him to attempt to reap among people who had not yet been prepared.

PRESENTATIONS POLARIZE

For years I lived with a very simplistic understanding of evangelism. I viewed it as a matter of being alert to opportunities to present the gospel to

147

a friend or acquaintance so that he could make an intelligent decision about whether or not he was going to open his life to God. Where the opportunity didn't naturally present itself, I would proceed to create one.

Dewey Johnson and I were classmates. His manner convinced me that if he wasn't already a Christian, a simple conversation would take care of it. So I began to watch for a chance to talk to him. But as the weeks passed, I realized no natural opportunity would ever come along. So I invited him to go fishing with me.

Afterward, as we sat and cleaned our fish, I began to talk to Dewey about the gospel. I had never been more mistaken about a person in my life. Dewey Johnson was far from being a Christian, and what's more, he didn't even want to talk about the subject. My attempt so polarized our relationship that further communication became impossible. Things were awkward between us from then on.

If I had only known at that time some of the things I've learned since then, it probably would have been a different story with Dewey. In this book I have developed the thesis that evangelism is a process including planting and cultivating as well as reaping. When we ignore this truth, when we persist in our attempts to reap where the soil is not prepared and the seed has not borne its fruit, polarization rather than conversion is frequently the result. The reason for this is obvious. Implicit in the gospel presentation is a call to make a decision. An insistent or an insensitive evangelist will inevitably force the nonChristian who is not ready to submit to Christ to back off, to create some distance between himself and those who are attempting to evangelize him.

SUCCESS STORIES TO THE CONTRARY

As you read this chapter, you are probably thinking about the people you know or have heard of who tell of how they put their faith in Christ the first time they heard the gospel, with no previous sowing or preparation. Perhaps it even happened that way with you. I am sure there are those exceptions, but it would hardly be wise to spend our lives in the pursuit of the exceptions. Also, a closer examination of an exception often reveals that it was, in fact, not an exception at all.

In reality, the sudden conversions we find in the New Testament came about as the result of considerable preparation. The Ethiopian eunuch was returning from a religious pilgrimage and was reading the book of Isaiah when he first heard the gospel (Acts 8:26-39). The first Roman convert, Cornelius, was described as a devout, God-fearing man who gave to the poor and prayed to God regularly (Acts 10:1-2). The Apostle Paul had, as his form of preparation, the heritage of sixteen centuries of biblical content and a powerful vision that struck him down and left him blind (Acts 9:1-9). In Philippi, where there was no synagogue, God prepared an instant harvest via an earthquake that would have cost a jailer his life had it not been for Paul (Acts 16:25-34).

It is so true that we are "God's fellow workers" (1 Corinthians 3:9). Where God has already made the preparations, we can and should proceed to reap. But very often what God has in mind for us to do as His fellow workers is to *prepare* the harvest. "Thus the saying 'One sows and another reaps' is true" (John 4:37).

The question, then, is not which one is right, proclamation or affirmation. Both have their place. Rather we need to ask, *which* do we use *when?*

Dawson Trotman, founder of The Navigators, used to pray that God would use him in the life of every person he met. That is a good request to emulate. If coming to Christ is a process, why not help every person we meet to move just one step closer to Christ? Some people are only a step away and it would be our joy to assist in the birth. Others are farther out, but the step we help them take would be just as significant.

Basically, our social relationships are of two kinds. There are the chance encounters with strangers, and there are the more permanent relationships with friends, neighbors, and colleagues. The passenger in the next seat is an example of the first. The neighbor who asks you to sign his petition is an example of the second kind. When we think of sharing our faith, it is important to keep this distinction in mind, even though our immediate objective is the same—to help people take the next step.

In the case of a casual encounter, we need to exercise discernment to determine a person's background and thinking. We should be prepared to explain the gospel, but should avoid doing injustice to the person by forcing a premature presentation, by pressing the issue unduly, or by being overbearing. In most casual encounters, our witness will be supplemented by the reinforcement of other influences God is bringing to bear. On occasion we will be able to leave a person with a clear understanding of the essential message. When we are led to do this, we can be assured that God will use that witness in a positive way.

In the case of our more permanent relationships, we must be acutely sensitive to the attitudes and emotions of others. The gospel is urgent news, but that doesn't mean we have to rush and push to get it across. According to 2 Peter 3:9, God is holding up the judgment of the world and the ushering in of His new creation until the stragglers cross the threshold. We can therefore assume that if God uses us to start something in someone's life, He also intends to bring it to fruition. Therefore, we need to evangelize the people in our daily world by reinforcing the relationships between us in the process rather than by polarizing them.

Most of us have only one sphere of friends and acquaintances. We can either see this sphere transformed into an increasingly fertile environment for the gospel, or we can exhaust it with a slash-and-burn approach. The intent of what I have defined as *affirmation evangelism* is to make the most of the opportunities our more permanent relationships offer us.

MINI-DECISIONS

I commonly hear people express a desire to know how to break into discussing the gospel with an acquaintance. As one put it, "I need to develop a positive, nonthreatening introductory statement, something that gets me into the subject with someone. What do you suggest?"

Usually what people are looking for is a one-step launch question—something that will carry them gracefully from a dead stop into an effective discussion about Christ in a single motion. In situations where God has already prepared the way, it's hard to go wrong at this point. Almost anything you say will do. Philip simply asked the Ethiopian man if he understood what he was reading. Peter asked Cornelius why he had sent for him. But most of the people we meet are neither reading the book of Isaiah nor have they had any recent visions. For the unprepared, there is no one easy step from where they are to where we want to go with them. This question of how to launch into the gospel in one step is equivalent to asking, How do I set the ball for a seventy-yard field goal attempt?

Rather than looking for a single step, it is better to think in terms of *mini-decisions*. If evangelism is a process, then our function is to accompany our acquaintances on the road to Christ, showing them the way. We must walk the road with them, a step at a time. So we think in terms of steps, or mini-decisions. We can diagram the process as follows:

DISTANCE FROM CHRIST   CONVERSION

When we see things from this perspective, our question changes. Rather than asking how to present the gospel so that this person who is a long way out will respond, we ask what needs to happen to draw this person to Christ.

We evaluate the resources at our disposal: God has made us light; we have the Holy Spirit; and we can pray. This is a formidable arsenal. Then we proceed, counting on God to effectively work as we use these resources.

The first steps toward Christ can begin with seemingly insignificant things: initiating a hello; doing small favors; borrowing and loaning things among neighbors; conversing over the fence. These grow into larger acts of friendship and hospitality such as a night out together, picnicking, etc.

As the distances are reduced, observe closely. Try to understand the needs and interests of your new friends. Don't try to build your witness on the problem side of their lives or you'll get off on the wrong foot.

Eventually you will begin to elicit from your friends some of the following "pre-conversion decisions" about you:

- He's okay.
- I'd like to get to know him better.
- I feel comfortable with him. He accepts me.
- I'm going to find out why he's so different.
- It seems that he gets his outlook on things from the Bible.
- He's a Christian, but he's okay.
- Being a Christian sure has its advantages.
- I like his friends. I envy their confidence.
- It might be interesting to look at the Bible someday.

Now our diagram looks like this:

When a nonChristian comes to the point where he is responsive to the idea of seeing what the Bible has to say, many of the major hurdles to faith have been overcome. The path that remains between his unbelieving state and faith in Christ becomes relatively smooth. This is because *the spiritual arsenal is now complete.* The Holy Spirit can now take up the sword that "penetrates . . . dividing soul and spirit . . . [and] judges the thoughts and attitudes of the heart" (Hebrews 4:12). For this reason, it is far more effective to first aim toward bringing the nonChristian to the point where he wants to examine the Bible with us. To have this as our first objective rather than thinking in terms of a single explanation of the gospel at an opportune moment offers some very large advantages.

If handled properly, our examination of the Scriptures together with the nonChristian *reinforces* rather than polarizes the relationship. Also, it allows us to lay a foundation of truth that will serve as a basis for faith. It gives the individual the time and freedom to fight and win the battle against his defiant will that has been saying no to God ever since physical birth. In short, the spiritual birth will be a healthy one.

So we add the following factors to our diagram:

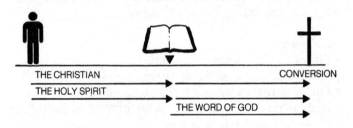

. . . AND MORE MINI-DECISIONS

Once the nonChristian has begun to examine the Bible with us, we can expect a new series of mini-decisions to occur. We might expect him to say, for example:

- The Bible isn't impossible to understand after all!
- The Bible says some important things.
- What the Bible says about life fits my experience.
- Jesus seems to be the key. I wonder who He really was.
- Jesus is God.
- I need to do what He says.
- I will believe in Him.

Central to successful evangelism among people in the mainstream is getting them to examine the Bible with us in a context of affirmation and acceptance. This is in contrast to the more common approach where we count on a single presentation to move a person from unbelief to faith. But what we are suggesting is probably new to many and therefore gives rise to further questions. Some of these are: How do I get people who don't even believe the Bible to want to study it? How can I keep their interest up so that they will continue week after week? What do I do with all the questions they are bound to ask that I'll never be able to answer? What about reaping? When and how do I do that? We will be addressing these questions in the following chapters.

SEVENTEEN

BRIDGING THE DISTANCE FROM INDIFFERENCE TO FAITH

Discovering Bridges of Common Interest

THE WORLD'S LEAST attentive audience would probably be found on the Friday afternoon flights between La Guardia Airport in New York and National Airport in Washington, D.C. These flights are always full of businessmen, many of whom make that same trip a hundred times a year. Invariably, before takeoff the stewardess comes on with the routine safety instructions. As she goes through her explanation, the inattention is absolute. She is endured, and everyone is relieved when she has finally finished.

She fails to hold the attention of her audience for two reasons. In the first place, nothing she says is news. Everyone aboard has already been through it countless times. In the second place, the dangers for which she is preparing the passengers are very remote. The felt need for what she has to say is just about zero.

What would it take for her to capture the attention of her passengers so that they would actually listen and finally learn how to use one of those oxygen masks? Suppose the plane developed serious mechanical problems at 20,000 feet and began to lose altitude. If that same stewardess would then repeat those same instructions to those same passengers under those emergency conditions, she would have everyone's total attention! People are motivated to learn to the degree that the subject matter is perceived as relevant to needs or wants.

The secularized person has quit listening to the voices of religion for similar reasons. He has concluded that no news (new information) will ever be forthcoming. The Christian claims and warnings appear hopelessly

153

redundant. If we are to recapture his attention, we must begin at the level of his felt needs and aspirations.

That is why Jesus said what He did to Nicodemus. Nicodemus had climbed as far as he was going to in the Jewish hierarchy. His achievements were his security. So when Jesus said, "You'll never make it unless you undergo a second birth," He had Nicodemus's attention. To a woman in the midst of her daily chore of hauling water, Jesus began talking about water. To a fisherman He talked about fishing. To the hungry He talked about bread. He began with the familiar, the daily concerns, and from these mundane matters He transported His listeners into new dimensions of understanding.

Apathy is the most difficult obstacle we can face. Apathetic people just don't care. They are indifferent. They are like the roadway in Jesus' parable of the sower (Matthew 13:4), which was so hard that when the seed was sown it bounced and then just laid there until the birds finally found it and devoured it. Hardness is not belligerence or toughness; it is indifference. She can be a sweet, fragile, 115-pound teenager—and still be spiritually hard!

Some people give the impression that they are indifferent about everything. They have seen it all and disbelieve it all. But that is only an impression. Everyone cares about something, and that something is our starting point. We can be confident that whatever the starting point, the ultimate word on it will be God's Word. So our objective is to begin with a person's felt needs and then lead him to the point where he sees that those desires of his, whatever they may be, are ultimately met in Christ.

STARTING POINTS

One obvious implication of what I've just said is that there is no single approach, no skeleton key that will unerringly unlock people's interest. Often we will need to forge new keys to fit particular situations. This is not especially difficult. We must begin by being observant and sensitive. Here are a few examples.

1. Young parents. For many Brazilians the family is still high on the priority list. If you ask a graduating university student in Brazil about his aspirations, he will frequently tell you he is looking forward to marriage and children. He wants a comfortable family life, and wants to be able to provide well for his wife and children. The Brazilian society is child-oriented. It is also basically Freudian.

At graduation the individual is often virtually impervious to the gospel. He is engrossed in other things. He is bent on getting into his profession, getting married, etc. But if we look in on this young family six or seven years later, we will find that life is not going exactly as planned. The family is feeling the consequences of their Freudianism. Mom and dad are now living under the dictatorial regime of their three-year-old, who has just stepped up his reign of terror to combat the recent intrusion of the newlyborn sibling.

The parents are at a loss. Afraid of damaging their child's psyche by disciplining him for his behavior, they elect to endure the pandemonium. But it's too much. They begin to take their frustrations out on one another, and soon the last vestiges of the earlier aspirations are dead.

Now there *is* a felt need!

We have picked up on this need by putting together a series of discussions on how to raise children according to the Bible. We find that many parents are at such a loss that even though they have ignored the Bible all their lives, they are eager to see what it has to say about child rearing. Although the Bible and Freud are in disagreement on almost every point, and although these parents would not be ready to recognize the Bible's inspiration, the Bible consistently ends up as the undisputed authority in our discussions. The experience of all parents tells them that what the Bible says is truth.

As I write this, my wife and I are helping an agnostic Jewish neighbor explore the Scriptures. She was attracted by our children, and has agreed to read the Bible because, in her words, "I want to have children that will turn out as yours have." We have found that instruction in child rearing serves as an almost irresistible bridge from indifference to keen interest for young parents.

2. University students. Had we started with the same individuals ten years earlier, they would have been totally indifferent to receiving instructions on child rearing. As students just beginning their university studies, their needs and interests would have lain elsewhere.

The first years of university life offer the long-awaited opportunity to get out from under the scrutiny of parents, brothers, aunts, and uncles. There's room to think, to question, to act. If there are any philosophical inclinations in a person, they will come to the surface at this stage in life. The student will look for some way to explain his existence and to justify his own behavior. So we have a different starting point.

In this case our bridge out of indifference might be along the lines of the following sequence of statements.

a. Man exists. Either he is here by chance, having evolved, or he is here by creation. If there is a Creator, He has to be intelligent and powerful. The question is, which of these alternatives is true?

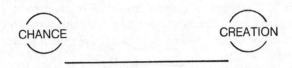

b. The equipment we have at our disposal to research the answer to this question is our five senses. Everything we know has been received through hearing, seeing, tasting, touching, and smelling.

c. If there is a God, and if He is Spirit, He would be beyond the range of these senses. He would go unperceived. Science, which researches only by extending the reach of those same senses, will never provide answers on God.

d. Therefore God would be unknowable—unless He somehow took the initiative to reveal Himself to man.

e. The basic claim of the Bible is that God *did* make Himself knowable by entering our time and space world.

f. Jesus of Nazareth claimed to be that revelation. Either He was who He said He was, or God remains unknowable. History records no other serious claimant to Deity.

g. This simplifies our search, reducing it to a single question: Who is Jesus? If He is who He said He was, we have answers to life. If we conclude that He isn't who He claimed to be, we also have our answer. In that case our answer would be that there are no answers.

Beginning with the possibility of this claim being true—that God could be seen, touched, and listened to in Jesus (1 John 1:1-2)—we have a basis for inviting the nonChristian to investigate the question, "Who is Jesus?"

3. The post-Christian. The above sequence is effective among people who are asking the existential questions. But among many of this generation, such questions are as good as dead. The secularized Europeans we described in chapter 1 would be an example of people who have given up on the big issues. They readily admit that they have no answers, but they are also quite convinced that no one else has any either. So, they reason, why bother to search? It's better to busy the mind with whatever happens to catch your attention.

To those of us who have been raised in the Aristotelian tradition of linear logic, these people are baffling—incomprehensible! But they are no exception to the rule. They, too, have needs and desires that can serve as bridges to Christ as effectively as any other. It's just that the bridge has to be quite different. It may not be built along a sequence of ideas at all.

For the secular European and his American cousin, relationships are of primary concern. There is a certain irony in this because although they place relationships at the top of their value system, they are, at the same time, unusually inept in this area. In part, their weakness is due to the fact that they were raised on bad relationships. Sensing that their spiritual inheritance went bankrupt before it ever got to them, they realize that the only thing that remains that can possibly give cohesion to life is other people. So the needs and desires in this area of relationships—love, affirmation, and acceptance—serve as ample footing for building their bridge to Christ.

The Bible has a lot to say about relationships, and discussions on the subject can be attractive and helpful. But in the case of this bridge, the practice is far more effective than the theory. Talking about love and acceptance is no substitute for the real thing. Simply move into a meaningful relationship. I've seen many people of this generation led into the Bible and on to Christ for no other reason than that they had been unconditionally befriended by the evangelist. The invitation to examine the Scriptures was accepted, not as a result of any overwhelming arguments or strong feelings of a need for answers, but simply because it represented one more opportunity to enjoy the love and warmth of that relationship. Logic, I'm convinced, is overrated as a persuader. It finishes a poor second to love every time.

These three illustrations of bridge building are intended to be just that: illustrations. I hope they will inspire some creative thinking on how to build bridges to fit the needs and aspirations of those you are seeking to win. There are many others, such as the pursuit of success, having a successful marriage, etc. Before going further, we should stop to ask ourselves two questions: (1) What are some of the felt needs and aspirations of the people I am desiring to reach? and (2) In what way could these needs and aspirations serve as bridges?

The next logical question, which we will address in the next chapter, is, How do we go about getting our friends onto these bridges, moving along toward Christ?

GOING TO THE PRIMARY SOURCE

Total Reliance on the Scriptures

THERE ARE PRIMARY sources and there are secondary sources. A primary source is an eyewitness. In the sciences, he is the person who does the experiments. He does basic research and surfaces new information. Secondary sources report on things that primary sources have seen and done.

Reliability is a problem with information of any kind, especially with any information that comes from secondary sources because they are never totally free from personal biases and subjectivity. Communicators do not have to intentionally lie to be misleading. As a person's own subjective perceptions are mixed with the facts he is reporting, distortions just happen.

The news media serve as an excellent example of how variable communication can be. Even if everything reported on a given issue is true, the simple act of choosing what to include and exclude, or the amount of time and space given to an issue, can determine favorable or unfavorable public sentiment.

Another example of variable communication is the broad range of history books. A quick comparison of a Mexican history book with an American history book, where the same events are recounted, reveals that frequently the heroes and the villains have changed hats. Bravery is alternately described as brutality, and an insignificant episode is interpreted as a great victory, depending on which country published the book.

When it comes to communicating the gospel to the secularized person, we strengthen our appeal immeasurably by letting him know we

159

intend to confine ourselves to an examination of the sole primary source that we Christians claim: the Bible. Although the average secularized person does not accept the inspiration or authority of the Bible, the idea of taking a look for himself at this famous book is likely to be attractive to him. It defines the parameters of the discussion for him, and for us. He thus feels that the odds are more even, that he will be free to think and decide for himself.

Frequently, the nonChristian fears being indoctrinated and manipulated. Christian books and tracts abound; they are in endless supply. Although many of them can be extremely helpful, all of them fall into the category of secondary sources. They are someone's perception of the primary source. As such, they are often viewed with suspicion by the nonChristian. He is never sure he is really getting the full story. Thus, the skeptical or wary nonChristian who keeps his distance will often respond favorably to an opportunity to do some original investigation—*if* the environment is right. So our goal is to create that right environment as we simultaneously lead the nonChristian to see the wisdom of taking time to personally research a subject of this magnitude.

GETTING USED TO THE IDEA

Most people automatically reject new ideas. Since it's part of human nature to resist change, whenever it's forced on us we react. This is because change is usually accompanied by a sense of loss. The familiar gives way to the unknown. Someone has described change as occurring in four stages: rejection, tolerance, acceptance, and assimilation. The first time we're confronted with something new, we tend to reject it. But after it is around for a while, we become tolerant of it. Then we begin to see its positive possibilities; we begin to accept it. From there it's a small step to assimilating the idea; we make it our own.

When a nonChristian is first introduced to the idea of examining the Bible, he will often reject it. So we introduce the idea without calling for a response. "Someday I'd like to show you how to read and understand the Bible on your own." Or, "Someday I'm going to invite you to our Monday night Bible study." "Someday" is vague, noncommittal. But by reading a person's reaction to such a statement, it is not hard to gauge whether that day should be arranged for the next week or the next month—or postponed until further notice.

After you repeat an abstract invitation of this sort several times, two things often begin to happen. First, your nonChristian friend has time to become accustomed and increasingly receptive to the idea. Second, he's beginning to wonder when you're going to get around to making your invitation good. The shoe is suddenly on the other foot. He's looking to you to keep your promise.

GETTING STARTED

Our immediate objective is to help a person begin to examine the Bible. From there on, our purpose is to lead him into an understanding of its central message: that Jesus is God and that one passes from death to life through faith in Him. This purpose can be summarized in two questions: (1) Who is Jesus? (2) What does He want of me?

The strategic importance of these two questions can easily be missed in the midst of the sixty-six books of the Bible with all of their diversity. As we invite a person to begin to examine the Bible on his own, we need to help him simplify his research task down to these essentials. The dialogue may go something like this:

A: If you're interested in examining the Bible, I'd like to help you get started.

B: I'd like to see what it says, but I think you need to know that I don't believe it the way you do.

A: That's fair enough. It's the only primary source we Christians have. If, after examining that source, you decide that it is not true, you have your answers. You can lay to rest your questions about God and go your own way. If, on the other hand, you find truth in the Bible, then you also have your answers. Either way you win.

B: That's fair enough.

A: Now, the Bible is different from other books. You don't just pick it up and read it from cover to cover. The Bible consists of 1,189 chapters, divided into sixty-six books. It was written by many different authors over a period of roughly 1,600 years. To sit down and read it through in order to research your questions would be the equivalent of going to a library with a question and reading your way randomly through the books on the shelves to get information. It would be better to get some help from the librarian. He can save you much time and frustration by helping you pull the right books off the shelf. That's what I'd like to propose to you: I'll help you find your way around.

B: I'd like that.

A: Okay, let's set a time.

We pick up the dialogue at the agreed-upon time and place. It's in a neutral, familiar spot, either in your house or in his. You have brought along an extra Bible, one with page numberings that are identical to yours. You are using a modern translation, intentionally avoiding the paraphrased versions. Explaining that the particular rendering of the passage isn't in accord with the original intent doesn't exactly build credibility in the Bible. Nor does it help to have to explain that "quit you like men" simply means "be courageous."

A: The Bible is divided into two parts: the Old Testament and the New Testament. The Old Testament has to do with things that went on before the time of Jesus Christ. The New Testament starts out with four accounts of Jesus' life by his contemporaries. Then there's a book that records the first years of the Christian movement. The remainder of the New Testament consists of letters written to the fledgling groups of Christians, or churches, that had begun to scatter out around the world in that first century AD.

The theme of the whole Bible, the Old and the New Testaments, is the same. It is that God is revealing Himself to man with the intent of rescuing him from his self-destructive rebellion. The basic claim of the Bible is that the man Jesus of Nazareth is the apex of that revelation.

The Old Testament was written to get the world ready for this revelation. The New was written to record the event and to explain its significance.

B: I follow what you're saying, but I can't promise I'll arrive at the same conclusions you have.

A: Of course not. All I'm asking is that you take a look. Whether the Bible is truth or not is beside the point. For now, the important thing is for you to understand that the Christian position stands or falls on this one figure, Jesus. If He does not prove to be what the Bible claims for Him, then Christianity offers no answers for anyone. Can you see that?

B: I see your point.

A: My proposition is to give you the opportunity to examine the Bible for yourself so that you can draw your own conclusions on the question of Jesus' identity.

B: Right!

A: As I said before, the New Testament begins with four books that we call Gospels. Three are eyewitness accounts of the life and teachings of Jesus, the other is by a physician. Why four? It is as if four people standing on separate corners of an intersection witnessed an accident. The four testimonies, although essentially the same, will vary according to where they were positioned and what

details especially caught their attention. By combining four testimonies, any event would be more thoroughly recorded. This is
the effect of the four Gospels. The sum of the four gives a quadra-
phonic record of Jesus' life.

I'd like to propose that we begin with the fourth Gospel, the
Gospel of John. John was one of Jesus' closest friends, so what we
have in this book is an eyewitness account by someone who
knew Him intimately. His account begins on page 1,137. Let's
begin by reading the first three verses.

B: "In the beginning was the Word, and the Word was with God, and
the Word was God. He was with God in the beginning. Through
him all things were made; without him nothing was made that has
been made."

A: Did you understand that?

B: No.

A: I don't blame you. Let's see if we can decipher the meaning. What
does *Word* refer to in this passage?

B: I don't know.

A: Look at verse 14.

B: "The Word became flesh and made his dwelling among us."

A: So evidently this "Word" became a human being. Who would that
be?

B: Jesus?

A: Right. Now reread the three verses putting *Jesus* in place of *Word.*
What is John claiming about Jesus?

B: That He existed in the beginning. That He was God. That He
created the world. But I can't agree with that!

A: I'm not asking you to agree, remember? My part is just to help you
understand what is written here. Would you agree that this is what
John is claiming about Jesus?

B: Yes, but I can't accept it.

A: Fine, let's go on. Could you read the next two verses?

And so it goes. Our purpose is to guide our nonChristian friend
through the book of John, helping him understand what the book says
concerning two questions: (1) Who is Jesus? (2) What does He want of me?

Our immediate concern is not to extract agreement or to win arguments; it is to produce understanding. We need to leave room for disagreement and doubt. It is the *Holy Spirit* alone who convicts of sin,
righteousness, and judgment, not us. It is the *Bible* that reveals the true
intents of the heart. We should leave these responsibilities where they
belong. Our part as we co-labor with God is to bring the nonChristian into

contact with these powers, and to love him as he struggles his way out of his rebellion and into faith.

A set of guideline questions for the book of John has been included in the appendix at the back of this book. They are not comprehensive, and with experience you will undoubtedly come up with additional questions that will serve better than mine. But I offer them as a start. It's usually best to try to cover one chapter of John at a time. Obviously, you'll not exhaust the contents of a chapter in an hour's discussion. But if you can't resist going into every little detail, you'll soon be studying by yourself again!

Now back to our dialogue. An hour or so has gone by, and we have just finished the first fourteen verses of the first chapter of John. We refer back to our original invitation: that we would help our friend research the message of the Bible for himself. At this point, as far as he knows, this is the first and last discussion the two of us will ever have on this subject.

A: That's enough to get you started. My impression is that you are getting a hold of the meaning of the text. How do you feel about it?

B: It's complicated, but, yes, I'm getting it.

A: It gets easier from here on as John begins now to narrate events in Jesus' life. Do you want to continue?

B: Yes.

A: Let's pick it up from here next time. In the meantime, if you feel like reading ahead, do it. Underline anything that strikes you as being especially interesting or significant, and put a question mark in the margin beside anything you don't understand. Let's get together again in a week or so and discuss your observations and questions.

KEEPING IT GOING

Rather than asking for a commitment to study through the entire book of John or even for a six-week commitment, it is better to take it one week at a time. The more loosely we hold people, the freer they will feel around us. If we establish expectations, and they don't fulfill them, there will be a sense of failure. We can avoid this simply by not expressing expectations or by not setting any standards. The continuing of the studies must depend on genuine interest in the subject and on the strength of the rapport or friendship between the two of us.

The importance of reaffirming our relationship in between the Bible sessions cannot be overstated! A fifteen minute drop-in visit or even a quick phone conversation communicates acceptance and interest on our part. Leisure time together is better yet. When you're with him, talk about him, about things that are of interest to him—sports or even the weather. But *don't* just talk about the Bible. We will soon wear thin if we are only conversant on the first chapter of John.

Sometimes the nonChristian is totally unabashed among his friends about his awakening interest in the Bible. More often it is the other way around. He struggles with feelings of embarrassment and fears of being ridiculed. We need to be aware of these feelings. Nicodemus came to Jesus at night because he didn't want his colleagues to know of his interest in this controversial man. Jesus, of course, realized this, but he didn't send Nicodemus away to come back when it was daylight. A person on his way to Christ is already battling with his inner demons. He doesn't need any additional enemies at the moment. So we need to be discreet and reassure him.

One way to honor this compunction of our friend is to be careful about where and when we meet to study. The location should be neutral and private. Church buildings are out because they are not neutral. Restaurants and offices are not private enough. Homes are good.

Many years ago, a friend and I conducted some evangelistic rap sessions in several fraternities on a particular campus. We got ourselves invited to conduct discussions. In most cases, the fraternity members would gather in the lounge and we would make our presentation, eventually throwing the session open for questions. Afterwards we would organize those who were really interested into study groups.

In one fraternity we decided to have the study in Jack Smith's room. It went great the first week—we thought. But we had taken the rest of the fraternity by surprise. The following week they were ready for us. Apparently they had spent the entire week getting ready for us!

Everything was normal for the first thirty minutes. Then suddenly a mocked-up radio program blared from a tape recorder placed just outside the door. There were a few phrases of music. Then came the commercials, more music, then more commercials. The commercials advertised such things as genuine John-the-Baptist road sandals and pictures of Jesus that glow in the dark. Jack Smith and the other fraternity brothers participating in the study were mortified. My feelings were more of frustration. Our study was being interrupted! As I look back on this episode, I can hardly believe we did what we did next. We continued to meet in Jack Smith's room! The other fraternity members fled the study, so it was only Jack and us. What could he do? We were using his room! The harassment continued. Finally, when Jack's social life was in ruins, he got up the courage to tell us he never wanted to see us again.

Somehow we justified what we did in the name of boldness. But the pressures that accompany being identified with Christ always come soon enough. We should be the last to contribute to them!

In this chapter we have treated the subject of getting started on a one-on-one basis. Very often this is where it all begins—with one individual. If we start out with the idea that before anything can happen we must organize a group of nonChristians, we could easily overlook the individual opportunities. Frequently these prove to be the greatest in the long run! But the approach we have described here can, of course, also be applied effectively on the small-group level.

NINETEEN

THE BIBLICAL BASIS FOR FAITH

Conscious Submission to God Through His Word

OUR OBJECTIVE IN going to the primary source is to bring people to faith in Jesus Christ. Mark Twain defined faith as "believing in something you know really isn't true." But a valid faith is just the opposite—it *must* be based on truth.

One of the most helpful definitions of faith in the Bible is found in Romans 4:21: "being fully persuaded that God had power to do what he had promised." Faith is the confidence that God will do what He has said He will do. Coming to faith then, means *knowing* what God has said and done, and then staking one's life on it. Faith in God is not a leap in the dark. It is a conscious, voluntary submission to His will for us.

Evangelism provides the nonChristian with the kind of input he needs to respond to God on the level of faith. For this we need to lay a base of truth. At what point can we know that has been accomplished? It is not always easy to evaluate.

In an unpublished paper on "The Doctrine of Sin in Cross-Cultural Church Planting," Wayne Dye described the efforts of a group of missionaries working among New Guinea highlanders. As they involved themselves with these primitive people, the missionaries became extremely concerned with the polygamy and betel-nut chewing they observed among the villagers—so much so that these two practices became the watershed issues for the Christian fellowship.

The villagers, however, felt other issues were more serious. To them, a long life depended more upon the avoidance of discord.

Dye reported one case where a number of converts had responded to

167

the missionaries' efforts. They were baptized and for several years they tithed, attended church, and obeyed the imported rules for Christian behavior. One day the village leaders went to the missionaries and said, "We ought to have done enough by now to repay Jesus for His death." Then they reverted to paganism.

What happened? Faith had not occurred at all. Something that *looked* like Christian faith had been constructed upon the highlanders' pagan presuppositions. Consequently, the villagers had gone along with the missionaries until they tired of it, then went their own way again.

In a case like this where the contrast is so sharp between Christianity and paganism, it doesn't require unusual perception to recognize what went wrong. But this same danger lurks wherever evangelism occurs, and it is often very difficult to spot.

I met Henrique in Curitiba, Brazil, in January of 1964. We met in an art store and struck up a conversation.

Henrique was one of the most brilliant men I have ever known. He was a voracious reader with a retentive memory. He could discuss any subject from Byzantine art to the genetic code as if he had finished a book on the subject the day before. Along with Portuguese, he spoke flawless English and Spanish. He also spoke German and French. He was twenty-one when we met, recently married, and the owner of a language school.

Henrique and I drifted from the art store to a restaurant where we had tea. His first question was, "What are you, an American, doing in Curitiba?" When I told him, he replied, "Fine. Convert me first, then we'll have a whole school we can go to work on." He meant it. He wanted me to explain the gospel right there, and he had decided to accept it even before he heard it. I held him off until the next day so we could sit down and work our way through the Bible. That next day Henrique made a decision. A few weeks later his wife followed suit. He and I saw each other every day for several years. A deep friendship developed. We became like brothers.

But I had known Henrique only a week or so when I spotted a dangerous weakness. I noticed it the first time we ate a meal together. He was uncontrolled in his eating. Alerted, I began watching for other symptoms of lack of self-control. They were present in the way he handled his money, in the way he ran his business, and in the urgency with which he smoked. I was scared. "The fruit of the Spirit is . . . self-control" (Galatians 5:22-23). But it wasn't there.

The Bible was still a novelty to Henrique, so he was busy devouring that. He was an audacious witness, but that too was still a novelty. I feared that when the newness wore off and continued progress had to depend upon a deeper level of motivation, we would be in trouble. We were.

When he ceased to open the Bible on his own, we began to do it together to compensate for his lack of personal discipline. Daily for over two years, he and I met over the Scriptures. Consequently, Henrique's life maintained a semblance of Christian behavior. But I never saw the Holy Spirit do anything about his basic problems. I grew irritated with God and asked Him why I had to do His part of the job as well as my own. That attitude didn't help either.

I couldn't sustain those daily transfusions indefinitely. So after a couple of years had gone by, I decided I had to wean him. Henrique would have to begin getting his nourishment from God himself.

When we returned to Curitiba after being away for a seven-month furlough, we found that Henrique's business had gone bankrupt, and he had divorced his wife and left town.

The last time Henrique and I were together was in a restaurant in Porto Alegre in 1971. His second career and his second marriage were disintegrating. In the course of our conversation he said, "You don't know how close you came to getting me to become a Christian back there in Curitiba!"

Henrique had been attempting to live the Christian life without being a Christian, and I had been trying to help him. How futile! Henrique had made a decision but I had not helped him lay an adequate basis for faith. Consequently, he and I spent two years perpetuating an illusion.

We must take care that faith is constructed on the only sure foundation, the rock of the living Word of God, incarnate and written (see Ephesians 2:20). Faith cannot rest on anything else without being compromised. It cannot be syncretized with other religious beliefs, or pagan or humanistic presuppositions. We come to God on His terms, not ours.

How easy it is to gloss over big issues with a few glib phrases, elicit a prayer, or some other action we interpret as "a decision," and move on, happy with our success. One of the challenges for the missionary is to discern whether those he is ministering to have actually put their faith in Jesus Christ, or are merely following the missionary himself. Sometimes an entire generation can go by before such a misplaced trust is discovered.

So wherever evangelism takes place, the witness should seek for a genuine response. Superficial, well-meaning decisions tend to sabotage the real thing. In Henrique's case, he had done everything I told him was necessary for conversion. So both he and I assumed a spiritual rebirth had occurred when it actually hadn't. When this happens, the effect will be either confusion, as in our case, or disillusionment.

When a person has tried our offer, and is expecting the promised benefits which never materialize, the end result is likely to be disillusionment. When I shared the gospel with a next-door neighbor while living in the United States, he replied, "Hell, I've been saved three times." He had tried it, but it hadn't worked, so he was into something else.

How do we avoid this?

MAKING A DECISION

Three elements of personality are involved in making a decision to become a Christian, or in making any significant decision for that matter. They are the emotions, the intellect, and the will.

For example, a young man meets a young woman. They are immediately attracted to one another. They both say to themselves, "Now there is someone I'd like to marry." At that point, if the emotions had their way, there would be a wedding. But the intellect intervenes, questioning the impulsive emotional response. Would we be compatible? What is she really like? Can I afford to support her? Both conclude it would be better to take some more time and answer a few questions before they proceed. So the two begin spending more time with each other. He eventually concludes that she is as beautiful on the inside as she is on the outside. Now his intellect has sided with the emotions on the idea of marriage.

But the final and heaviest vote remains to be cast—that of the will. It stops the march toward the altar with the questions, "Am I willing to give up this lifestyle for another? What about my freedom—is it worth the trade? Am I willing to assume the added responsibility?" The marriage will occur only when the *will* finally agrees with the emotions and the intellect. And so it is in coming to Christ.

Isn't this the message of the parable of the sower?

> "When anyone hears the message about the kingdom and does not understand it, the evil one comes and snatches away what was sown in his heart. This is the seed sown along the path. The one who received the seed that fell on rocky places is the man who hears the word and at once receives it with joy. But since he has no root, he lasts only a short time. When trouble or persecution comes because of the word, he quickly falls away. The one who received the seed that fell among the thorns is the man who hears the word, but the worries of this life and the deceitfulness of wealth choke it, making it unfruitful. But the one who received the seed that fell on good soil is the man who hears the word and understands it. He produces a crop, yielding a hundred, sixty or thirty times what was sown." (Matthew 13:19-23)

The difference in the response is in the difference in the soil, not in the seed. Four kinds of soil. Four different responses.

1. There was the seed sown on the path. The path was hard. There was not enough loose soil there to produce even an emotional response. We all know people like this. Indifferent, they seem not to care about spiritual things. These are the most difficult of all to attempt to win. Such people may be cultured and gracious, but impervious to the Word of God. Their only hope is for God to break up their hardness, thus changing the consistency of the soil, and preparing it to receive the good seed. With people like this, the place to begin is with intercession. God does break up their hardness as we pray. I've seen Him do it often, and it's always impressive.

2. Then there's the rocky soil. This person hears and initially receives the word with joy. He responds emotionally, but lacks an adequate basis for faith, so his response is short-lived. What happened? These people do their thinking *after* making a decision. They have second thoughts about what they have done and feel embarrassed over their gullibility or impulsiveness. Very often they will avoid those who were responsible for leading them to the decision.

In such situations, the parable explains, there was no real understanding in the first place. The intellect had not been satisfied that what was being decided could stand up to closer scrutiny. For some reason, the person just wasn't mentally ready for a binding commitment to Christ.

3. Some seed falls on the thorny soil. Here the seed does germinate. It looks good. Surely this time there's life! But other seeds lie unnoticed in this same soil. They are "the worries of this life," and the "deceitfulness of wealth." They are other concerns and ambitions. The will is harboring other commitments which in time choke off the person's response to the gospel.

Why does a person like this make a decision to become a Christian at all? He may make a decision simply because he has run out of arguments against the gospel. He can no longer come up with any good reasons why he shouldn't become a Christian—even though he really doesn't want to. It's usually not very difficult to destroy a person's arguments against the gospel. Often when someone finds himself in this position, he simply says, "You win." He gives in to the truth, but he doesn't submit his life to Christ. His will remains intact.

Have you ever stopped to reflect on how easy it would be for God to prove His existence to every breathing soul? Or take Jesus—why didn't He go back to the temple in Jerusalem just one time after He rose from the dead to give just one discourse, and personally confront those who had killed Him three days earlier? Instead of doing that, He limited Himself to visiting those who already believed. Had He returned to the temple, the whole world would have acknowledged His messiahship. Why didn't He do it? I believe it was because He wasn't interested in the kind of response such an act would have encouraged. The world would have capitulated to His sovereignty against its will. There would have been no faith, no love, just a grudging admission as to the truth of His message.

The day will come when what I have just described will happen, but it will be the Day of Judgment.

Another reason a person will make a decision to become a Christian, while at the same time insisting on keeping his own will intact, is that he thinks he can make it work that way. But he can't. We come to God on His terms or not at all.

Jesus went through a phase of popularity in his three-and-one-half years of ministry. Masses of people followed Him everywhere. They liked what He had to say. They were fascinated by His miracles. They wanted to make Him king. Judging by outward appearances, Jesus was highly successful. But rather than being impressed by the response, He deliberately stung the multitude with a series of very hard statements that offended them and drove them back to their homes (see John 6:25-66).

What was the issue? The people were following Him for the wrong reasons. He told them that unless they were prepared to accept Him as the only source of eternal life, they had nothing in common with Him. Although they liked Jesus, they weren't ready to give Him a central place in their lives. Offended by His demands, they went their way.

The will has always been the greatest hindrance to personal faith. That is because man's basic problem ever since the Fall has been rebellion. Satan told Eve, "You will be like God" (Genesis 3:5). That was an attractive offer! Rebellion is insisting on being one's own god (see Isaiah 53:6).

God is limited in what He can do with a rebellious individual. He created us in such a way that He cannot violate our freedom of choice. This fact is reflected in an appeal God made to His people: "Why will you die, O house of Israel? For I take no pleasure in the death of anyone. . . . Repent and live!" (Ezekiel 18:31-32).

Often we evangelize those around us as if ignorance were the main obstacle to faith. It is an obstacle, but a secondary one. Imagine how easy it would be to evangelize your city if the task merely involved informing the ignorant! But salvation means submission to Christ. There can be no other way.

4. The fourth soil is the good soil. "It is the man who hears the word and understands it." We know he's good soil because he's faithful. Where there's fruit, we know there's life.

How do we know when spiritual life has been created? How do we know when a baby has been born? Life speaks for itself. Becoming a Christian is equivalent to receiving the Holy Spirit (see Romans 8:9). Can it be possible for the Creator of all that exists, the One who possesses all power and wisdom, to slip into a life and remain there unnoticed? The proof of spiritual life is not merely in being able to give the right answers to certain questions. It is in the evidence of the fruit of the Spirit: "Love, joy, peace, patience, kindness, goodness, faithfulness, gentleness and self-control" (Galatians 5:22-23).

Assurance of salvation for the young Christian comes from the same source. "This is how we know that he lives in us: We know it by the Spirit he gave us" (1 John 3:24).

TWENTY

THE DYNAMICS OF CONVERSION

The Christian, the Holy Spirit, and the Scriptures

WE HAVE CONCLUDED that the basic obstacle to faith is rebellion, not ignorance. If this is true, the means God uses to draw man to Himself will bear it out. As we saw earlier, God influences nations and works through circumstances and events to prepare people for His message. Beyond this, God has other influences at His disposal: the Holy Spirit, the Scriptures, and the Christian. These are the three basic means God uses in His work of reconciliation.

We have already discussed how God employs the Christian on three levels—through the witness of his life, through the collective witness of Christians, and through each one's verbal witness. In this chapter, we will examine the other two influences: the Holy Spirit and the Scriptures.

THE HOLY SPIRIT

The need to get something going was almost overwhelming as we began our ministry in Curitiba, Brazil, in 1964. There we were with all the trappings family living implies. On one occasion, at the height of my frustration, I wrote in my journal, "I am a full-fledged missionary now. I have a house, a car, and a camera. The only thing missing is a ministry."

We were foreigners, strangers in town, and didn't know a soul. I found myself casting about for something I could do, some activity that would justify my existence to myself.

I soon discovered it's not hard to find things to do if you are not choosy. Opportunities began opening up, but as I considered them, God

175

convicted me with an unsettling thought from Matthew 15:13. It dogged me everywhere I went and still does. Jesus said, "Every plant that my heavenly Father has not planted will be pulled up by the roots."

How simple it is to get into some activity out of a misplaced sense of duty, or because we were asked and couldn't say no, or because it was something we just felt like doing. I realized that if God was not committed to what I got myself into in Curitiba, eventually my efforts would be pulled up by the roots. Nothing would remain. Considering the options, I elected to turn down the opportunities I was contemplating and live with my tensions. God was going to have to make the first move. My dependence on the Holy Spirit reached a new level of desperation. I reviewed some promises in Isaiah 45:13-14. For six months I began every day by opening my Bible to those verses, praying, and claiming those promises for our ministry in Brazil.

Jesus said, "Apart from me you can do nothing" (John 15:5). If the Holy Spirit is not committed in tangible ways to what we are doing, we should find out what's wrong or give it up. After He had risen, Jesus told His disciples to go to Jerusalem and lock themselves in a room to wait for the Holy Spirit to be sent. That was all they were capable of doing until the Holy Spirit arrived on the scene.

THE HOLY SPIRIT IN CONVERSION

In John 16:7-11, Jesus described the role of the Holy Spirit in the reconciliation process. He said He would send the Holy Spirit to His disciples and that when He came, He would convict the world of guilt in regard to three things: sin, righteousness, and judgment. These are exactly the three things needed to change the consistency of the soil of a person's heart in order for it to receive the good seed, which is the Word of God.

Jesus expanded on these three things with three cause-and-effect statements: "In regard to sin, because men do not believe in me; in regard to righteousness, because I am going to the Father . . . and in regard to judgment, because the prince of this world now stands condemned" (John 16:9-11). The cause-and-effect relationship of these three phrases is not immediately apparent.

What does the Holy Spirit's convicting a person of his sin have to do with not believing in Jesus Christ? It has everything to do with it. *Unbelief is the root of all sin.* It is synonymous with rebellion. In Luke 16 we read about the rich man who, finding himself in hell, became concerned about his brothers. So he asked that Lazarus, the beggar who once lived by his front door and who also had died, should be sent to his brothers on earth to warn them. Abraham's reply to this request was shocking: "They have

Moses and the Prophets [the Old Testament]; let them listen to them. . . . If they do not listen to Moses and the Prophets, they will not be convinced even if someone rises from the dead" (Luke 16:29,31).

Here again we are reminded that the basic problem with man is not ignorance, but rebellion. When people don't believe the gospel message when they come to understand it, it is because they don't want to. So God sends His persuader, the Holy Spirit, to convict man of his sin.

What about the second phrase? Jesus said the Holy Spirit would convict men of guilt "in regard to righteousness," because He was "going to the Father" (John 16:10). What is the relationship here? Simply this: Jesus is the perfect standard of righteousness. His life defined righteousness. While He was physically present in this world, man's unrighteousness was laid bare. This is supported by His statements, "I am the light of the world," and "You are going to have the light just a little while longer. Walk while you have the light, before darkness overtakes you" (John 12:35). When Jesus left this world, He sent the Holy Spirit to take over this function. Today, the Spirit is the one who measures the dimensions of true righteousness in a person's heart, to show him how far he falls short.

What about the third phrase, "in regard to judgment, because the prince of this world now stands condemned" (John 16:11)? What is the cause-and-effect relationship here? We live on a fallen planet that is plagued by sin. This whole creation is coming into judgment. Satan, the prince of this world, has been mortally wounded.

Meanwhile the nonChristian lives and acts as if both his achievements and his possessions will somehow last forever. One of the things the Holy Spirit does for the nonChristian is to make him aware of the precariousness, futility, and brevity of his life.

The Holy Spirit convicts of sin, righteousness, and judgment. What a relief to discover that this responsibility has been assigned to Him, rather than to us!

THE SCRIPTURES IN CONVERSION

The Bible is our authority. It is able to stand on its own against the unbeliever. Our job, as a witness, is not to defend it, but to give it an opportunity to work.

But what do we do with the nonChristian who refuses to accept the authority of the Scriptures? The secularized person's position implies either unbelief or a rejection of the authority of Scripture. Then what?

We should not allow ourselves to get drawn into discussions over the inspiration and authority of the Bible. Not that this is not an important issue, but it's just not the right place to begin. The truths of the gospel have their sequence and we cannot deal with them out of that sequence any more than one could put a roof on a house that hasn't been framed up.

We have a friend, Jorge, who became a Christian. Then his fiancée, Elisa, accepted Christ. Elisa's German father, who was still a loyal supporter of the Third Reich, was aghast. He came to our house to find out who we were and what we were doing with his daughter. He was so angry that as he crossed our living room he didn't see a large wooden coffee table in the middle of the room. He smashed into the table so hard he upset it. In his rage, partly because of what had happened to his daughter and partly because of the pain in his shin, he announced loudly that he was going to begin a study of the Bible from cover to cover to disprove its credibility. He was going to begin in Genesis and work his way through, and record all the errors and contradictions he discovered.

Of course, he never made it. Every question he raised remained inconclusive. He gave up somewhere in the deserts of Leviticus and Numbers. Meanwhile, his daughter Elisa grew into a strong Christian.

Almost all the people we have ministered to over the years have not at first been willing to accept the authority and inspiration of the Scriptures. Nonetheless, only rarely have I had to discuss the subject, whether among nonChristians or with those we have brought to Christ. About the only useful information we have had to supply has been of a historical nature, the origins of the Bible, how the Scriptures came into existence, and when they were written.

Since the Bible *is* authoritative, it assumes its rightful place as the new Christian is exposed to it. Gradually, unconsciously, he acknowledges its supremacy. This happens because the Bible is truth. The Bible brings light and truth to bear on the issues it addresses. When it considers man, life, society, and the world, its words ring true.

But the Scriptures go one step further. They uncover the fallacies and inconsistencies in our personal philosophies. "The word of God is living and active. Sharper than any double-edged sword, it penetrates even to dividing soul and spirit, joints and marrow; it judges the thoughts and attitudes of the heart" (Hebrews 4:12).

What else can the nonChristian do when confronted by the living, mind-revealing, and prophetic capacities of the Scriptures but concede they are indeed authoritative? He will either submit to Christ, or admit he's just not willing for Him to rule in his life.

WHERE TO BEGIN

What is the starting point? Where do we begin if we are to bring about this kind of response? The answer to this question depends entirely on the hearer's starting point. Where is he in his understanding? What does he accept? What does he know?

Whatever the case, as we saw in chapter 3, the entire Christian message can be summarized with two questions. Our aim is to begin studying the Scriptures with a person at whatever point we find him in relation to these two questions. They were the questions Paul asked Jesus when he was struck down by a vision on the road to Damascus: "Who are you, Lord?" and, "What shall I do, Lord?" (Acts 22:8,10).

Put another way, the two questions are, "Who is Jesus?" and "What does He want of me?"

WHO IS JESUS?

The Bible builds its case on one historical figure, Jesus of Nazareth. He said, "If you really knew me, you would know my Father as well. From now on, you do know him and have seen him. . . . Anyone who has seen me has seen the Father" (John 14:7,9).

The basic affirmation of Christianity is that God is knowable because He has taken the initiative to bridge the gap between Himself and man. This is critical because if it were not true, man would be left to make his own way to God with only his five frail senses to go on. He would get nowhere. In short, either Jesus was God, or God is unknowable. In that case, we would all be lost in a sea of relativism.

According to the Scriptures, God has revealed Himself in various ways throughout history, consummating the process in Jesus Christ. "In the past God spoke . . . through the prophets at many times and in various ways, but in these last days he has spoken to us by his Son. . . . The Son is the radiance of God's glory and *the exact representation of his being*" (Hebrews 1:1-3, emphasis added).

"The exact representation of his being." You can't believe God exists? Then who was Jesus? What about the justice of God? Do you have problems with it too? Then look at Jesus. What was His sense of justice like? What about the problem of evil in the world? How did Jesus deal with evil? Is the Bible the inspired Word of God? What did Jesus say about it?

Until we settle this basic question regarding the person of Jesus, we cannot speak conclusively to any other particulars. But when we arrive at the conclusion that Jesus is God, we discover that many of our other questions, that once seemed so insoluble, suddenly become either redundant or easily understood.

The Bible brings people to this conclusion about Jesus. John said his Gospel was written "that you may believe that Jesus is the Christ, the Son of God, and that by believing you may have life in his name" (John 20:31).

Jesus took the unbelieving Jews to task for missing the point as to the basic intent of the Scriptures. He told them they diligently studied the Scriptures "because you think that by them you possess eternal life." But, He added, the intended purpose of the Scriptures is to "testify about me" (John 5:39).

So the first function of the Scriptures in leading a person to conversion is to answer the question, "Who is Jesus?" As we answer this question, the next one grows in importance.

WHAT DOES JESUS WANT OF ME?

Obviously, if the nonChristian draws any conclusion about Jesus other than that He is God, this second question is irrelevant. But if the conclusion is that He is who He claimed to be, every other concern in his life is eclipsed by this question: "What does He want of me?"

If the incarnation is true, if God actually became man, this fact must be of utmost significance to every man on earth. Consequently we must ask, "What do You want of me?"

For the nonChristian, the answer is narrowed down to a single word: believe.

On one occasion, the multitude that followed Jesus asked a question very similar to the one we are discussing here: "What must we do to do the works God requires?" Jesus answered, "The work of God is this: to believe in the one he has sent" (John 6:28-29).

I'll never forget the day I understood the answer to this first question, "Who is Jesus?" The only logical response I could think of was to put the answer to the second question into action immediately. I acquired a notebook and spent weeks combing the gospels for every command I could find. With two-thirds of the notebook filled, I despaired. I realized I could neither live up to it all, nor even keep track of it. I hadn't understood the dynamic nature of my subject matter. The Bible is a living book that speaks to life as we live it. The Bible comes alive through the promptings of the Holy Spirit according to our individual needs.

The fact is, we never outgrow either of these two questions. Continued progress in the Christian life comes as a result of further insight into Jesus Christ. "Who is He?" and "What does He want me to do?" are the first questions for every occasion in life. They are also the primary questions we ask as we daily read the Scriptures.

In this chapter we have discussed how God employs a certain division of labor in the ministry of reconciliation. *Christians*, individually and collectively, bear witness by their life and word. They bring the nonChristian within hearing range of the Scriptures. The *Scriptures* reveal the truth and testify of Christ. The *Holy Spirit* convicts, draws the person to repentance, and gives life.

Following is an example of how these three functions work together.

THE EXAMPLE OF ABRAHAO

Abrahao was an agricultural student at the University of Parana in Brazil. His purpose for being in school was not as much to get an education as it was to stimulate political unrest. He was a Communist. It happened that his roommate in the student boarding house where he lived was a new Christian. His name was Jark. Abrahao ridiculed Jark unmercifully until finally, in frustration, Jark invited Abrahao to one of our open studies. Abrahao had gotten what he wanted, the opportunity to cause one more disruption.

Abrahao sat in a corner of our living room where the study was taking place, apparently disinterested in everything that was being said. Suddenly, as the discussion was finally winding down, and everyone was becoming more interested in having coffee than in what was being said, Abrahao's hand went up. He asked the discussion leader a well-placed question. The leader paused to regroup his thoughts. As he did so, Abrahao's hand went up again. He fired a second question. Now there were two questions to cope with. The leader became confused. The pause lengthened. Abrahao moved in with two or three more questions, one on top of the other. Finally, as the leader sat struggling with his confusion, Abrahao said, "See, you don't know what you're talking about. You can't answer my questions."

In the following weeks, Abrahao never missed a meeting. He did his best to create as much confusion as possible. I entertained the idea of asking him not to attend any more discussions, but I decided to make one last attempt to get through to him.

After our next study, as Abrahao and I were chatting, I asked him, "Abrahao, what kind of odds will you give me?"

He asked what I meant. I went on, "What kind of odds will you give me that I am right and that you are wrong—that God does exist?"

He laughed and replied, "None!"

Then I said, "Do you mean to tell me you have examined all known knowledge and have researched everything unknown, and that you have scoured the universe, and now you stand before me saying, 'Relax, there is no God'?"

He replied, "I wouldn't say that."

I said, "Then you have to admit there is a possibility that I am right and you are wrong."

He conceded. I then pressed him: "What odds do you give me? Twenty percent?"

He said, "No."

I bargained for fifteen, ten, and finally said, "You must at least give me five percent."

He asked me what I was getting at. I replied, "If I'm right and you're wrong, you're dead. And since there is that possibility, the only rational thing for you to do is to check it out to see which of us is right."

He asked, "How do I do that?"

I replied, "Go to the original sources. Anyone doing serious research bypasses the secondary sources (what other people have said about a subject) and examines the original data."

He asked, "What are the original sources?"

I said, "The Bible."

He said, "I don't believe the Bible."

I said, "That gives you an advantage over me. The Bible is the only original source we Christians possess. If you can disprove the Bible, you win."

He asked, "What are you proposing?"

I explained, "The Bible is a thick book with fine print. You don't read it like any other book—from start to finish—because it is really a library of sixty-six volumes. You are going to need help in knowing which book to pull off the shelf first. My offer is to show you where to look and to help you understand what it says."

Abrahao accepted my offer and we set a date for our first meeting.

I introduced him to the Gospel of John. We started by my asking him to read the first three verses: "In the beginning was the Word, and the Word was with God, and the Word was God. He was with God in the beginning. Through him all things were made; without him nothing was made that has been made" (John 1:1-3).

I asked Abrahao if he understood what was being said. He didn't. I asked him, "What does the word *Word* refer to?"

He didn't know, so I referred him to verse 14: "The Word became flesh and made his dwelling among us."

With a little help he realized the passage was talking about Jesus Christ. When he understood that the Bible claimed Jesus was eternal and that he had created all things, he was ready to fight. I defused his arguments by saying, "I'm not asking you to believe or to agree with what is written here. I just want to make sure you understand what it says. Do you?"

He replied, "Yes, but . . ."

I said, "Good, let's go on to the next paragraph."

As we worked our way through the next passages over the following weeks, Abrahao didn't appear to budge an inch. He assigned every claim about Christ to legends or exaggerated accounts. I stuck to the single objective of helping him understand what the Bible was saying about who Jesus was. Thus, in spite of his rebellion, our meetings, though always electric, were debate-free.

Meanwhile, my friends and I prayed that the Holy Spirit would accomplish His work of persuasion.

After a few months, I began to spot signs of change. Abrahao quit disagreeing with the Scriptures. He began to see the relationships between one passage and another. He gradually changed from being a generally negative person to being positive. He volunteered to spend his summer vacation working on a government-sponsored project for the poor. When the summer was over, he returned as an old friend, no longer as an adversary. Without a word we went back to studying the Gospel of John.

Finally, I could contain my curiosity no longer. He was so changed! As we sat down to study John 13, I said, "Okay, Abrahao, what's happened?"

He replied, "Yeah, it's true."

"What's true?"

"Jesus is God."

"So?" I pressed him.

"Well, I guess I'm a Christian now. But," he went on, "I need to tell you one thing. I'm politically active, and I've taken a position which is against our government. I'm also anti-American. My friends criticize me for seeing you."

I said, "Go on."

He said, "That's it. I just thought you should know."

"Do you think it makes any difference with me?"

"No."

Then I said, "I'd like to show you a verse." It happened to be in the chapter we were about to study. We turned to John 13:13: "You call me 'Teacher' and 'Lord,' and rightly so, for that is what I am."

I asked Abrahao, "What does it mean if Jesus is our teacher?"

His reply was perfect. "It means what we think and believe must come from Him. We refer our ideas back to Him."

"Do you accept that?"

"Yes."

"What does it mean for Jesus to be Lord?"

Again his reply was excellent. "It means that He's the boss."

"Do you accept that?"

He said that he did.

We never did discuss politics or economics. Abrahao and I were now under the same teacher and under the same authority—Jesus Christ. Both of us were responding to the same call: "Be worthy citizens of the Kingdom."

What is the lesson from this illustration?

Our job is to help a person *understand*. The burden of proof is not on us, but on the Scriptures. The responsibility to convince lies with the Holy Spirit, not with us. We are responsible to be faithful to that person by maintaining his exposure to the Word of God until a final decision is made, for or against.

I have a Christian friend who is one of those beautiful people who attracts every person he meets. He always seems to say the right thing at the right time. He witnesses with ease wherever he goes, and leaves people hungry for more. When we first became friends years ago, I thought, *Here is one person who is going to make an impact.*

It never materialized. He's beautiful like a butterfly, but you can never count on a butterfly to land on the same flower twice. Bringing a person to Christ from far away requires perseverance and tenacity. It means establishing and maintaining a relationship as he goes through the throes of resistance. At times, it is only that relationship that prevents the nonChristian from rejecting the Holy Spirit and running away.

Obviously, this is costly. It costs hours as well as emotional and spiritual energy. If we are not convinced of the eternal worth of the individual, we'll never do it.

SUMMARY

God's means of communicating with unreconciled men and women are the Holy Spirit, the Scriptures, and the Christian. Each has a specific function. The Christian testifies to what he has seen and heard (see 1 John 1:1-3). He brings the nonChristian into contact with the Scriptures. Then the Holy Spirit does the convincing. It is through the "living and active" Word of God (Hebrews 4:12) that an individual is born again.

It is important to keep this division of labor clear in our minds. For us to attempt to do the work of the Holy Spirit or that of the Scriptures is futile. If a person is convinced by the Spirit of God, and spiritually reborn through the Word of God, we can be confident of the kind of new life that has been created. It will bear fruit. As for us, we have had the privilege of making the introductions.

TWENTY-ONE

GUIDING SOMEONE THROUGH THE SCRIPTURES
Questions Are Our Most Valuable Tool

A GOOD QUESTION is the best possible teaching tool. Because Jesus was the foremost Teacher, no one could ask questions the way He could. Frequently, with a single question He penetrated to the core of even the most controversial issues.

"Which is easier: to say . . . 'Your sins are forgiven,' or to say, 'Get up, take your mat and walk'?" (Mark 2:9)

"Show me a denarius. Whose portrait and inscription are on it?" (Luke 20:24)

"But what about you? . . . Who do you say I am?" (Matthew 16:15)

"John's baptism—was it from heaven, or from men?" (Mark 11:30)

Jesus' questions made an impact. They drew from His listeners conclusions they would never have faced up to otherwise. A study of the gospels for the purpose of observing Jesus' use of questions and their effect on others is in itself a course in communication.

Communication takes place whenever understanding is transferred from one person to another. It is not what we manage to *say* to someone that is important; it is what is *heard*, what sinks in, that matters. The use of questions is especially effective in communication because this harmonizes with the way our natural thought processes work. As we think, we constantly pose questions to ourselves: What do I need to do next? When can I work that in? At what percentage point does the other option become favorable?

The sciences are structured on hypotheses and research. A hypothesis is a statement that serves as a question. Research either confirms, disproves, or modifies the hypothesis. As we repeat this testing process, we make progress in our understanding.

I have entitled this chapter "Guiding Someone Through the Scriptures." "Guiding" is more descriptive of what we should do in the course of evangelizing than either "telling" or "teaching." Our purpose is to guide the nonChristian into the Scriptures in search of truth. We must recognize that his basic assumptions and values are not Christian. Some reconstruction must go on at this primal level of assumptions before he comes to faith, and this reconstruction takes time. It involves discoveries and reformulations on his part. Much of this will be subliminal, but it will take place. We need to be patient guides during this process.

If we limit our understanding of evangelism to telling (declaring the propositions of the gospel) or to teaching (giving instructions regarding the body of truth), we will not have the staying power needed to work with people who must make a full 180-degree turn in their personal presuppositions and values. Such people need room to think in a stimulating, accepting environment. Learning to ask the right kinds of questions is a key to meeting these needs.

Generally we don't give much thought to asking questions. We're usually more concerned about being able to *answer* the questions non-Christians customarily pose. In fact, Christians often fall prey to two misconceptions. They are the two sides of a single coin, which go like this: (1) I'm not qualified to get involved in evangelism because I can't seem to answer people's questions, and (2) I'm ready for anybody because I've learned the answers to the top ten questions nonChristians ask.

These miss the point because they assume that it is our answers to questions that are the most important. We need to know how to deal with questions, but we do *not* need to know all of the answers. In reality, the ability to ask questions is more important in guiding someone through the Scriptures. We'll see why as we move along in this chapter and consider *how to ask and how to answer questions.*

HOW TO ASK QUESTIONS

We are prepared to lead a Bible study only when we have formulated a few questions that will draw the other person into discovering the relevant truths of a passage. The ability to do this presupposes, of course, a fair understanding on our part of what the passage says and means. That will take some work, especially the first time around.

In chapter 15 we talked about the importance of making evangelism a team effort. We will need that team at this point because few of us have the initiative or discipline to persevere week after week in Bible study when left to ourselves. Hence, one of the first activities you might do together could be to study the book of John, or whatever book you choose, chapter by chapter. You would study with two purposes: to understand the text for yourself and to formulate questions to use with others.

Questions can have three functions. They can (1) *launch* a discussion on a subject, (2) *guide* a discussion, and (3) serve to *summarize* what has been said. The following are examples of launch, guide, and summary questions:

Launch: What observations did Nicodemus make about Jesus?

Guide: How did Jesus respond to these observations?

Summarize: What can we conclude from this dialogue about our human abilities to understand spiritual matters?

The questions on the book of John in the appendix are mostly launch questions. You will find that as you actually get into the discussion of a passage, you will be able to improvise most of the guide and summary questions. It is helpful to bear in mind that questions can serve all three of these functions. It is possible, with a proper use of questions, to move the discussion into deeper levels of communication.

There are a number of rather standard *guide* questions that are frequently useful. Some of these are,

- Why do you think he said that?
- What do you think he was getting at?
- What else do you see in this verse?
- Why do you say that?
- What do you mean?
- Why do you think he uses the word _____ here?

There are also some basic *summary* questions that you could use:

- How would you summarize the main idea of this paragraph?
- How would you say this in your own words?
- How would you summarize the idea we've been discussing?

We have described three *functions* that questions can have in a discussion. There is also a variety in *kinds* of questions. There are questions for,

- *Understanding:* What does it say? What else?
- *Interpretation* or *Clarification:* What does this mean?
- *Justification:* How did you arrive at this conclusion?
- *Direction:* Mike, what do you think?
- *Comparison:* Where did we see this same idea before?
- *Application:* How does this affect us?

A WORD OF CAUTION

We began this chapter by saying that questions are the best possible teaching tools. But they can also be used as weapons. In careless hands they can kill or maim communication in a minute. This is because questions are seldom neutral. A question is also a statement. The statement behind the old question "When did you quit beating your wife?" is obvious. But there is also a statement behind an apparently innocuous question such as "How does this chapter apply to you?" With one or two similar questions we can checkmate the person we're studying with at any time. It might go like this:

- What does this chapter say about you? (This chapter talks about you!)
- Would you agree that what it says is true? (You must change!)
- What do you think you should do about it? (You must change now!)

With a few well-placed questions of this sort, what started out as an accepting environment with time and room to think is transformed into a verbal war game. And we have just ended it by pinning our quarry to the wall. It's so easy to do, but it will happen only once!

The wise thing to do is to restrict our application questions to those of a more general nature, such as "Did you learn anything about yourself in this chapter?" Then stop; back off. Give the other person the room he needs to make his 180-degree turnabout. He'll get there.

HOW TO ANSWER QUESTIONS

When a nonChristian begins to study the Bible with you, one of his biggest unspoken questions will be, "To what degree will I be able to express what I really think with him? What will be the reaction if I express my true doubts and questions?" The person will first send out some rather "safe" trial questions. How we react to these questions will affect the level of communication between us from then on. If we respond with dogmatism (which is a form of insecurity) or with defensiveness (which is another form of insecurity), the nonChristian will quickly understand the rules of the game and will proceed accordingly. He will either operate within our limitations—or he will disappear. But if we demonstrate an attitude that encourages the expression of doubts and questions, our effectiveness will be far greater.

QUESTIONS ARE WELCOME

Even more effective than *asking* a good question is *being asked* a good question by the person you are guiding. When the discussion of a passage is conducted on the basis of the questions the other person raises, the relevance of the discussion increases. So we should give the nonChristian the first chance. After reading a paragraph, we first ask him what questions come to his attention. Sometimes he doesn't really understand enough to ask a question, but often he comes up with enough to carry the discussion. If, after he has had his opportunity, an important truth remains unaddressed, we can come in with our own questions.

When we approach our guiding session in this way, we create a climate where all questions—even questions unrelated to the text—are free to flourish. These are the questions the nonChristian has carried for years but has never had the freedom or opportunity to raise before. It is important to give these questions a genuine welcome when they come up. They may scare you to death when you don't have a notion of how to answer them, but you can worry about that later. The important thing is to receive the nonChristian's questions positively.

THREE KINDS OF QUESTIONS

Why do people ask questions? The motive is not always a desire to learn. They may not even want an answer. Sometimes questions are asked with the intent to trap or embarrass. We'll call these *captious questions.* Or a person can ask a question in an effort to escape, to justify his own actions, or just to buy time. We'll call these *self-defense questions.* Then there are straightforward questions that are truly motivated by a desire to know and learn. These are *honest questions.*

Questions need to be answered according to their intent. As this writer artfully put it, "Do not answer a fool according to his folly, or you will be like him yourself. Answer a fool according to his folly, or he will be wise in his own eyes" (Proverbs 26:4-5). In other words, if we miss the intent or fail to perceive the motivation behind a question, we will fall into the other's trap. To try to give an honest answer to a captious question is to play the fool.

There are many illustrations of these three kinds of questions in the dialogues recorded in the Gospels. It is instructive to observe the way Jesus responded to questions. Rather than taking a question at face value, He responded according to the motives of the questioner. In a dialogue in Luke 10:25-37, we have examples of how Jesus handled both a captious question and a question asked in self-defense.

"On one occasion an expert in the law stood up to test Jesus. 'Teacher,' he asked, 'what must I do to inherit eternal life?'" This was a captious question. Rather than seizing it as an opportunity to teach, Jesus countered with a question. "'What is written in the Law?' he replied. 'How do you read it?'

"He [the expert in the law] answered: '"Love the Lord your God . . ."'; and, "Love your neighbor as yourself."'

"'You have answered correctly,' Jesus replied. 'Do this and you will live.'" People who ask captious questions are not looking for information, so Jesus gave this person none. He only reminded him of what he already knew. But that was enough to put the aggressor on the defensive.

"But he wanted to justify himself, so he asked Jesus, 'And who is my neighbor?'"—a self-defense question.

This time Jesus replied with a story, the parable of the good Samaritan, which He typically concluded with another question: "'Which of these three do you think was a neighbor to the man who fell into the hands of robbers?'

"The expert in the law replied, 'The one who had mercy on him.'" Self-defense questions are frequently very much like this one, in which the legalist attempted to split hairs over who constitutes a neighbor. Such questions are raised in an effort to evade personal responsibility or to justify oneself. Jesus' final reply, "Go and do likewise," certainly did nothing to restore the man's equilibrium. He probably felt devastated as he came away from that exchange.

But Jesus had all the time in the world for those who came with honest questions. "When he was alone with his own disciples, he explained everything" (Mark 4:34).

Jesus is an impossible act to follow. But we can take some lessons from Him. We can either weary ourselves in vain preparing and expounding our irrefutable arguments and apologetics in response to insincere questions, or we can separate out the questions that come our way, taking the serious questions seriously and not allowing the others to disturb us. We need to realize that even if we could satisfactorily answer the captious questions, it would make little difference in bringing the questioner closer to Christ! So our responses need to be in accord with the *intent* behind the questions.

UNDERSTANDING THE INTENT OF A QUESTION

If we are successful in creating an affirmative environment for the non-Christian, he should feel the freedom to raise all sorts of questions. He may test you with probing questions before asking *honest* questions. Often the intent of a test question is not malicious as in the case from Luke 10. Rather, the questioner wants to see if it will be safe for him to ask his more serious questions. It serves as a trial balloon. It is not easy, nor is it necessary, to identify the intent of every question. But there are a few simple guidelines that, if followed, can help sort out the questions for us.

WHAT DIFFERENCE WILL IT MAKE?'

When the nonChristian asks a question, you need to ask *yourself*, not him, several questions: "What difference will it make if I answer this question? What will he do if I give him a satisfactory answer? Will he accept it and build on it? Or is this question more of a general statement of rejection than anything else?"

If, after asking yourself these questions, you conclude that the non-Christian's question deserves an immediate answer, and if you feel you are prepared to answer it, go ahead and deal with it.

One characteristic of the honest question is that the questioner is willing to wait for his answer. It won't bother him if you say, "That's a good question but I don't know how to answer it at the moment. Let me study it this week and I'll show you what I find out the next time we get together." The person who is trying to test or trap you, however, will want his answer on the spot. But we've already seen how, when the motives are not right, our best answers won't make any difference anyway.

WRITE THE QUESTIONS DOWN

Questions that arise out of the text you are studying are usually honest questions, which should be treated as they come up. But since nobody has all the answers, inevitably some questions will arise that we won't know how to answer. That won't bother the other person if it doesn't bother us. To say "I don't know, but I'll try to find out" will build credibility rather than undermining it as we might fear. We should write such questions down, then come back with the answers when we have them.

Questions that are unrelated to the text, that come out of the blue, are the ones that require closer scrutiny. For example, what if someone suddenly asks, "If Jesus is the only way, what will God do to the heathen who have never even heard His name?"

There might be one of several motives behind such a question. It could be asked in a captious manner, in which case the question is not really a question at all. It is simply a statement trying to justify the person's unbelief by saying that God is not just.

Or, the question could be asked in self-defense. Perhaps the discussion is getting too close to home for comfort. The person needs time and space. He senses either you or the Holy Spirit closing in on him, and he's not ready for that. So he throws in a difficult question to halt the advance. Sometimes the person really does need that space, and you should allow him to have it. If the intent is similar to that of the legalist's question, "Who is my neighbor?" we should not give an answer.

It's not difficult to avoid being caught in a diversionary tactic of this sort. You can say, "Now that's an important question and we'll get to it. Let me write it down." Have the person repeat it so you can record it. By writing a question down, you communicate that you are taking the other person seriously, listening to him, and respecting his concerns and doubts.

The next time you meet, you need to be sure you have that piece of paper with you. As you begin the session, take it out and place it on the table before you. This will communicate a great deal. It will say, "I've not forgotten your question. We'll get to it, and if you have any similar questions, they are welcome too!"

QUESTIONS HAVE A SEQUENCE

Frequently it is impossible to answer a particular question for the simple reason that it has been asked out of sequence. For example, how can we discuss the justice of a God whose existence is in doubt? So we need to communicate the idea that questions have their sequence to the person with whom we are studying. This helps him understand why we are postponing answering some of his questions, and it makes him feel free to add new questions to his list.

By recording extraneous questions as they come along rather than attempting to answer them immediately, we are able to retain control of the direction of the dialogue. We can decide when and how to deal with these questions. Thus, we can neutralize the wrong motives present when a question is first raised. The desire to trap or test us fades as we consistently demonstrate love and acceptance. As the relationship grows, the nature of the questions will change.

There are important exceptions, of course, to this idea of responding to questions according to their sequence. Frequently, it becomes apparent that a particular question is, in fact, blocking the road to progress toward

Christ. Even though we may not have had the time yet to lay the foundations for an answer, we may realize that the questioner really needs some kind of an answer before he can go on.

On such occasions, our response could go something like this: "I can see this is an important question to you, so I'll try to show you what the Bible says in answer to it. I wouldn't be surprised if the answer doesn't satisfy you [he has not yet conceded to the authority of the Scriptures], but just for your information, this is what the Bible says about this question."

Whether the person accepts or rejects the answer we give in this situation is secondary. The important thing is to answer the question from the Bible.

STICK TO THE BIBLE

When studying with people who don't believe the Bible, it is especially important to consistently use nothing but the Bible.

Our position is: "You're not ready to accept the authority of the Bible? That's understandable. One of the reasons we're sitting here together is to give you the opportunity to judge for yourself whether the Bible speaks the truth or not. So I'll try to keep my own opinions out of the discussion. We'll consider my personal opinions to be no better than anyone else's. When you ask a question, I'll try to restrict myself to showing you what the Bible says in response."

Any other position eventually serves to undermine the authority of the Bible. Once we mix opinions, whether our own or those from secondary sources or traditions, with truths from the Bible, we create a second authority: man himself! Whenever this occurs, man eventually ends up having the last word.

This attitude of letting the Bible speak for itself must be based on our own deep confidence in the Bible. Since it is the truth, it is authority. As such, it is fully capable of taking care of itself. As it addresses the issues of life and as it speaks of man and his society, it always rings true. As this occurs again and again, the nonChristian, usually subconsciously, simply begins to concede to the Bible's authority.

THE WATERSHED QUESTION

There is one key question that, when answered, unlocks the answers to most of the other questions. Many of the previously impossible questions become easy, if not redundant. This watershed question is, of course, the one we raised in chapter 3, that of Jesus' identity.

Jesus' identity is the premise upon which our other answers are constructed. For example, until a person acknowledges the deity of Christ, he is faced with an unresolvable dilemma when it comes to his relationship with God. This dilemma is described in Luke 7:29-30: "The people . . . acknowledged that God's way was right, because they had been baptized by John. But the Pharisees and experts in the law rejected God's purpose for themselves, because they had not been baptized by John."

One group said God was just; the other said He wasn't. Those who said He was just had been baptized by John; those who said He wasn't just hadn't been baptized by John. But what did John's baptism have to do with a person's position on God's justice? It was a baptism of repentance. To repent means to conclude that you are in the wrong. We have to come to that conclusion before we can admit that God is right.

In other words, if God is just, I am not just. But if I am right, then God is wrong. Since I'm not ready to admit I am wrong, God has to be the one who is wrong. Therefore I must find some injustice in Him. This is where the questions about the destiny of the heathen or the severely retarded child frequently have their origin. It is the reason why man, after he himself has transformed this world into a hell, blames God for the mess. Either we must find something wrong with God, or we must assume the blame ourselves. But if we assume the blame, we also sentence ourselves to judgment with our own words.

When we settle the question of Christ Jesus' identity, we can bring ourselves to the point where we face up to our own injustice. It would be quite valid to translate Romans 1:17, "In the gospel the *justice* of God is revealed."

You question God's justice? Examine Jesus' life. Was He ever unjust? No. But also, in Him, there is deliverance from our own unjustness. We can face up to it.

Once this is understood, the remaining questions almost answer themselves.

- You have a question about God's existence? That question is redundant now that we've identified Jesus as God.
- What is God like? Look at Jesus.
- What are the origins of the world? What is man? What is life all about? The answers to these and similar questions are found in what Jesus had to say about these things.

SUMMARY SUGGESTIONS

As you grapple with the matter of guiding someone through the Scriptures, here's some practical advice.

Things to Do.
- Remember that "telling is not teaching."
- Remember that your job is to guide into the discovery of truth.
- Rely on the Scriptures by letting the Bible assert its own authority and letting the Bible reveal the truth.
- Use questions as your primary teaching tool.
- Learn to handle philosophical questions.
- Learn to capitalize on serious questions.
- Allow the person you are guiding to think and discover the answers.
- Keep conflict between the individual and the truth, not between the individual and you.
- Be aware of and sensitive to feelings and apprehensions.
- Make the individual comfortable.
- Control the characteristics of the study.
- Control the make-up of the group.
- Keep a list of difficult questions, and answer them in their logical sequence.
- Avoid arguing in defense of the Bible.
- Avoid debating on any subject.
- Avoid giving the answers, especially dogmatic answers.
- Avoid feeling threatened by the strength of the opposition or by your own lack of knowledge.
- Avoid defending philosophical positions.
- Avoid insisting on agreement.
- Avoid judging behavior.

Results to Expect.
- The Bible will assume its authority.
- The Bible will overpower with truth.
- The Holy Spirit will do His part, both revealing and convicting.
- The identity of Christ will become evident.

TWENTY-TWO

A TIME TO SOW, A TIME TO REAP

Patiently Aware of the Process

"AS FOR YOU, you were dead" (Ephesians 2:1).

Our ministry is to the dead. That's what evangelism is: working among the dead. But death is repulsive. It is ugly. We want to get away from it so we don't have to look at it.

So it is with the spiritually dead. Their behavior is often ugly and embarrassing to us. We feel offended by the things they do and say. We're anxious to get them converted so that they can clean up their act. But the world is not a nice place to live in, and often the people of the world are neither respectable nor nice to be around. Nevertheless, it is precisely to these people that we are sent.

Jesus said, "It is not the healthy who need a doctor, but the sick. I have not come to call the righteous, but sinners to repentance" (Luke 5:31-32). Later He communicated the same idea in His parable of the wedding banquet. According to this parable, when the upper social set began to make excuses, the king sent out his servants to stand on the street corners to gather in the poor, the crippled, the blind, and the lame. Thus the wedding hall was filled with many social rejects (Luke 14:15-24).

It is so easy to judge others, to measure others by our own criteria for acceptable behavior. But what realistic expectations should we have for people who are spiritually dead, who come to us maimed and blinded? What expectations should we have for the person who was abandoned when he was eleven years old? What about the man who has to overcome his resentment against his religious father who left him to clean up the financial and moral mess when he skipped town with his mistress?

197

Repeatedly in the Old Testament, God says He punishes the children for the sins of the fathers to the third and fourth generations. Anyone who has spent much time around people of the world understands the terrible truth of this sad legacy. There is a law of cause and effect: like father, like son (Exodus 20:5). Aberrant behavior is the norm for those we are sent to win. This decadence has been passed on from parent to child. Thus, we should be neither shocked nor offended by what we encounter.

We are so given to judging others. It is so easy to carry judgment and criticism in our hearts against the nonChristian. We feel so virtuous when we condemn the husband who abandons his wife and emotionally cripples their children in the process. Instead, we should weep. The dead are dead. They are under the spell of "the ruler of the kingdom of the air" (Ephesians 2:2). That is the reality of the situation. We must be cognizant of the distance and the difference between the living and the dead if we are to have the tolerance and patience necessary to accompany someone in his pilgrimage out of the dominion of darkness into the light and life of the Kingdom of God's Son.

For the great majority of people, the road to Christ is long. Although He is near, man is so very far. Belief systems have to be turned around. Many people have to do a total about-face. James Engel summarized the belief system and the presuppositions that commonly prevail among what he calls modern man:

> God, if He exists at all, is just an impersonal moral force.
> Man basically has the capacity within himself to improve morally and make the right choices.
> Happiness consists of unlimited material acquisition.
> There really is no objective basis for right and wrong.
> The supernatural is just a figment of someone's imagination.
> If a person lives a "good life," then eternal destiny is assured.
> The Bible is nothing other than a book written by man.[1]

The contrast between a system of belief such as this one and the Christian position defines the distance that needs to be reckoned with as we take the gospel to this generation. This vast distance is not going to be closed by confrontation, debate, and rebuttal. We do not win people by proving to them that they are wrong. Rather it is the beauty and superiority of Christ that makes them realize there is a better way. But such a realization takes time. My own experience is that frequently the nonChristian will spend a year or more becoming acquainted with Christ through the Scriptures before spiritual birth occurs. But such births after an adequate spiritual gestation period are always healthy. The babe lives.

A TIME TO SOW
Sustaining Interest While Planting and Cultivating

How do we sustain interest? How do we keep a person coming back for more, week after week, when he's not even a Christian?

We have already given several answers to this question. It is the love and acceptance. It is the absence of manmade norms and expectations. It is our refraining from using the person for our own personal success. It is the opportunity we offer him to take an honest look at the primary source. It is the steady prompting of the Holy Spirit through the Word of God. These are the basic factors that keep people interested. But there are other lesser, perhaps more technical, things to keep in mind as well.

1. *Watch the tempo of your Bible discussions.* Frequently, someone will tell me, "Man, we went until midnight in our discussion last night. They didn't want to quit."

It may be true that they didn't want to quit. But the next day they will undoubtedly be sorry that they didn't, as they wearily drag themselves through the day. Next week they'll think twice about whether they have the physical and emotional energy to go through another similar session. Don't let a discussion drag on. Quit while you're ahead, before people want you to.

Observe this principle as you work through a chapter. Keep moving. Don't try to wring the last drop out of every question. Be the first, not the last, in the group to decide it is time to go on to the next paragraph.

In short, don't bore people.

2. *Keep your content relevant.* When the people you are guiding through the Scriptures comment on how profound you are, it is probably not a compliment. They are really saying they are having a hard time making sense of what you're talking about. Truth, in its essence, is simple.

Discussions become tedious when we belabor the theoretical or the doctrinal side of things. They become alive when we succeed in correlating what the Bible says with everyday experience.

Content must speak to the hearer. It is not necessarily what catches your attention in a chapter that is important, but what is relevant to the hearer. There can be a large difference between your needs and interests and his.

3. *Take no-shows in stride.* Don't take offense when the nonChristian cancels out at the last minute or simply doesn't show up. It is an inevitable part of the dynamic of the process. The nonChristian is ambivalent about the time he's spending studying the Bible. He wants to continue, and yet he doesn't! As he begins to understand the implications of the Christian message, this ambivalence frequently evolves into a real inner struggle. This is progress.

One of my friends, as he gives his testimony describing his pilgrimage of several years toward Christ, tells of how he stood me up. He would be on his way over to where we met, looking for the slightest pretext for changing his plans. Often he would simply decide to stop and have a beer with a friend rather than going on.

When this would happen, I'd let a couple of days go by. Then I would drop in on him at the bank where he worked. We'd go have coffee together and spend a few minutes chatting. I would never ask him why he hadn't shown up. (I already had the answer to that.) And he would never offer any explanations. As we'd say goodbye, I'd ask, "How's Thursday night, after the evening news?" So it went.

We should respond to no-shows with acceptance. We get back on track by touching base—in person, if possible. Touching base is important no matter how well things seem to be going. A quick visit or even a phone call confirms the friendship and prepares the way for the time when the struggles begin.

4. *Preserve the affinity in group situations.* Recently, a lot of debate has been generated over what is being referred to as "homogeneity." Donald McGavran was the first to expound what he calls the *homogeneous unit principle.* Essentially what he is saying is that people don't like to gather with others who are different in any major way. Therefore, a church will not grow if it is heterogeneous. Those who disagree claim that McGavran's principle is based on pragmatism rather than on the Bible. The Bible, they point out, teaches that all are one in Christ, that there are no real walls of human differences between people. McGavran's defense claims that the other side suffers from idealism.[2]

To talk about the fellowship of Christians is one thing. But to have any expectations along this line for the lost is quite another. We began this chapter by saying that to evangelize is to work among the dead. Christian love can only come from people whom the Holy Spirit has restored to life and made whole. According to the Bible, it is more realistic for us to expect attitudes of resentment and conflict from the nonChristian.

Enigmatically, although it is often this unique oneness among Christians that captivates the nonChristian, he himself is incapable of behaving in the same way. He may be inspired by our comments about God being no respecter of persons and about the Body of Christ being one. He might agree that these ideas are true and right. But they will do nothing to alter his dislike for the new couple we are trying to integrate into the group.

Frequently, simply because of a lack of affinity, the nonChristian will drop out. He'll just disappear without causing a ripple. It's a very relevant fact that we will not successfully sustain interest among people arbitrarily grouped together without due consideration for natural affinity.

5. *Maintain a good group balance.* It should be obvious that an evangelistic Bible study should favor the nonChristian rather than the Christian. But I've frequently seen three or four Christian couples attempt to gang up on a nonChristian couple or two. This is almost always extremely intimidating for the nonChristians. They become self-conscious about their ignorance of the Bible and fearful of asking their real questions. They are afraid that their questions will appear stupid, or that they will be rejected if they reveal their deeper disagreements with the Christian position. Not wanting to be disagreeable, they often simply choose not to verbally disagree. Real communication becomes almost impossible in such a context.

A good study should be informal, casual, and nonthreatening. The atmosphere should be one of acceptance—low-key and relaxed. Under these conditions, a lot of strange ideas will be expressed. But that's good. It's essential that freedom of expression exist, that there be room for incomplete and erroneous conclusions. We don't have to set everything straight at once. But where the group is made up predominately of Christians, someone will inevitably be unable to resist. Someone will turn to a chapter and verse to "set the record straight." The nonChristian's interest will not be sustained for very long when the thinking process is consistently stifled in this way. This potential stumbling block leads us to a final suggestion for sustaining interest.

6. *Hymns and prayers are out.* So are sermonettes. It is sometimes difficult for people who have been raised in a church environment to perceive how they come across to the nonChristian. Often they do things automatically without even stopping to question their propriety—things that strike the non-religious person as very strange.

For example, when I open my Bible in private, I have formed the habit of stopping to pray first, asking God to help me understand it. When I'm finished, I usually find myself praying again, this time asking God to help me make what I just learned a part of my life. But I neither open nor close a study with a nonChristian with prayer. I refrain from this for two reasons. First, the nonChristian is unable to participate in talking to someone whose existence to him is still in doubt. But more importantly, opening or closing a discussion with prayer is viewed as a religious form by the nonChristian, and that is usually enough to formalize the discussion! It changes the environment.

You should pray before and after your discussions, but do it on your own, in your heart—to God, not as a subtle sermon to the nonChristian. If you feel like singing, do that the same way. To the non-religious, a hymn and a prayer and a sermon equal a church service. So we should be sure to discuss rather than lecture, lead rather than teach, and we should do our singing and praying in our hearts to God.

In chapter 20 I discussed the fact that three elements of personality are involved in making a decision to become a Christian, or in making any significant decision, for that matter. They are the *emotions*, the *intellect*, and the *will*. The emotions contribute the desire, the intellect provides the reason, and the will commits the person to action. A decision that is made solely on the basis of emotions or merely as a result of intellectual assent—any decision that does not include the commitment of the will—is a non-decision. Such decisions fail the tests of time and pressure. Our stereotype New Year's resolutions illustrate this point.

In making a decision to become a Christian, the involvement of the will is fundamental. This is because it was our will that got us into trouble with God in the first place. Adam's sin was an act of headship. Conversion is laying down our arms and coming out with our hands up. It is submitting again to God's sovereign rule over one's person. As we saw in chapter 3, this is the meaning Jesus gave to the word "believe." To present conversion as anything less is to misrepresent the gospel.

Whatever overt response a person makes to express a decision to become a Christian (whether it is a prayer, a testimony, or a request to be baptized), it must be a reflection of an inner transaction with the Holy Spirit. More often than not, as we evangelize people in the way we are describing it, this transition occurs when we're not around. We'll know when it has happened by the changes in the person's attitudes and life. Sometimes the first signal is a sudden change in pronouns. Rather than "you Christians," the person speaks of "we Christians." Or the first indication may be a voluntary testimony.

Although we cannot bring about the inner transformation from death to life, we can do a lot to assist in the process.

As we move along through the Scriptures with a nonChristian, his attitude usually begins to change. In the beginning, his questions and responses may reflect unbelief, doubt, or even belligerence. But there will come a time when the rejection is gone. The intent of his questions will change. This means he is proceeding on from the initial question, "Who is Jesus?" to the next question, "What does He want of me?"

When this shift in attitude occurs, it is time to sharpen the focus on the essential message. We need to give the person a summary of the gospel and a clear definition of what he needs to do by way of response. He needs to be made aware of the fact that there is a decision to be made.

Frequently, after a few weeks, as we sit down to study, I will suggest that rather than going on to the next chapter we should do something different this time. I tell the person that I'd like to show him an illustration summarizing the central message of the Bible. I then proceed to show him the *Bridge Illustration.* This illustration shows how Christ is the bridge over the chasm separating death from life. If we're studying the book of John, I use verses from that book as our basis. I cross-reference the main points with passages in other parts of the Bible in order to clarify what we're saying and to demonstrate the harmony of the Bible. (This illustration is included in the appendix, page 248.)

My purpose in using this illustration at this point is not to call on a person to make a decision. Rather, it is to plant the idea of deciding in his mind. So, when we are finished, instead of asking him, "Where would you place yourself on the diagram?" (he has already mentally done that), or, "Do you see any reason why you shouldn't make the decision now?" (he probably *is* intellectually persuaded), I say, "This illustration summarizes the central message of the Bible. Fold this page up and keep it in your Bible and we'll refer back to it as we go along." From that time on, we use this diagram to summarize our discussions. At the end of each discussion, we take it out and talk about how the content of the chapter we just covered fits into the overall picture.

Summarizing the gospel in this way has several significant effects:

• It facilitates an understanding of the Bible because it provides a basic framework to which the parts can be related.
• It seeds the inner thought that a decision needs to be made.
• It clarifies what a person must do by way of response.

As one person with whom I've studied put it, "Every day when I get up in the morning, I ask myself the question, 'Is today the day I'm going to cross that bridge?'" It is helpful for the person who is on his way to Christ to understand what we have said in this section about the place of the emotions, the intellect, and the will in the decision-making process.

Several years ago, a friend wrote to me from another country where he was just getting started as a missionary. In his letter he told me that he had been studying the Bible with five nonChristians for several months, but that he was about to give up on them. They had come to the point, he said, where they all understood and accepted the truth of the gospel. But none of them had submitted to Christ. Since they openly admitted they were just not willing to make that decision, he was ready to give up on them and move on. He wanted to know what I thought.

In my reply I congratulated my friend on getting those people to the place where they understood the real issue so clearly. I said that in the final analysis the will is always the issue, and that when a nonChristian can admit this fact we should celebrate rather than become discouraged. That's progress. My friend stuck with that group, and eventually they became the foundational people for his ministry in that country.

It often helps a person when we say, "Just to clarify where we are, my impression is that you have just about satisfied your questions on the intellectual level. The real issue now is whether or not you're going to let God have your life. Would you say this is the case?"

Intellectual questions usually don't survive for long. Even with someone coming out of agnosticism or atheism, the intellectual questions are frequently satisfied in a matter of a few weeks. But the will is a different story. It can hold out indefinitely.

WHEN DO WE GIVE UP?

God will not override a person's will. Man can persist in saying *no* right down to the end. I suspect a person can give God a final *no*, and that God will accept that decision and leave him alone from then on. We need to be sensitive to God's leading on this point.

The whole process we have been describing must be borne along with prayer. We pray our way through every discussion. We look to God in prayer to do whatever is necessary in a person's life to bring him to Christ. God's responses to these prayers are observable. We take our cues from God on how long to persevere with someone, staying in there as long as God does, but no longer. Our cue to desist is when an individual quits fighting and makes peace with his decision to not allow God into his life.

MAKING THE ASSIST

The problem with a premature decision is that it puts words into people's mouths. They think they've done something they in fact have not. It's hard work to act like a Christian when you're really not one. No one can keep it up indefinitely, and eventually a person has to quit.

But procrastinating over a decision is equally dangerous. People who know better often die in their sins. Sometimes people just need a gentle shove. It might go like this:

A: We've been examining the Bible for six months now. How's it going? Where would you say you are in your progress toward Christ?

B: I'm understanding a lot more now.

A: What, in your opinion, needs to happen yet for you to become a Christian?

B: I'm not sure. I guess I just need to decide to let Christ come into my life.

A: Are you willing to do that?
B: Yes, I think I am.
A: Would you know how to go about it?
B: I think so.
A: How would you feel if we settled the issue together right now? Or would you rather do it on your own?

AVOID THE TIME PANIC

Mother O'Leary's cow has had a great influence on evangelism in America. The cow kicked over a lantern, starting the great Chicago fire in which many people perished. D.L. Moody was conducting evangelistic meetings in the city when the fire took place. Moved by the tragedy, he announced that he would never again preach without giving an invitation. Many ministers picked up on Moody's commitment, and on the level of personal evangelism many of us now labor under an exaggerated sense of urgency. Often we fear that if the person doesn't make a decision on the spot, he never will. We fear that when he goes his way, still undecided, he will probably be struck by a car—and then his blood will be on our hands.

But anxieties of this sort come from a false sense of responsibility. I am not the Lord of the harvest; *God* is. It is the Holy Spirit who draws people to Christ. We can be confident that He will preserve and complete His work in those who are on the way, responding to Christ.

The gospel is urgent news, but that doesn't mean we should be in the kind of time panic that can be so destructive in its results! I have a friend who was led into a response at the age of eight under the kind of pressure we are talking about. For the next fifteen years he went through an incredible inner struggle. Finally, at age twenty-three, he was able to recognize that the necessary inner transaction had never occurred. So we need patience. We need to believe that God will bring about conversion in its proper time.

SUMMARY SUGGESTIONS

Throughout the course of sowing and reaping in the harvest field, we should keep certain basic practical guidelines in mind:

Things to Do.
• Accept the nonChristian as he is. Be a genuine friend.
• Maintain friendly contact between sessions, but don't overdo it. One friendly contact between sessions is usually sufficient.
• Keep it simple. Focus on the two basic questions.

• Keep the group homogeneous if it is a group study.
• Be sensitive about when to introduce the idea of the need for an eventual decision.
• Allow time for the "decision" idea to ferment.
• Make the actual "assist" after the Holy Spirit has done His work.

Things to Avoid.
• Avoid attempting to reform the nonChristian.
• Avoid letting sessions drag on. It is better to quit too soon, leaving the people hungry.
• Avoid letting cancellations bother you. Respond with acceptance.
• Avoid worrying that progress is slow. Just keep the person in the Scriptures.
• Avoid being impatient for a decision. Remember that it takes time to overcome a rebellious will. Let the Holy Spirit do His work.

Results to Expect.
• God will accomplish His purpose.
• The conversion will be genuine.
• Follow-up will be automatic as you continue.

NOTES:
1. James F. Engel, *Contemporary Christian Communications* (Nashville: Thomas Nelson Publishers, 1979), page 75.
2. Engel, page 98.

TWENTY-THREE

ENLARGING YOUR CIRCLES OF OPPORTUNITY

Capitalizing on New Relationships

INHERENT IN MAN is a craving for involvement in things of significance. There is nothing more significant or more adventurous than participating in the purposes of God—sharing in finishing His work. His work has to do with people.

This book is written on the assumption that healthy Christians desire meaningful involvement with people in evangelism. It also assumes that such involvement is within our reach. Jesus expressed feelings of personal fulfillment after talking to the Samaritan woman. "I have food to eat that you know nothing about. . . . My food," said Jesus, "is to do the will of him who sent me and to finish his work" (John 4:32,34). Jesus had been fed well by His conversation.

As Christians, we have a natural concern for evangelism. But most of us have some personal adjustments to make if we are to become meaningfully involved with nonChristians. I have described these adjustments relating to the work of evangelism in the preceding pages of this book. Here they are in review:

- We should overcome our inertia by committing ourselves to action and changing our living patterns.
- We should gain an understanding of the people of our time and learn to relate to them accordingly.
- We should acquire new skills in communication.
- We should get our nonChristian friends involved in ongoing exposure to the Scriptures.

207

DON'T SPEND YOUR LIFETIME STARTING OVER

Once we are moving in these areas, we don't want to lose our hard-won momentum. Evangelism should become a continuous, integral part of our lifestyle. Often our first crisis in this area comes as a result of our success. Our nonChristian friends have come to know Christ. What is the next step? Do we begin all over again making new acquaintances and building new relationships so that once again we can sit down with a nonChristian over an open Bible?

A lifetime of repeating this lengthy and laborious process would be difficult to live with. In fact, if this kind of repetition is necessary, then we are certainly doing something wrong, failing to capitalize on the natural opportunities inherent in each situation. Usually, when initial relationships have been established and people begin to respond to Christ, one relationship leads to another. The succeeding concentric circles of opportunity can continue almost indefinitely.

We need to use wisdom, however, if our opportunities are to expand in this way. It is our challenge to help the new Christian integrate into the Body of Christ in such a way that he preserves his communication with his peers and family in the process.

The new Christian meets the church. The new Christian's first exposure to the local church can be a very delicate encounter! On one occasion, I was invited to address this subject at a conference for missionaries of a particular denomination. They explained their situation as follows: "We are relatively successful in evangelism. Our difficulty lies in getting converts into our churches. We lose most of them at that point." This is one of the most common difficulties the Church encounters around the world.

The degree of success in bringing new Christians out of the world and into our existing churches depends on a number of factors: the spiritual vigor of the local fellowship; the relevance of the forms of the local church to those who are coming in; the nature of the evangelism employed; the background of the people coming to Christ; and the distance between the church's "culture" and the culture of the new Christians.

I marvel at the apparent ease with which first-century churches incorporated their new converts. The churches were very indigenous or "grassroots." These early churches were natural to the culture in which they flourished. They met primarily in homes. Once the initial beachhead was established through the apostolic effort, the churches grew because of the influence of the believers on those around them. Structures, or forms, were relevant because they were created in response to immediate needs. It is interesting that the New Testament doesn't even address the question of how to get converts into a church. To be converted was to be in!

Perhaps we need to make a 180-degree turn in our thinking on this matter, particularly in situations where the distances are really great between two cultures, or even between two subcultures. Should we continue to think in terms of taking the new Christian to church, or should we think of bringing the church to him? The church is not a physical structure; it is people. It consists of Christians relating in such a way that they help one another live the Christian life. A church building is not required to meet the spiritual needs of a body of new Christians.

If we think "people" when we think "church," then we can have the necessary flexibility to incorporate those we win, without dislocating them at all. As more of their kind come to Christ, and as they are supported and ministered to by people sent out by the church, their needs begin to be met. Whether this arrangement is provisory or becomes permanent, it offers two immediate advantages. First, the new Christian has plenty of time to mature spiritually in surroundings that he has already accepted. With this maturity, he will gain a tolerance for further adaptation. Second, in leaving him where he is, we are not cutting him off from his natural network of relationships.

So I'm suggesting that we not be in a hurry to tie new Christians into our congregational structures, especially those converts coming out of a highly secularized context. I am also saying there will be situations where the distances will be so great that we should simply accept the fact that new wineskins will be needed.

Expectations on Christian conduct. By insisting on conformity in gray areas of conduct, we might quickly terminate the new Christian's communication within his old network of relationships. Thus, we must differentiate between behavior that is nonnegotiable (what is right and what is wrong) and behavior that has no hard-and-fast ethical guidelines.

The Bible instructs us on several categories of behavior. Certain things are always right. Whatever the situation, if you do these things your behavior will be correct. Galatians 5:22-23 gives us a sample list: love, joy, peace, patience, kindness, goodness, faithfulness, gentleness, and self-control. There are no laws against any of these characteristics. So the first category of behavior consists of those qualities the Bible specifically identifies as right behavior.

Then this same passage specifies certain behavior as always wrong. No matter what the situation, it's wrong. Sexual immorality, impurity, hatred, discord, jealousy, fits of rage, selfish ambition, envy, drunkenness, and so on, are out (Galatians 5:19-21). They have no place in the life of any Christian at any time.

Although certain matters of conduct are clear-cut, there is an in-between category of "disputable matters" (Romans 14:1). These are areas the Bible does not specifically address—matters such as what day to worship or what foods to eat. What constitutes proper behavior in this case is determined by several variable factors. Sometimes it might be wrong to do a particular thing. But at other times that same action might be right. The Bible leaves it up to the individual believer to decide *what* is proper for him, and also *when* and *where*.

This rather open arrangement is considered too ambiguous and risky for many church bodies to contemplate. Conformity of behavior is easier to live with. Nonconformity, we reason, tends to engender judgments and conflicts. Thus, we find it safer to define a position on the more bothersome, doubtful issues, and then we ask everyone to fall in line. The Bible instructs us *not* to handle doubtful issues this way, but we do it anyway (Romans 14:1-4,22; Colossians 2:16,20-23).

According to Romans 14, one of the signs of a healthy fellowship is a loving attitude toward diversity of convictions on those matters of personal behavior that are relative and not absolute. The mature know the Kingdom of God does not consist of eating and drinking. Consequently, they accept the various behavioral choices on doubtful issues without judging. They know that, in the end, all accounts will be settled individually before God Himself. So, they make room for the scrupulous and accept the uninhibited as well. Their own behavior is ruled by the laws of love and moderation (Romans 13:10, 1 Corinthians 9:24-27).

In a group where these principles prevail, there will be room for new Christians to be accepted as they grow into their own convictions. This makes for greater maturity in the long run (Hebrews 5:14).

How we handle this matter of doubtful things will heavily influence the nature and extent of our outreach. Frequently, new Christians are cut off from their nonChristian peers when they conform to the extra-biblical standards that their newly adopted Christian community imposes on them. Because of such rules, new Christians suddenly discover that their old friends are off-limits. When this happens, we are back to where we started, looking for new threads that will lead us into new relationships, etc.

CO-LABORING WITH OUR SPIRITUAL CHILDREN

We are able to have an ongoing, fruitful ministry among people in the mainstream only to the degree that we are able to extend our witness into the network of relationships of the people we have already reached. We must not inadvertently and unnecessarily cut off communication within this network.

While it is vitally important to help the new Christian coming from the world to integrate into a body, this must not be done in a way that severs his relationships. It is obvious that coming to Christ means a break with the past, a new beginning. But this is a repudiation of the *works* of the past, not the *people* of the past.

As our opportunities expand, with one relationship leading to another, we need to co-labor with those we are ministering to. We need their help, and they need ours.

NonChristians can be great evangelists. This is an overstatement, but it makes the point. Frequently, people who are discovering the Bible for the first time and are on their way toward Christ show a fresh, uninhibited enthusiasm over their new discoveries.

One new Christian with whom I'm currently involved brought at least a dozen people around before he himself believed. He often brought his friends with him to our studies. Then, with his typical lack of inhibition, he would inject articulate questions and doubts about God and about this world He has created. This was distressing only to the person trying to lead the discussion. His guests, rather than being driven to doubt by his performances, were made to feel at home. Unintentionally, he was expressing their questions as well.

People don't need to know much before they can begin to influence others. Philip brought Nathanael to Jesus with three words: "Come and see" (John 1:46). The Samaritan woman did the same with her neighbors: "Come, see a man who told me everything I ever did. Could this be the Christ?" (John 4:29).

We shouldn't overlook the potential for outreach the nonChristian can offer. We should encourage him in this by affirming his efforts and by being careful to respect the needs and feelings of his friends when he brings them around.

New Christians can be very bad evangelists. For some reason, once a person crosses the line of belief, he frequently goes through a period when he loses this ability to draw others in. Things get awkward. The new Christian can be very overbearing and dogmatic among his friends, and especially with his family. He tends to say too much, press too hard, and he can't understand why everyone in the world can't see something that has become so obvious to him. He tends to forget that it took him many years to see it himself.

Much permanent damage can be done in the first few weeks of a person's Christian life. He can burn off his communication with his peers. Then, smarting from the ensuing rejection, he can conclude that evangelism is something to be carefully avoided in the future.

Thus, new Christians need coaching. They need to be made aware of the things mentioned here. They need to be encouraged to share their faith, but they also need help in what and how much to say. They, too, need to learn that evangelism is more than the verbal witness. If they have been brought to Christ through the process of *affirmation* that we have been describing, it will be easier for them to understand that the same kind of process is necessary among their peers.

Extend your friendship. When a person coming to Christ realizes that you will extend your love and acceptance to his friends without seizing the first opportunity to assault them with the gospel, then he will want to bring them around. But until he is sure it is safe, he won't.

We should be prepared to keep social occasions strictly social and not to think in terms of using them as bait for a session in the Bible. I had to blunder on this one a number of times before one nonChristian finally confronted me, charging me with being deceitful. We get much further with people when we are honest and up-front with our intentions. A social occasion should be a social occasion. When we intend to open the Bible with people, our invitation should communicate this intention.

We should not feel the evening was wasted when the dinner conversation didn't lead into a verbal witness of some kind. If we are light, the non-verbal witness will be communicated. Mini-decisions *will* be made, and once there is some foundation of confidence, the relationship will support the weight of the verbal witness. This building of confidence will take far less time among our friends' friends, because we will in a sense be hitchhiking on longstanding relationships.

A word of caution is needed at this point. We are talking about extending the outreach of the gospel throughout the spheres of influence of those we reach. We need to be careful of the form this takes. The temptation is to usurp the opportunities as our own, to make the process a simple extension of our own evangelism. In fact, the new Christian will often initiate this himself, bringing his friends for us to evangelize. But to do this evangelism ourselves would be to miss the greatest opportunity inherent in the situation, that of multiplying our ministry by training the new Christian in evangelism. We need to make sure that he is always involved in the process as a co-laborer, assuming more and more direct responsibility as he matures. As the concentric circles of opportunity expand, the number of evangelists multiplies accordingly.

Provide a bridge into the gospel. Evangelism in Ephesus took a fascinating form. Paul began in the synagogue. When the conflict with the

Jews became too heavy, he moved to a neutral location, taking his disciples with him. He conducted daily discussions in the school of Tyrannus for two years (Acts 19:8-10). The result was that "all the Jews and Greeks who lived in the province of Asia heard the word of the Lord." What were those discussions like? How were they conducted? What did they talk about? We'll never know. We only know that they were dynamic. Otherwise the whole province of Asia wouldn't have bothered to listen.

It is useful to observe that these daily discussions provided a forum where people could come and listen, interact, go away and think—and then come back for more. Certainly the discussions became known by word of mouth from those who had come to faith or were on their way. The ongoing exposure to the gospel had a cumulative effect in the region.

Only an unusually gifted teacher could attempt to do something as far-reaching as Paul's teaching in Ephesus. But we can achieve a similar effect, at whatever level the abilities of our little band of kindred spirits permits. The school of Tyrannus was essentially a neutral place (in contrast to the synagogue) where interested people could receive an ongoing exposure to the message.

There are ways in which we can provide a similar opportunity, even on a one-on-one basis. For example, we can maintain an open-door attitude toward the friends of the people with whom we are currently involved in the Scriptures. So what if someone new drops in at chapter 5? A quick review that brings him up to date will benefit everyone.

Another way to create an environment where young Christians can help bridge the gap between their friends and the gospel is to conduct a series of three or four open discussions on some deeply felt need (see chapter 17). If it is beyond your abilities to do this among yourselves, invite someone in to teach. It would be better, however, for you or someone in your group to go to a person who can give you the help you need to prepare to do it yourself. This would be an opportunity for you to learn and develop.

Pick an area or topic of interest. Study it; read up on it. Take your time, and when your thoughts are in order and in communicable form, then proceed. Invite a number of nonChristians equivalent to the present number in your group, and maintain that ratio.

Begin with a twenty- to thirty-minute presentation designed to give a foundation of biblical thought on the subject and to stimulate discussion. Discussion is stimulated by creating tension—positive tension, of course. Good questions create this kind of tension. Have a few guide questions prepared to keep things moving, and then be ready with a closing summary. When you're done, break for coffee and an informal time together. Here are some possible topics:

- God and history: What does the Bible say about current events? About the future?
- What does the Bible say about marriage? About the family? About child rearing?
- What is success? How is it achieved and maintained?
- Biblical principles of financial management.
- Interpersonal relationships.

The purpose of open discussions like these is not to bring people to the point of decision but to bring them to see that a relationship with God is fundamental to living and understanding life. Such discussions should motivate people to respond to our invitation to go on to examine the Bible further with us. One of the positive effects of these discussions will be that we have provided our new co-laborers with the assistance they need to draw their friends into a meaningful exposure to Christians and to the Christian message.

EPILOGUE
Unity in Diversity

THIS BOOK HAS focused on one of the essential functions of the Church: evangelism. Since it is impossible to isolate evangelism from its adjoining functions of establishing, edifying, and equipping Christians for the ministry, I fear that I have raised as many questions as I may have answered. This is due to the fact that I have limited the scope of this book not only to evangelism but also to a particular form of evangelism, one that meets two basic needs: (1) the need to communicate the gospel to the people who are caught up in the mainstream of our society, those who are being carried in the opposite direction, away from Christian presuppositions and values; and (2) the need for a concept of evangelism that provides meaningful, ongoing involvement for the average Christian among his peers. The questions raised have contextual answers.

I would like to think that after reading these pages the reader's reaction will be, "I can do that! With a little help from my friends, I can do it." I hope this book gives enough guidance and answers enough questions to bring the reader to this conclusion.

This book raises questions about the implications of our success in reaching unbelieving people in the mainstreams of our society. Generally, we're not accustomed to such people coming into the Body of Christ. How do we minister to these people whose needs and values are so different from our own? How do we accommodate this kind of growth into the Body?

For now, let's press ahead, concentrating on bringing these questions upon us! The fruit of our labors will transform what are now theoretical

215

questions into real needs. This will enable us to define them accurately and resolve them biblically and practically. Necessity fathers creativity.

A FINAL WORD

After investing fourteen long years in ministry among the Gentiles, the Apostle Paul returned to Jerusalem to consult with the men in leadership there (Galatians 2:1-10). He did this, he said, "for fear that I was running or had run my race in vain."

Isn't it strange that Paul, after experiencing God's great blessings on his efforts, worried that it could all prove to be in vain? What were his misgivings? He had no doubt about his message! He had just finished saying, "If anybody is preaching to you a gospel other than what you accepted, let him be eternally condemned!" (Galatians 1:9).

Paul's doubts were over how his brothers were feeling about what he was doing. He wanted to be sure they understood and accepted his relatively off-beat ministry among the Gentiles. He wanted their approval and support. He was inquiring about *unity* because he was well aware of the destructive power of disunity. He knew it could snuff out everything he had labored to build.

Unity is not uniformity. In this encounter, Paul and Barnabas agreed with Peter, James, and John that the most effective thing would be to maintain the diversity. "They agreed that we should go to the Gentiles, and they to the Jews" (Galatians 2:9). So there was diversity in what they did and how they did it, but there was unity of mind and purpose regarding their overall mission.

We have been talking about taking the gospel to a diversified and diversifying world. There are countless cultures and subcultures among the more than five billion people in the world, and many trends within each of these cultures! To go as a Church to this world and to cope with this diversity without making unwholesome judgments and comparisons will take a miracle of God's grace.

On the individual level, we want to commit ourselves to maintaining an attitude of humble submission to our pastors, spiritual overseers, and brothers as we move into the spheres of ministry we have examined in this book. To do otherwise is to run the risk of laboring in vain. Wherever love does not prevail between brothers, we essentially deny the gospel. We rob it of its credibility and power, destroying the very thing we have purposed to build. Jesus said, "All men will know that you are my disciples, if you love one another" (John 13:35).

TWENTY-FOUR HOURS WITH JOHN

FROM A STRICTLY historical point of view, Jesus of Nazareth was the most remarkable person in all human history. Whatever people's opinions of Him may be, almost everyone would seize an opportunity to spend a day with one of His closest friends.

The Apostle John was among Jesus' three closest friends. He was in on everything. Frequently it would be just the four of them together: Jesus, Peter, James, and John. John saw Jesus, touched Him, heard Him speak. Together they walked the hot dusty roads—conversing, perspiring, and experiencing hunger and thirst.

John's record of his experiences with Jesus, the Gospel of John, is divided into twenty-one chapters. This Bible study is a total of twenty-four lessons. Two of the chapters are so long that I divided each of them into two lessons. Also, I have included a summary study with an illustration that summarizes John's central message, which happens to be the central message of the whole Bible. These twenty-four studies offer us an opportunity to spend twenty-four hours with John.

As you, the leader, guide the nonChristian into this adventure with John, it will be important to keep certain things in mind. We have already discussed most of these points in this book, but we will review them here.

1. Remember that your part of the process in evangelism is to love the individual and help him understand what the Bible says. Leave the rest to the Holy Spirit and the Word of God.
2. Fortunately our job is not to defend religion—not even Christianity. In

217

fact we don't have to defend the Bible, the creation story, nor God's existence.

3. Since the primary issue for the nonChristian is the matter of Jesus' identity, this is where we want to focus our attention in these studies. We can summarize the scope of our emphasis with just two questions: (a) Who is Jesus? and (b) What does He want of me?

4. Don't feel you need to rigidly follow the questions I have provided here. Discussions never go quite the way we intend. The objective is not to cover all the material; it is simply to help the other person understand what each chapter says.

5. Maintain a sense of progress. If you ever want to get rid of someone, just take a month to plod through a chapter with him. Try to get through a chapter at every meeting.

6. On the other hand, remember that most of the questions listed are *launch* questions. You will need to make up your own *guide* and *summary* questions according to the way the discussion goes (see page 251).

7. You don't want to walk into an evangelistic study with this book in one hand and a Bible in the other. I have always felt uneasy about using any printed materials while studying with a nonChristian. To them, the printed page often smells of indoctrination. It's better to write out the questions and cross-references you intend to use on a separate piece of paper, or in the margin of your Bible. This, I find, contributes to the spontaneity of the discussions.

8. Throughout the studies you will find notes, as well as cross-references. These are to help you understand the passages and deal with questions raised by your study. You don't need to make sure that your group learns everything in the notes. Be selective in what you explain, so that your friend doesn't feel that he is ignorant or that you are preaching.

9. Seldom will it take all twenty-four studies for a nonChristian to come to faith. How long it takes depends on the distance the person is from Christ and the nature of the obstacles he has to overcome. So what do you do if a person comes to faith while you are studying chapter 6? You go on to chapter 7.

   The whole Christian life can be summarized in our two questions: Who is Jesus? and, What does He want of me? All of us would do well to dedicate our lives to answering these two questions.

   So when a person comes to faith in the midst of these studies, just keep going. Rejoice with him over his spiritual birth, and then proceed, paying special attention to the second question: What does He want of me? The Gospel of John contains some of the greatest "follow-up material" ever written.

10. Remember that at the beginning your friend is committed to you for only one study at a time. Even in later stages only you will be aware of the extensiveness of the process.

This material is intended as a guide for you, not for the other person. He probably should not even be aware of its existence. This will give you the freedom to select what you need out of these studies. Use your own judgment in deciding what and how much you will use.

STUDY #1—JOHN 1:1-14

Read 1:1-14.

1. What is John referring to when he speaks of the "Word" in verses 1-3 and 14? (See 1 John 1:1-3.)

2. Why do you think He is described as the Word?
Note: The function of a word is to transmit an idea. I say "pencil" and you know what I mean. I say "God" and what comes to your mind? From where did you get this concept of God? Jesus Christ is the "word" for God. (See John 1:18.)

I am limited to the range of my five senses. Could God exist beyond them? Of course. If He remained beyond them, knowing Him would be an impossibility. Before I can know Him, He must take the initiative and give us the "Word." This is the claim made here about Jesus.

Whether we are ready to accept this claim or not, we must admit that as long as the possibility of God existing beyond our senses stands, the position of atheism or dogmatic agnosticism is untenable. Nobody knows enough to be either!

3. What are some qualities you see attributed to the Word in verses 1-5 and 14?

4. In verses 4-9, light is used as another analogy to describe Christ. What, to you, are some implications of this analogy? (See 3:19-21; 8:12; 12:35,36.)

5. John 1:9 says every person is illuminated by Christ. In what sense do you think John means this?
Note: All people are created by Him. All have *life* from Him. But man has abandoned this source of life and has fallen into darkness. There are still traces in man of his noble origin, but they are merely the remains of what he once was. What does remain?

A certain God-consciousness—Everyone has a certain knowledge of God, in the same way that something may be known about an artist by seeing his works. (See Romans 1:18-21.)
An innate sense of morality—Everyone has an idea of how life should work: the "internal laws." (See Romans 2:14-15.)

These two elements explain the existence of religions and philosophies: a "God" notion and a standard of morality of which this God is the guardian. However, it is only by returning to the Light that man can be illuminated and thereby reoriented. Life is in Him. We understand life—our own and others'—by coming to the Light.

6. According to John 1:11-13, how does one enter God's family?
Note: It does not happen through
• heredity
• self-effort
• the efforts of another (pastor, priest, etc.)
Only God can give life.

7. What do you think it means to "receive Christ"?
Note: In 1:12, "receive" and "believe" are synonymous. In 3:36, the opposite of believing is rebellion against God—not accepting His authority over our lives. What do you conclude from this? Believe implies submission. (See Revelation 3:20.)

STUDY #2—JOHN 1:15-51

Read 1:15-28.
1. What claims do John the Baptist and John the writer make about Christ in verses 15-18?
Note: The writer of this Gospel never names himself. In chapter 1 and elsewhere, "John" refers to John the Baptist, a well-known, radical prophet of Jesus' day.

2. What do you know about the Law Moses gave (1:17)? Why do you think it was given?
Note: The Law wasn't given to be kept but to reveal sin for what it is. Like an x-ray, it doesn't cure anything; it simply reveals the problem. (See 5:45; Romans 3:19-20, 7:7; Galatians 2:16, 3:24.)

3. According to John 1:23, how do you understand the primary role of John the Baptist? (See also 3:26-30; Luke 3:4-14, 7:29-30.)

Note: John the Baptist announced the imminent arrival of the Messiah, calling on men to make their way straight—a way that had been twisted by centuries of self-will and religious traditions. If they didn't do this, they wouldn't recognize the Messiah.

4. How could the people of Israel straighten their way of living?
Note: Repentance means a change in mentality, a desire to leave your current way of life in order to enter into a relationship with Christ. Notice that the change came first, then the baptism. John's baptism was the sign that the individual had indeed repented (Luke 3:4-14).

Read John 1:29-34.
5. Why do you think Jesus is called the "Lamb of God"? (See Isaiah 53:4-7, Hebrews 10:1-14.)
Note: The Old Testament sacrifices are illustrations of the need for the single, sufficient sacrifice of Christ.

6. What do you think are the implications of John the Baptist's declaration in John 1:33 that Jesus will baptize with the Holy Spirit?
Note: Being a Christian is not merely following a certain philosophy, or becoming a part of a religious system, it is a relationship between two persons: Jesus Christ and the individual (1:12, 3:5-8, 4:23-24). This baptism doesn't involve water.

Read 1:35-51.
7. This section teaches the story of how five people first encountered Christ. Each one came by a different means. Who are the five, and what was it that prompted each to believe in Christ?

STUDY #3—JOHN 2

Read 2:1-11.
1. What do you think Jesus' attendance at the wedding indicates about Him? (See Matthew 11:16-19.)

2. Do you find Jesus' solution to the problem of no wine at the wedding believable? Why or why not?
Note: What claim was made about Jesus in John 1:3? It would be hard to imagine the Creator appearing on earth without revealing His power over His creation. Christ, fully understanding the nature of matter and having power over it, could command the elements of creation at will (Hebrews 11:3).

3. Notice in John 2:11 that John describes the event as a "miraculous sign." He consistently uses this phrase to refer to Jesus' miracles (3:2, 4:54, 6:14, 6:26, etc.). Why? What is the function of a sign?
   Note: Signs serve to inform.

4. What does the sign tell us about Jesus?

5. How do you understand this conversation between Jesus and His mother (2:3-5)?
   Note: "Woman" was an expression of endearment. What Jesus said could be paraphrased as follows: "We are not of the same world. What is a problem for you is nothing for Me. I'll take care of it. I have time for such things before My 'hour' comes."

6. What "time" do you think Jesus is referring to in 2:4? (See 7:6; 12:23,27; 17:1.)
   Note: His death was not a futile and unforeseen tragedy. It was the reason for the coming. The "miraculous signs" contributed to setting off the chain reaction that inevitably led to His death.

Read 2:12-22.

7. What do you suppose prompted Jesus to act the way He did when He cleared the Temple (2:13-17)?
   Note: The Passover was one of the principle religious feasts of the Jews. They came to Jerusalem for celebration and spiritual cleansing. However, the temple merchants were exploiting the situation by selling animals and exchanging foreign currencies for the temple currency—all for profit. Jesus accused them of soiling God's name. He told them, in so many words, "Don't use My Father's name to promote your dirty business!" (See Romans 2:24.)

8. How can Jesus' anger be justified? (See Romans 1:18.)

9. The Jews demanded He show His credentials for such authoritative actions. What do you learn about Jesus from His answer (John 2:18-22)?

10. Why do you think His resurrection would constitute the ultimate credential? (See 1 Corinthians 15:12-19.)

Read John 2:23-25.

11. Why do you think Jesus did not respond to the people in 2:23, even though it says they believed in Him?

Note: Real belief implies commitment. Their acceptance of Jesus did not go that far. (See 12:42-43, James 2:19.) A faith in which the individual reserves the right to run his own life is not faith at all. (See John 3:36.)

STUDY #4—JOHN 3

Read 3:1-14.

1. What stands out to you about Nicodemus's observations concerning Jesus (3:1-2)?

2. Jesus corrects Nicodemus in verse 3. When, according to Jesus, is someone qualified to understand the things of God? (See 1:12-13, 1 Corinthians 2:7-16.)
   Note: Jesus said that Nicodemus could not come to any meaningful conclusions about the things of God without being "born again."

3. How did it become evident that Nicodemus did not understand spiritual matters (John 3:4,9)?
   Note: God speaks on a spiritual level. Man interprets Him on human terms and finds it difficult to conceive of anything beyond those terms. For example, imagine a world of blind men attempting to comprehend the color red. Their failure to comprehend it does not preclude its existence. To "see" the Kingdom of God, one must acquire spiritual senses.

4. How do you understand "born again" in 3:3-8?
   Note: Being reborn implies:
   • a person was dead in some sense and is now alive in that area. The Holy Spirit makes a formerly dead spirit alive (Ephesians 2:1-9).
   • a person has a new parent. Believers are born of God (John 1:12-13), so they now have their Father's spiritual "genes."

5. Why do you think Jesus insists that one must be born over again before he can see God's Kingdom (3:3,5,8)? (See also Ephesians 2:1-9.)
   Note: You must have an alive spirit with the Father's spiritual "genes"—His traits and some of His abilities—to have the spiritual senses for seeing His Kingdom.

6. What do you suppose being "born of water" means (John 3:5)?
   Note: Jesus was probably referring to the baptism of John here. (That was the only kind of "water" Nicodemus was acquainted with.) How

ever, this does not imply that one must be baptized to be saved. John's baptism was unique, a symbol of repentance already in effect. (See Luke 3:7-14.)

The water didn't bring about the change; the repentance did it. Repentance is necessary if spiritual birth is to take place (Isaiah 55:6-7, Luke 13:1-5). Jesus was saying to Nicodemus, "Do what John the Baptist has said. Do an about-face, leaving your old way of thinking; then permit the Holy Spirit to enter you, giving you a new life."

By itself, John's message of repentance was not complete. It was not sufficient for spiritual life without the additional part of being "born of the Spirit." (See Acts 19:1-7.)

Read John 3:14-21.

7. The word *believe* appears several times in verses 15-18. What is the relationship between believing and being born again?

8. For what purpose did God send Christ (3:16-21)?

Read 3:22-36.

9. How does John the Baptist describe himself and his work (3:27-30)? What qualities characterize the man?
Note: He is a model for those who would witness about Christ. He doesn't call attention to himself, but describes himself as "a voice" (1:19-23) or as the best man at the wedding (3:27-30).

10. According to 3:31-36, what must take place in order for a person to come to the conclusion that this message about God is the truth?

11. What did you learn about your relationship with God from our discussion of this chapter?

STUDY #5—JOHN 4

Read 4:1-18.

1. What do you learn about Jesus from these verses?
Note: It was rare for a rabbi to condescend to talk to a woman, let alone to a Samaritan woman.

2. What do you think Jesus meant by "living water" (4:10)? (See Isaiah 44:3-4, John 7:37-39.)

3. What claims did He make about the very special water?

4. How do you understand this "thirst" Jesus talks about?
Note: The innate human dissatisfaction is strong.

5. How had the woman previously tried to quench her thirst?
Note: She had been drinking at the wrong fountain—the fountain of promiscuity (4:17-18). (See also Isaiah 55:1-2.)

6. Why do you think the woman did not understand what Jesus meant by living water?
Note: She was thinking in the natural plane, whereas Jesus was speaking of the supernatural (John 3:4; 6:26,34).

Read 4:19-30.
7. As soon as the Samaritan woman perceived that the conversation was heading toward religion, she tried to keep it from becoming personal by employing a very common tactic. What was it (4:19-20)?
Note: She tried to draw Jesus into a general discussion on religion, but one that didn't focus on her.

8. How did Jesus handle her evasive tactic (4:21-24)?
Note: It's not the religious system, or the forms, or the creed that makes the difference. God's new temple is the individual, and that is where the worship is to take place (1 Corinthians 6:19).

9. What do we learn about Jesus from His declaration in John 4:26?

10. What decision did the woman face?

11. What happened to her waterpot?

Read 4:31-42.
12. Why was Jesus no longer hungry (4:31-34)?

13. What is the harvest (4:35)? (See also Matthew 9:36-38.) Who are the harvesters (John 4:36-38)? (See also 2 Corinthians 5:18-20.)

14. What conclusion did the townspeople come to about Jesus? What was the basis of their thinking (John 4:39-42)?

Read 4:43-54.
15. How do you interpret Jesus' reaction to the royal official's request? Compare the official's attitude with that of the official in Matthew 8:8.

16. Why do you think Jesus answered the request in spite of the man's imperfect faith?

STUDY #6—JOHN 5

Read 5:1-18.
The most ancient known documents do not include verse 4. This suggests that it may have been interpolated later to explain the phenomenon of the pool.

1. Why do you think Jesus chose that particular lame man out of the multitude of diseased people (5:7)? (See also Luke 19:10.)

2. Did the lame man demonstrate any faith? Why might this be significant?

3. Why do you suppose Jesus asked, "Do you want to get well?" (John 5:6). Why wasn't that a stupid question?

4. Imagine being a paralyzed beggar waiting thirty-eight years for an improbable cure. Yet Jesus spoke of "something worse" (5:14). What could it be? (See Matthew 16:26.)

5. Is it possible to quit sinning? (See Romans 7:14-20.) Why did Jesus tell him to stop? (See Romans 3:19-31, 7:21-25.)
Note: Imagine how the man felt when he found himself sinning again after Jesus' warning. But he had to try to stop on his own to be convinced that he couldn't stop. It usually takes such a stubborn, independent attempt before we try God's way. The man had to realize that it was impossible for him not to sin unless he changed his very nature. He had to be born again (John 3:3).

6. Why did Jesus deliberately violate the sacrificial laws (5:16-18)? (See also Matthew 12:1-14.)
Note: Centuries of tradition had obscured what the Old Testament actually taught regarding the Sabbath. Jesus was merely giving the Sabbath its proper interpretation. One of the characteristics of tradition is that it eventually becomes authoritative. (See Mark 7:6-9.)

7. What do you observe about Jesus from John 5:17-18?

Read 5:19-30.
8. What observations can you make about Jesus' relationship with His

Father (5:19-23)? (Compare 8:28, 12:48-49, 14:10.) In what sense was He dependent on His Father?

9. What do you see Jesus promising in 5:24? How does one receive these promises?

10. How would you reconcile 5:29 with the teaching that spiritual life comes through faith and not works? (See 6:28-29, 15:5.)
Note: The life must come first, for it is the life that produces the works.

Read 5:31-47.
11. Jesus presented five witnesses who attested to His deity (5:31-39). Who or what were they?
Note:
• Jesus Himself
• His own works
• John the Baptist
• The Father
• The Scriptures

    It is possible to isolate these witnesses, casting doubt on them individually. But when they are called to the stand together, although they do not prove the divinity of Christ with human proofs, they become irrefutable.

12. What obstacle to faith do you observe in 5:44? (See also 12:42-43.) How does this still hinder people?

STUDY #7—JOHN 6

Read 6:1-31.
1. What motivated the multitudes to follow Jesus (6:2, 14-15,26-27)?
Note:
• Their physical needs (6:2)
• Politics (6:14-15)
• Material gain—free bread (6:26-27)

2. Do you think these same things motivate people to be religious today?

3. How did Jesus react to these people (6:26-29)?

4. What do you think it was that disqualified them from being real followers of Jesus?

Note: They refused to accept the significance of the signs. They were interested only in the utilitarian side, what Jesus could do for them.

5. What do you think Jesus was really trying to teach the crowd when He fed them (6:27)?

6. Jesus attached a second meaning to both that bread and the manna Moses gave the Israelites. How would you explain that second meaning? (See Isaiah 55:1-2.)

Read John 6:32-58.
7. What do you think Jesus was implying when He referred to Himself as "the bread of life" (John 6:35,51)?
Note:
• He is from above—the supernatural world (6:38,41,42).
• He gives life to the world (6:33).
• He satisfies our hunger and thirst (6:35).
• He is eternal (6:51,54).

8. How can a person get some of this "bread" (6:51-58)?

9. What do you think Jesus means by "eat my flesh and drink my blood"? *Note:* It is an individual act. A person must take Christ as the "staff of life." (See Galatians 2:20.) This chapter is not referring to Communion. With whom did Jesus break bread at the Lord's Supper? For what purpose? (See Luke 22:14-23.) The Lord's Supper was intended to provide a permanent remembrance of the hour of His death. Jesus told the multitude in John 6 that they had to eat and drink of Him for a very different reason. What was it?

10. Why is it impossible for Jesus to be merely a teacher or a philosopher and say what He says in 6:35-38?

Read 6:59-71.
11. Why didn't Jesus try to smooth things over when He saw that His followers were offended by what He said (6:60-66)? (See also Matthew 15:8-9, Acts 28:26-27.)
Note: The people were only superficially accepting Jesus. He wanted all or nothing. He did those people a favor by sending them away. They had long been under the illusion that they were "followers of Christ." But Jesus' nonnegotiable terms are, "Give Me your whole self or forget it!"

If Christianity were something we were making up, of course we could make it easier. But it is not. We cannot compete, in simplicity, with people who are inventing religions. How could we? We are dealing with Fact. Of course anyone can be simple if he has no facts to bother about.[1]   —C.S. Lewis

12. When Jesus asked His twelve disciples why they didn't leave along with everyone else. Peter summed up their position (John 6:68-69). What was his answer?

13. What do you think he meant by that?

14. Have you learned anything new about being a follower of Jesus Christ through this Gospel?

STUDY #8—JOHN 7

The theme of this chapter is the controversy that continually went on over the question "Who is He?"

Read 7:1-52.
  1. List the factors that contributed to the people's bafflement on this question, as indicated in the following verses:
  • John 7:14-15
  • John 7:19-20
  • John 7:25-27
  • John 7:31
  • John 7:40-44
  • John 7:46-49
  • John 7:52

  2. To what extent did their confusion result from their preconceived notions about the Messiah? Where do you suppose these preconceptions originated?
  Note: Ignorance of the Scriptures and/or failure to understand them (Luke 24:25-27); religious traditions (Mark 7:6-9).

  3. Do you think people have similar misconceptions to deal with today before they can come to understand Jesus Christ? What are some of those misconceptions?

  4. What clues do you find in this chapter that suggest Jesus was divine?

Note:
- John 7:15-16,46—His wisdom
- John 7:28-29—What He Himself claimed to be
- John 7:31—His signs
- John 7:33-34—His prediction of His resurrection
- John 7:37-39—His claims to give life to others
- John 7:41-42—The prophets

5. What impresses you about the offer Jesus makes in 7:37-39?
   a. To whom did He make it?
   b. What kind of thirst was He talking about? (See 4:13-14, 6:35; Isaiah 55:1-3.)
   c. Exactly what was He offering? (See John 14:25-26, Romans 8:9.)
   d. How does one respond to this offer? (See Revelation 3:20.)

6. The guards were impressed with Christ's words. How did the authorities try to diminish this impression (John 7:48-49)?

7. What point was raised by Nicodemus, and how did the authorities react to it (7:50-52)?

8. What attitude would you say characterized the authorities? How does this attitude affect objective thinking? (See Psalm 10:4.)

9. What do you think about Nicodemus?

STUDY #9—JOHN 8

Read 8:1-11.
1. Why do you think the Pharisees took this woman to Jesus?

2. What do you observe about Jesus' attitude toward the woman caught in adultery? (Did He approve of what she had done? Then why didn't He condemn her?)
   Note: Was it that He closed His eyes to her sin? (See John 3:16-18, 1 Peter 3:18.) Jesus paid dearly to be able to offer her the pardon she needed. He took the woman's place. (See 2 Corinthians 5:21.)

3. What stands out to you about Jesus' attitude toward the Pharisees?
   Note: He tried to help them see that they were no different than the woman. But their case was more difficult. She knew she had a problem; they didn't. (See Matthew 9:10-13, 21:28-32.)

Read John 8:12-20.
4. In 8:12, Jesus made another of His "I am" assertions. How do you understand His claim to being the "light of the world"?

5. If Jesus is the light of the world, what could this imply for you? (See Ephesians 5:8-15.)

Read John 8:21-38.
6. In John 8:24,28,58 we see more "I am" statements. To what was Jesus referring? I am *what?* He said that after His crucifixion people would know the answer to the question of His identity (8:28). What is the answer? (See Romans 5:8.)

7. a. What was the main reason for the conflict between Jesus and His enemies (8:23)?
   b. Why do you think this is so hard to accept?
   Note: To admit that Jesus is God is to admit one's error and need for change. (See Luke 7:29-30.)

8. Jesus talks about truth and freedom (John 8:31-36).
   a. What do you think He means by "truth"? What is a truth?
   Note: A truth is something tested and proven. Jesus said in John 14:6, "I am the truth." Either this was the ultimate expression of egotism—or He was right!
   b. How can we determine whether He was right or wrong when He made this claim (8:31-32)?
   Note: We must put Him to the test—on His terms.
   c. Jesus offered a spiritual maxim on freedom: Committing sin results in slavery (8:34). What do you think this means?
   Note: The person who says, "I am free to do whatever my inner voice suggests," soon finds himself enslaved to what he sought to be free to do. (See Mark 7:14-23.) It is impossible to do or be what we really desire to do or be.
   d. Why do you suppose the Jews couldn't perceive their spiritual slavery (John 8:33)?
   Note: People in spiritual slavery can't see it because the bondage itself blinds them. (See 9:39-41.)
   e. What must happen before a person can be really free?
   Note: Submitting to Christ requires an unconditional surrender (Luke 14:25-33). We must fully submit before He can do anything for us. Example: The sick must submit to the surgeon so that he can do whatever is necessary to produce the cure.

Read John 8:39-59.
   9. Why did Jesus say that the Jews who rejected Him weren't sons of God (8:42)? How did He support that assertion (8:37-47)?

   10. Do you think it is possible to believe in God and not believe in Christ? Why? What are the characteristics of one who knows God and of one who doesn't?

   11. What were the Pharisees thinking at this point about Jesus' identity (8:48)?

   12. What was the basis of this judgment?

   13. How did Jesus answer them (8:49-59)?

   14. In summarizing this chapter, list the main reasons why it is of primary importance to establish a relationship with Jesus Christ.

STUDY #10—JOHN 9

The miracles that Jesus performed were "signs" that pointed to the spiritual truths He sought to teach. The story of this blind man is an example of this. By curing him, Jesus revealed what true blindness is and who is truly blind.

Read 9:1-12.
   1. What was the disciples' evaluation of the blind man (9:2)? Why do you think they thought that way? (See 9:34.)
   Note: That was the common religious explanation of the day.

   2. What was Christ's evaluation of the blind man (9:3)?
   Note: He saw him as an opportunity to contribute to God's works. How does Christ interpret suffering? (See Luke 13:1-5, Romans 8:18-20.) The suffering we see in the world is a consequence of the Fall. Those who believe participate in the damage just as those who don't believe. (See 2 Corinthians 12:8-10.) Suffering is an opportunity for us to experience God's participation in our lives.

   3. What do you observe happening among the neighbors after the man was cured (John 9:8-12)?

   4. Why do you think the ex-blind man's explanation did not satisfy them?

5. According to Jesus, what are the "works" of God (6:28-29, 40)?

Read 9:13-34.
6. How many times did the ex-blind man have to tell his story? Why?

7. Why was it so hard for others to accept the healing?
   - The neighbors (9:13)
   - The parents (9:22)
   - The Pharisees (9:16-19,24,29-34)

8. The neighbors, not satisfied, took the case to the theologians. What conclusion did they arrive at after examining the case theologically?

9. Why did their arguments fail to shake the ex-blind man?

10. Who was in a better position to discuss the subject: the ex-blind man or the theologians? Why?
   Note: Imagine trying to explain color to a world filled with blind people. You couldn't prove that it exists. The blind could even offer theoretical proofs as to why color can't exist. This simple beggar with eyesight would know more about color than the greatest intellectual ever could.

11. Who finally won the argument? On what grounds?

12. Why do you think the man's parents took the attitude they did?

Read 9:35-41.
13. What do you learn about becoming a Christian from this story?

14. Why couldn't the Pharisees do the same as the blind man?

15. Why is there more hope for those who admit blindness than there is for those who don't (Luke 5:30-32)?

16. Look at the purpose for which Christ came (Luke 4:16-22). Do you see a parallel between the miracle in John 9 and this statement of purpose for His coming?

STUDY #11—JOHN 10

In this chapter we see Jesus as He describes the true leader and the false leader. The Scriptures frequently use a sheep-shepherd analogy in discussing leaders and followers. Why? *Note:* Sheep can't survive without a shepherd. They are helpless.

Read 10:1-18.
1. This portion gives a parable and its explanation. What do you think is the main point of the parable?
Note: Christ is the only one who takes a personal interest in man to the point of giving His life for him. (See also Psalm 100:3, Luke 15:4-7, Romans 8:31-39, 1 Peter 2:24-25.)

2. What are the characteristics of a mercenary leader (John 10:12-13)? Whom would he represent?
Note: He's not interested in the well-being of the individual. He's a professional, so to him man is a means to an end. For this reason, when there is a crisis this type of leader leaves a person to his own plight.
Read Ezekiel 34:1-31. Observe what this passage says about:
a. The mercenary (verses 1-10)—the poor leader
b. The faithful shepherd (verses 11-16)—the good leader
c. The sheep (verses 16-31)—the kind of sheep the good leader is interested in.

3. What lessons do you learn about man from the sheep analogy? (See also Isaiah 53:6, Matthew 9:36.)

4. What do you observe about Jesus from His picture in John 10:7 as the "door" for the sheep? (Compare 14:6.)

5. How would you describe the relationship Jesus desires to have with people who are His, based on His sheep-shepherd analogy?

Read 10:19-42.
6. In the remainder of this chapter, the perpetual question, "Who is this Jesus?" reappears. In what ways does Jesus assert His deity in this section?

7. Jesus talks a lot about believing in Him. Take a look at 1 John 3:1-2 (or 2 Peter 1:4; or Romans 8:16-17,28-30). What does Jesus offer to those who believe—who make the commitment to heed His Word?
Note: Christ came to earth as the only begotten, the firstborn among many children of God who will share in a great eternal inheritance.

8. John 10:27-29 describes the security enjoyed by those who belong to Christ. What is the individual's part in this? What is Christ's part?

9. Have you arrived at a personal conclusion on the question raised by the Jews (10:24)? What is the basis for your conclusion? What implications do you see for your life?

STUDY #12—JOHN 11

Read 11:1-17.

1. Observe that Jesus deliberately delayed responding to His friends' urgent request for help. The result was that Lazarus died before Jesus arrived. Why do you think Jesus did this (11:3-6,11-15)?

2. What do you think Jesus is communicating with His analogy of walking by day and walking by night (11:9-10)? (See also 8:12, 9:4, 13:27-30.) *Note:* Whoever doesn't orient himself by God walks by night.

Read 11:18-27.

3. What do you think are the implications of Jesus' assertion, "I am the resurrection and the life" (11:25)? *Note:* Read 1 Corinthians 15:12-19. *His* resurrection is the key to the resurrection He has promised *us.* (See 1 Corinthians 15:35-49.) What will be the nature of our resurrection?

4. What must happen to a person before he can share in this promise (John 11:25-26)? (See 12:24-25.) *Note:* Two grains of wheat may look exactly alike on the outside, but one may have the germ of life inside it, and the other may not. (See Romans 8:9-11.)

Read John 11:28-46.

5. Since Jesus knew that He would soon raise Lazarus from the dead, why do you think He wept (11:31-35,41-44). (See also Luke 19:41-44.)

Read John 11:47-57.

6. What were the two different reactions to the miracle?

7. Normally unbelief is attributed to encountering things that are intellectually unacceptable. But on this occasion the unbelief appeared in the face of irrefutable evidence. What motivated the Jewish leaders to reject Jesus (11:47-48)? (See also 12:9-11,42-43.) *Note:* The reasons were political and personal.

8. Could these motives still constitute an obstacle to faith today?

9. What was the human rationale used by the high priest, Caiaphas, to justify the plan to put a good man like Jesus to death (11:49-50)?

10. How did this perspective coincide with God's eternal plan (11:51-53)? *Note:* (See also Isaiah 53:1-12, Acts 2:22-23.) Jesus' death was not an accident, nor a defeat at the hand of His enemies. It was the fulfillment of God's plan for the salvation of man.

STUDY #13—JOHN 12

Read 12:1-11.
1. Note who among the Twelve was the treasurer (12:4-6). Why do you suppose Jesus gave the job to the only thief in the group? *Note:* Judas needed an opportunity to see himself as he really was, so that he could realize his need for a Savior. (See Romans 7:7-8.)

Read John 12:12-19.
2. What led the crowd to give this demonstration (12:17-18)? *Note:* Jesus rejected the people's earlier attempts to involve Him politically (6:14-18). Why, then, did He submit on this occasion? He was forcing a showdown. (See 11:27-57.) By this act He demanded that the Jews make up their minds about Him; "Either accept Me as the Messiah or kill Me!" It was the last sign. (See Zechariah 9:9.)

Read John 12:20-36.
3. How would you state Jesus' central purpose in life from these verses?

4. Jesus said, "The hour has come for the Son of Man to be glorified" (12:23). What do you think He was referring to? (See 12:27,32.)

5. Why do you suppose He referred to His death as His "glorification"? *Note:* See John 17:4-5, Exodus 33:18-19. By the life He lived, Jesus revealed His Father's attributes to the world, glorifying His Father. Now Jesus' death would reveal His identity and His purposes to the world.

6. Who is "the prince of this world" (John 12:31)? (See also Luke 4:5-7.)

7. What would be some of the implications of this? (See Romans 8:18-22, 1 John 5:19.)

8. What do you learn about Jesus' death from His illustration about the grain of wheat (John 12:24)? How did His death bear much fruit? (See

Romans 5:15-19, 1 Peter 2:24.) Why is this death indispensable? (See Luke 9:23-25.)

9. In the subsequent verses, Jesus extends this principle of death as a prerequisite of fruitfulness to us as well. How do you understand this?

Read John 12:37-50.
10. Why is it that some people can't believe in Him?
Note: What happens to those people who choose the world's value system or refuse to give up their prejudices and their spiritual callousness? (See Acts 28:25-28.) Does John 12:38-40 suggest that it is impossible for some people to be saved? (See 2 Corinthians 3:15-16.)

STUDY #14—JOHN 13

Read 13:1-20.
1. In 13:1-16, we have the account of Jesus performing a symbolic act in order to communicate a spiritual principle to His disciples. What do you think He is teaching them? (See also Luke 22:24-27.)

2. Why do you suppose it was so difficult for Peter to let Jesus wash his feet (John 13:6-9)? (See Matthew 16:13-17.)

3. The washing obviously has a second meaning (John 13:8-11). What do you think it is? (See Titus 3:5.)
Note: We are made clean at salvation (1 Corinthians 6:11). We need the daily cleansing by Christ because our feet are constantly contaminated by the dust of the world (Romans 12:1-2).

4. Jesus makes two assertions in John 13:13. What are their implications for you?
  a. What does He mean by being our "Teacher"? Can you accept Him on this condition? (See 6:68-69.)
  b. What does He mean by being our "Lord"? Can you accept Him on this condition? (See Matthew 7:21.)

5. What other lesson was Jesus communicating to His disciples by washing their feet (John 13:14-17)? What might this mean for us in practice?

Read 13:21-38.
6. What do you think motivated Judas to betray Jesus? (See John 12:4-6; Matthew 26:14-16,47-50; 27:3-10.)

7. What command did Jesus give His disciples in John 13:34-35? Why did He say it was new? (See Leviticus 19:18, Matthew 22:34-40.)
Note: Until this time the Jewish rule was to love your neighbor as yourself. Now Jesus gives us a new dimension for comparison: "as I have loved you." (See 1 John 3:16.)

8. What do you think it is about the love Jesus describes that makes those who practice it so unique (John 13:35)? (See 1 John 4:7-12.)

9. Do you think that Peter was sincere when he made the verbal commitment that he would give his life for Christ? If Peter was sincere, then why do you think he failed? (See Matthew 26:40-41, John 15:5, Romans 7:18-25.)

STUDY #15—JOHN 14:1-14

Read 14:1-14.
1. As you have no doubt noticed, one of the most prevalent themes in Jesus' teaching is eternal life. In the first four verses of this chapter, He elaborates on the nature of this life. What do you observe about eternal life from this passage? (Compare 1 Corinthians 15:35-50.)

2. What do you learn about Jesus from John 14:6?
a. What did He mean by, "I am the way"? (See Ephesians 2:1-10.)
b. What did He mean by, "I am the truth"? (See John 8:32.)
c. What did He mean by, "I am the life"? (See 1 John 5:11-12.)

3. Jesus tells His disciples they have already seen God the Father. Philip, not understanding, takes exception to this, asking Christ to show them the Father. Jesus responds by reaffirming that they indeed have already seen the Father. In what sense is this true? (See John 5:19,30; 8:28; 12:49-50; 14:11.)
Note: What was the origin of the things Jesus said? What was the origin of His works? Whose will did He obey?
How, then, did Jesus go about revealing the Father to His disciples? In seeing Him they saw the Father.

4. What implications do you think there are for us of this interdependence between Jesus and His Father?
Note: God is knowable. Whatever questions we may have about Him are answerable by examining Jesus. For instance, is God just? Look at Jesus. Was Jesus just? (See Hebrews 1:2.)

5. How would you describe Jesus' relationship with His Father? (See John 14:10.)

6. In what way is this a pattern for the relationship between Christ and those who believe in Him? (See 14:10, 15:5.)

7. We now have our definition of a Christian. What is it? (See Romans 8:9.)

8. According to your understanding, how does a person enter this kind of a relationship with Christ? (See Romans 10:9-13.)

9. What resource did Jesus offer in order that great things could take place in our lives (John 14:12-14).

STUDY #16—JOHN 14:15-31

Read 14:15-20.
1. In this passage Jesus begins to make it clear to His disciples that He will soon leave them. What do you learn about the Holy Spirit from this passage (14:16-17)? (See Romans 8:9-17, 1 Corinthians 2:10-12.)

2. How do you understand the apparent paradox in Jesus' words here? He said He would send someone to them (John 14:16-17); He then said He Himself would come to them (14:18-20); then, He said not only He, but also His Father, would inhabit them (14:23).

Read 14:21-31.
3. In 14:15,21,23 Jesus describes the nature of the relationship He desires to have with those who are His. How would you explain what Jesus says in these verses?

4. What promise is made to those who, out of love, obey Christ (14:23)?

5. Why is obedience a necessary requirement to a more intimate understanding of Christ? (See Matthew 11:28-30.)
Note: If we're not willing to "try it His way," He can't help us.

6. What does the Holy Spirit do for the Christian (John 14:26)?

7. What differences do you think His presence could make in a person's life? (See Romans 8:14-17, 8:26-27; 1 Corinthians 2:12; Galatians 5:22-23.)

8. In John 14:27, Jesus says the peace He offers is different from that of the world. How would you describe that difference? (See also Philippians 4:6-7.)

STUDY #17—JOHN 15

Read 15:1-8.

1. Jesus compares His relationship with the Christian to that of a vine with its branches. In what ways does He say we are like branches of Him?

2. What are the implications of Jesus' claim that He is the true vine (15:1)? (Compare Luke 6:43-45.)
Note: He is the only kind of vine that produces true life.

3. If Christ is the vine and the Christian is the branch, what fruit does the Christian produce?
Note: Christ produces after His kind. His personality is reproduced in the Christian. (See 1 Corinthians 13:1-8, Galatians 5:22-23.)

4. How do you interpret what Jesus says about the branch that does or does not produce fruit (John 15:2,6-7)?
Note: Producing is inevitable for a branch that is joined to the vine. That which is fruitless is cut back, and even that which is fruitful is trimmed so that more fruit will grow. Although this may be a painful process, it is positive. There is a correlation between suffering and fruitfulness. (See Romans 5:1-5, Hebrews 12:4-13.)

5. What is the secret of producing fruit?
Note: "Remaining," "abiding," or living in dependence on Christ is the key. Jesus modeled this dependence in His relationship with His Father. (See John 5:19,30; 8:28-29.) He desires to have the same kind of relationship with us (15:5).

6. According to 15:8, what is the purpose of the branch that bears fruit?

7. Why does bearing fruit glorify the Father? (See 14:7, 17:4.)
Note: Christ's function on earth was to glorify His Father—to show who and what the Father is. A true disciple will serve the same function.

Read 15:9-27.

8. According to 15:9-27, what can the person who is dependent on Christ expect in return?

Note:
- Because we are recipients of Christ's love, we know Him better. Of what does His love consist? He sacrificed Himself (15:13); He sought intimacy (15:15); and He took the initiative (15:16).
- Peace.
- Joy.
- Loving others as He loves them, becoming their true friends, and thereby assisting them to become His disciples as well (15:12-17).
- A new relationship with the world: conflict (15:18-20). Why does the world hate Christ and His disciples? Because they are different (15:19); because they don't know God (15:21); and because He reveals their sin (15:22-25). What are two ways of changing this particular attitude of the world (15:26-27)? Answer: The work of the Holy Spirit and the testimony of the disciples' changed lives.

STUDY #18—JOHN 16

This is the last of four consecutive chapters in which Jesus devotes His full attention to teaching the Twelve. All of this teaching took place in the last few days of His life. Since He was preparing them for His departure, we can be sure He devoted those hours to underlining the things of greatest importance.

By way of review:
- What attitudes did Jesus teach His disciples (chapter 13)?
- What provision did He promise them in the light of His imminent departure (chapter 14)?
- What is the key word in chapter 15? What does it mean?

Read 16:1-11.

1. Now, in chapter 16, Jesus continues on the same theme, talking about the provisions He has made for continuing to assist His followers after He departs. Notice in verse 7 that He even claimed that they would be better off after He was gone. How could that be true? (See 14:16-20, 1 Corinthians 2:11-16.)

Note: The intimacy of all human relationships is limited by physical separation. Jesus said that He had to leave, thereby discarding His physical limitation. But He emphasized that He would return to cohabit our bodies. When this happens, we enjoy a greater level of intimacy with Him than even the apostles did while they walked with Him.

2. a. What do you learn about what the Holy Spirit will do for the person who does not believe (John 16:8-11)?

Note: In 16:8-11, the word *because* occurs three times. In each case, the word *because* is followed by a dependent clause, intended to explain the primary clause. At first glance these dependent clauses appear to explain nothing. But how should we understand these verses?

b. What does the word *sin* mean in verse 9?
Note: In this case, sin refers to a deliberate refusal to believe in Christ. (See Isaiah 53:6; John 3:36, 5:40.)

c. According to 16:10, how is "righteousness" (justice) obtained?
Note: By Christ's return to the Father. (See John 11:51; Romans 5:18, 8:31-34; 1 Peter 3:18.)

d. According to John 16:11, who is under "judgment"?

e. Who rules the world? (See John 12:31, Matthew 4:8-10.) The Spirit of God convinces the individual that he is on a shipwrecked planet that has no future. (See 2 Peter 3:7.)

3. What does Jesus promise that the Holy Spirit will do for the Christian (John 16:13-15)?
Note: He will guide the Christian into all truth. (See 1 John 2:27.) And He will glorify Christ (enhance our understanding of Christ). (See Ephesians 1:17-19.)

Read John 16:16-33.

4. Jesus foresaw a crisis in the lives of His disciples.
a. What was this crisis (16:16-22)?
Note: While they suffered and cried, the world would rejoice.

b. What would bring on this crisis?
Note: His departure.

c. Why would His departure from them bring about the crisis?
Note: The disciples would behave like cowards, their faith would disintegrate, and they would feel embarrassment as if they had been victimized by a charlatan. (See Mark 14:27-42.)

d. What good would come out of this crisis (John 16:22-23)?
Note: The disciples would become steadfast and mature. While they were in the depths of their despondency, they would realize the reality of Jesus' resurrection. Then they would become indomitable. No one could destroy the resulting joy.

e. Do you think crises are important for us? Why? (See Deuteronomy 8:2-3, James 1:1-4, 2 Corinthians 7:8-10, Hebrews 12:4-13.)

5. It is in this context that Jesus offers us the ultimate in terms of spiritual resources. What is it (John 16:24)?

6. Why do you think God answers prayers made in Jesus' name (16:26-27)?
Note: Those who are His have family rights as God's children. (See Ephesians 5:14-15.)

STUDY #19—JOHN 17

Read 17:1-5.

1. In verse 3, Jesus describes eternal life in rather unusual terms. How do you understand this description?
Note: Eternal life is not just a state of being. It is also an eternal relationship with God the Father and with Jesus Christ. (See 1 John 5:11-12.)

Read John 17:6-19.

2. In verse 4, Jesus told the Father that He had finished the work He had given Him to do. What work do you think He was referring to?
Note: He multiplied Himself by eleven. (See Luke 6:12-13, John 15:16.)

3. Why was this work so important (17:18)? (See Matthew 28:16-20.)

4. What do you find in John 17:6-19 that describes what Jesus did to prepare these men for the work He had in mind for them?
   • He transmitted the Scriptures to them in such a way that they could believe and live in accordance with them (17:6-8).
   • He was with them (17:9-13).
   • He prayed for them—that they would be able to withstand the pressures of a world that thought and acted differently than they did (17:9-11).
   • He took care of them so that they wouldn't lose their way (17:12-17).
   • He entrusted them with His mission (17:18-19).

5. Describe what you think their relationship with the world was to be like. Why do you see it this way?

Read 17:20-26.

6. What stands out to you about unity from these verses? Why is it so important?

7. In this chapter Jesus has revealed His strategy for getting His message to the world. What is it? (See Matthew 9:36-38, 2 Corinthians 5:18-21.)
Note: The means was the multiplication of workers.

8. In what ways do you think you could participate in this work? What might be your part?

STUDY #20—JOHN 18

Jesus knew from the beginning that He was to be killed. Indeed, He knew His death was central to the purpose for His coming into the world. (See 2:4, 3:14-15, 12:27.) Jesus controlled the circumstances and the timing of His death (11:53-54) until His work was finished (17:4) and until those who rejected Him had ample opportunity to observe and listen to Him.

Read 18:1-9.
1. Why do you suppose the religious authorities needed Judas's assistance? *Note:* Judas was familiar with the secluded spots Jesus and the disciples frequented (18:2). The arrest had to be discreet because Jesus was popular with the crowds. (See Matthew 26:3-5,14-16.)

Read John 18:10-27.
2. What do you make of Peter's behavior? In 18:10, armed with one of the two swords the Twelve had in their possession, he attacks a band of soldiers. A few minutes later he is defeated when a young girl merely asks him a question. How would you explain his going from courage to cowardice so quickly? (See Matthew 26:31-35, Luke 22:31-34.)

3. What personal lesson can we draw from Peter's experience? (See 1 Corinthians 10:12-13.)

Read John 18:28-40.
4. What argument do you think Jesus' accusers used with Pilate to get Him tried under the Roman system rather than under the Jewish system (18:33-37)? (See Mark 15:1-15.)

5. How do you understand Jesus' response to the charge that He was presenting Himself as the King of the Jews? *Note:* He affirmed that He was a king, but that His Kingdom was not a political order such as the Jewish nation (John 18:36).

6. What is the significance of His claims to kingship? (See Philippians 2:5-11, Colossians 1:13-14, Revelation 19: 11-16.)

7. What was the real reason that the religious authorities demanded Jesus' death? (See John 19:7, Matthew 26:63-66.)

Note: It was because of His claims concerning His identity. He claimed to be God. Accepting Him as such would have meant accepting Him as King. That would have meant personal submission.

8. What do you think Jesus meant when He said that His purpose for coming into the world was to "testify to the truth" (John 18:37)? (See 1:14; Colossians 1:15-17, 2:3.) *Note:* We can know the otherwise unknowable because He revealed it to us. We can know God.

9. What do you make of Pilate's question, "What is truth?" Why do you think he asked it?
Note: "As long as I am searching and haven't made up my mind, I'm not responsible." (See 2 Timothy 3:7.)

STUDY #21—JOHN 19

Read 19:1-16.

1. In this section we have the final interaction between the religious authorities and Pilate before Jesus is sentenced to death. What, in your opinion, was the driving motivation of the religious authorities?

2. What do you think was going on in Pilate's mind?

Read 19:17-30.

3. When Jesus perceived that He had fulfilled His mission, He said, "I thirst." What kind of thirst was this? (See Mark 15:33-37, Galatians 3:13.)
Note: It is significant that the One who offers living water (John 4:13-14) died thirsty. He assumed our thirst.

4. What was "completed" (19:28)? (See 12:24-27.)

5. Death on a cross was usually caused by asphyxia (lack of air in the lungs). In order to make the death faster, the Roman soldiers broke the victims' legs. No longer able to expand their lungs by pushing up with their legs against the cross to raise themselves, they soon suffocated. Why didn't the Roman soldiers break Jesus' legs (19:31-37)?

6. What really caused Christ's death (other than the crucifixion itself)?
Note:
• Carrying the burden of our sins. (See 2 Corinthians 5:21.)
• His own decision. (See John 10:18.)

This chapter brings us to the climax of Jesus' life. His death was not a disastrous reversal of events, as most of His followers and enemies believed. On the contrary, prophets had been speaking of it in detail for centuries, and Jesus Himself, from the beginning of His ministry, spoke of "this hour" as being the very purpose for His appearance among us. This shows us that the crucifixion of Jesus is basic to God's eternal plan for mankind. Compare the details of this chapter with some of the prophecies of the event.

7. a. What details are prophesied in Psalm 22 that are fulfilled in John 19?
   b. What does this psalm reveal to you about Jesus' sufferings that John 19 does not?

8. a. What details do you find foreseen in Isaiah 53 that were fulfilled at Christ's death?
   b. What significance do you observe Isaiah giving to Christ's death?
   c. What would you say is the significance of Christ's death (Romans 5:6-11)?
   d. How do you feel His death can make a crucial difference in one's life?

STUDY #22—JOHN 20

Read 20:1-18.
1. What do you learn about Jesus' followers from their initial reactions to the empty tomb? Why do you think they reacted the way they did? (See also Luke 24:1-12,19-27.)

2. What evidence did the disciples have for Christ's resurrection?
   Note:
   • The stone was removed (John 20:1). The tomb carved out of rock was sealed with a circular stone weighing several tons. Such a stone could be set into position by rolling it down a ramp, but it could not be easily removed. Notice that the door was not opened to let Christ out but to let the disciples see that He was gone.
   • The empty tomb. The burial cloth had been laid aside (20:3-8).
   • The presence of angels (20:12-13).
   • The prophecy of Christ Himself and of the prophets. (See Luke 24:25-27.)

3. None of this evidence persuaded the disciples to believe. What did it take (John 20:16)? (See Luke 24:25,31; 2 Corinthians 3:16; 4:3-4.)
   Note: It took understanding, sight, given by God.

4. Notice the new relationship between man and God in John 20:17. Jesus refers to God for the first time as "My Father and your Father" and "My God and your God." How did His resurrection bring about this new relationship?

5. What other implications do you see in the resurrection of Jesus? (See 1 Corinthians 15:12-19.)

Read John 20:19-23.
5. a. In this paragraph we find the risen Christ sending His disciples on a mission. What do you understand that mission to be?
   b. What resources did He leave them with to accomplish it?
   c. What do you think are the implications of this mission for our lives today?

6. How do you understand the special authority Jesus gave His disciples in 20:22-23? (See Romans 1:16-17; 2 Corinthians 4:5-7.)

Read John 20:24-31.
7. a. In 20:24-29 we have the well-known story of Thomas the doubter. How did Jesus handle Thomas's doubts?
   b. Why doesn't He continue to handle our doubts with similar dramatic manifestations? (See 20:29. See also Matthew 12:38-39, Luke 16:31, John 4:48, 1 Peter 1:8-9.)

8. What do you learn about the purpose of the book of John from 20:31? How does one acquire this life?

STUDY #23—JOHN 21

Read 21:1-14.
1. Peter is perhaps the dominant character in chapter 21, as much by his actions as by his part in the conversations. What can we discover about the kind of man he was from the chapter? How would you describe him?

2. When Jesus first met Simon, He nicknamed him Cephas (Peter), which means "rock" (John 1:42). Why do you suppose He did that?

3. Peter made a lot of blunders in the course of his association with Jesus. (See Matthew 16:21-23, 17:2-6.) How do these add to the picture of the kind of person Peter was?

4. It was Peter who denied Jesus. (See Mark 14:27-31,66-72.) This denial was the last thing that had happened between Jesus and Peter before these events of John 21 took place. How do you think this affected Peter's response to Jesus here in John 21?

Read 21:15-23.

5. A very interesting dialogue takes place between Jesus and Peter in 21:15-19. Why do you think Jesus asked Peter virtually the same question three times? (See Mark 14:27-31.)

6. What do you think Jesus' responses meant? (See Isaiah 40:11, Acts 20:27-31.)

7. Do you think Peter got the message? (1 Peter 5:1-4, 2 Peter 1:12-15.)

8. "Follow Me" was almost the first thing Jesus said to Peter. (See Mark 1:16-18.) It was also just about the last thing He said to him (John 21:19-20). Why is this second invitation more significant than the first? How was following to be different from that point on?

9. What verse or thought in this chapter do you find most personally challenging?

STUDY #24—THE TWENTY-FOURTH HOUR WITH JOHN
(The Bridge Illustration Based on John's Gospel)

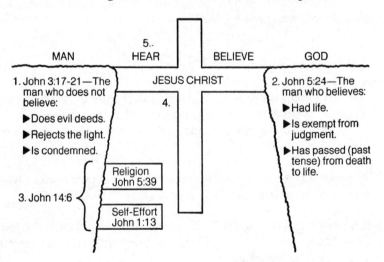

1. Man is separated from God and is under judgment because of sin (John 3:17-21,36). (See also Romans 3:23, 6:23; Hebrews 9:27.)

2. The many statements made by Jesus about eternal life indicate there is a solution to this separation (John 5:24).

3. Man attempts to build his own bridges (1:13), but Jesus declares Himself to be the only Way (14:6). (See also Ephesians 2:8-9.)

4. Jesus is the Way because of who He is: God (John 1:14); the Lamb (1:36) . . . and because of what He did: He died (6:51; see also Romans 5:8); He rose from the dead (John 11:25).

5. Jesus calls on us to act on this message—to hear and believe (5:24). Synonyms: receive (1:12); be reborn (3:3); drink (4:13). (See also Revelation 3:20.)

Summary Question:
What permanent effects do you think the study of this book has had on your life?

NOTE:
1. C.S. Lewis, *Mere Christianity* (New York: Macmillian Publishing Company, 1943, 1945, 1952), page 145.

TWELVE TYPES OF UNDERSTANDING QUESTIONS

1. *Synonyms:* "What are some words or phrases that mean the same thing as _____?"
2. *Definitions:* "How would you define _____?"
3. *Differences:* "What do you think is the difference between _____ and _____?"
4. *Similarities:* "In what ways would you say that _____ and _____ are alike?"
5. *Opposites:* "What do you think is the opposite of _____?"
6. *Relationships:* "What do you think is the relationship between _____ and _____?"
7. *Examples:* "What are some examples of _____?"
8. *Why:* "Why does this verse say _____ when several other passages emphasize _____?"
9. *Explain:* "How would you explain verse _____? How would you explain _____'s change of attitude?"
10. *Extremes:* "Which one of these do you feel is the most (or the least) _____?"
11. *Quantity/Quality:* "How significant do you think _____ really is?"
12. *How:* "How is _____ of any value today?"

INTEGRITY - opposite of
selfishness doing what
is right even when it
is to your disadvantage

p.114 → words that need
         definitions

EVERYONE CARES ABOUT
SOMETHING AND THAT
SOMETHING IS OUR
STARTING POINT. Q 154

WHO IS JESUS?
WHAT DOES HE WANT OF ME?